GREAT GOLF COURSES OF THE WORLD

Tall pines filter late-afternoon sunlight at Pinehurst, N.C's., famous No. 2 Course (overleaf).

GREAT GOLF COURSES OF THE WORLD

By William H. Davis and
the Editors of Golf Digest

Copyright © 1974 by Golf Digest, Inc.

Published by
GOLF DIGEST
A New York Times Company

297 Westport Avenue
Norwalk, Connecticut 06856

Book trade distribution by
Harper & Row
10 East 53rd Street
New York, New York 10022

First Printing

ISBN 0-914178-06-7

Library of Congress Catalog Card Number: 74-77084

Manufactured in the United States of America

contents

Foreword

2.
NORTH AMERICA

3.
BRITISH ISLES

4.
THE WORLD OF GOLF

5.
COURSE DIRECTORY AND CHARTS

foreword

Golf, inseparable as it is from nature, is a game of infinite variety and beauty. Capturing these dimensions in words and pictures is the ultimate objective of this book.

While the outline for *Great Golf Courses of the World* was continually revised almost until the day it went to the printer, there was never any question that we wanted it devoted primarily to courses that we have come to know as "great tests of golf." (See page 12, "The Test of Greatness.")

On a biennial basis, *Golf Digest* names "America's 100 Greatest Tests of Golf" (see pages 38-42), but we ruled out the idea of describing them in 1-2-3 order in this book. We felt that from a reader interest point of view, greater prominence should be given to the most famous, or the most frequent sites of the Open Championships of the United States and Great Britain. The United States Golf Ass'n and the Royal and Ancient Golf Club of St. Andrews have always applied demanding criteria to the selection of Open courses. Not only are they great tests of golf, but their greatness has been enhanced and popularized by the events that have taken place on them.

The book is divided into five parts, the first of which explains how we arrived at a definition of a "great golf course," and gives some specific examples. Within the parts that follow, arranged geographically, there are sections devoted to special categories of golf courses. For example, we devote one section to "Other Great Tournament Courses," like the Augusta National which will never host a tournament other than the Masters. Top-rated Pine Valley, the fabled New Jersey masterpiece that hosts no spectator golf tournament, is also featured in a special chapter.

Within the first pages of the book, we photographically feature each of the top 20 of "America's 100 Greatest Tests" in one way or another. While I can recall no lists of best U.S. golf courses other than the *Golf Digest* biennial selections, there have been occasional efforts to name the nation's great golf holes. The most memorable was Dan Jenkins' *The Best 18 Golf Holes in America,* published in 1966. The most recent was "My Favorite 18 Holes" by Arnold Palmer, a three-part television series aired about the time this volume was nearing completion.

It is natural that most of their selections, listed on the next page, came from great tournament courses. Although only four holes are chosen by both Jenkins and Palmer, 11 of the courses are named by both. We take a look at all of them in this volume.

The tone for *Great Golf Courses of the World,* with its emphasis on well-designed golf courses, is set by Herbert Warren Wind in Part 1 on page 16. His piece, "The Architect Makes the Golf Course Great," is the longest selection in the book and is used almost as it originally appeared in a two-part series in *Golf Digest* in 1966, with minor revisions.

The volume contains 147 pages of four-color photographs and a dozen or so of black and white. We would have preferred to use even more, but, as many amateur and professional photographers learn, capturing good golf course pictures is a frustrating quest. The configuration and nuances of most golf holes are not always perceived by the camera's eye. Even when a cherry-picker or helicopter is handy, the film often gains perspective but loses contour. Says photographer Tony Roberts, who went on a couple of expeditions to shoot golf scenics for us, "You can't plan to shoot anything until you get there. You simply have to find a photographable scene and shoot it at the right time of day. It can take a lifetime." Clearly, Tony arrived at Prairie Dunes, Hutchinson, Kan., at the right time (see page 13).

John de Garmo, a New York advertising man who excels at both golf and photography, claims, "On a golf course you cannot photograph substance, only mood." Of all his pictures, he is proud of only a handful. One of them is pictured on the last page of this book.

No doubt our most frustrated photographic contributor is Tom Crow, former Australian golf champion who now lives in southern California where he makes a small, quality line of golf clubs. A few years ago, he graciously accepted the assignment of naming the best courses in Australia and gathering pictures of them for this volume. On his first try for pictures he commissioned a professional photographer who had never taken golf course photos. The results were so "disastrous" that Tom scheduled a visit to the branch offices of his company, Precision Golf Forgings, personally photographing golf courses in Sydney, Melbourne, Adelaide and Brisbane. The resulting transparencies were lost in the mails between Australia and the United States. With additional help from his company offices, he arranged for, or personally took, a whole new series of pictures, the third try. The results (pages 210-216) comprise the first four-color pictures of the better Australian golf courses ever published in one book.

From the onset, we knew we did not want *Great Golf Courses of the World* to be primarily a guide book for the traveling golfer. Numerous volumes of this nature have been published over the years in the United States and in foreign countries. Some are very useful. However, in their quest for completeness and in their desire to provide basic facts on as many different facilities as possible, they often leave the reader with too much to choose from and too little in the way of recommendation. As stated earlier, our primary purpose is to take readers through the portals of the truly great golf courses they might never get to see, to let them enjoy vicariously the flavor and beauty of the world's great courses whether or not they ever visit them. Only as a secondary objective have we dealt with courses available to the vacationing golfer.

Within Part 2 on North America, we devote a special section to "Resort Golf." In it we feature the top resort areas of the country and give pictorial emphasis to outstanding courses within each area. Some are among *Golf Digest's* 100 Greatest Tests of Golf. While others fall short of this distinction, all of those photographed are superior by resort course standards and provide the book with functional and geographical balance. Together with Part 5, the "Places to Play Directory," it furnishes a guidebook that will uniquely answer the needs of most traveling golfers. Part 5 is based on material which has appeared each year in the *Golf Digest Annual* and which has grown to include over 900 courses in the key resort areas of the world. We have included locator maps and essential information about each course. Following Part 5 is a special section in which the course charts for five of the most famous courses in the world appear in full color.

Our hardest task was in making selections for *Great Golf Courses of the World* outside the United States, where fewer courses meet the same tests of greatness as do the great championship courses of the United States and the British Isles. To help accomplish the task, we relied heavily upon our friends among prominent players and golf writers in foreign countries.

In terms of space allocation, we kept in mind the relative importance of the game in different

DAN JENKINS:

Course	Hole No.	Yardage
Merion G.C. (East), Ardmore, Pa.	1	360
Scioto C.C., Columbus, Ohio	2	436
Olympic Club (Lake), San Francisco, Calif.	3	220
Baltusrol G.C. (Lower), Springfield, N.J.	4	196
Colonial C.C., Fort Worth, Tex.	5	459
Seminole G.C., N. Palm Beach, Fla.	6	388
Pine Valley G.C., Clementon, N.J.	7	570
Prairie Dunes C.C., Hutchinson, Kan.	8	424
Champions G.C. (Cypress Creek), Houston	9	538
Winged Foot G.C. (West), Mamaroneck, N.Y.	10	191
Merion G.C. (East), Ardmore, Pa.	11	378
Augusta Nat'l G.C., Augusta, Ga.	12	155
Dunes G. & B.C., Myrtle Beach, S.C.	13	560
Cherry Hills C.C., Denver, Colo.	14	460
Oakmont (Pa.) C.C.	15	453
Oakland Hills C.C. (South), Birmingham, Mich.	16	408
Quail Creek G. & C.C., Oklahoma City, Okla.	17	459
Pebble Beach (Calif.) Golf Links	18	530

ARNOLD PALMER:

Course	Hole No.	Yardage
Merion G.C. (East), Ardmore, Pa.	13	129
Laurel Valley G.C., Ligonier, Pa.	18	470
Olympic Club (Lake), San Francisco, Calif.	16	600
Baltusrol G.C. (Lower), Springfield, N.J.	4	196
Southern Hills C.C., Tulsa, Okla.	12	447
Seminole G.C., N. Palm Beach, Fla.	15	528
Medina (Ill.) C.C. (#3)	2	192
Firestone C.C. (South), Akron, Ohio	16	625
Champions G.C. (Cypress Creek), Houston	14	430
Cypress Point Club, Pebble Beach, Calif.	17	375
Augusta Nat'l G.C., Augusta, Ga.	13	475
Augusta Nat'l G.C., Augusta, Ga.	12	155
The Country Club, Brookline, Mass.	11	445
Cherry Hills C.C., Denver, Colo.	17	529
Oakmont (Pa.) C.C.	15	453
Oakland Hills C.C. (South), Birmingham, Mich.	16	408
Bay Hill Club, Orlando, Fla.	17	238
Pebble Beach (Calif.) Golf Links	8	425

regions of the world, guided by the following chart of the world's top nations, listed in order according to the estimated number of golfers and golf courses.

Country	No. Courses	No. Golfers*
United States	11,956	13,550,000
Great Britain	1,662	694,500
Australia	1,324	336,711
Canada	1,250	900,000
Japan	800	1,100,000
New Zealand	370	90,000
South Africa	360	50,000
Ireland	320	89,550

*Statistics come largely from the national golf associations of each nation, and tend to exclude casual golfers. For example it is estimated that in Japan 10 million people practice the game.

Separate chapters of the book are devoted to each of the nation's listed, with picture selections from many others. It should be noted that Sweden, France, Germany and India are the next most important nations in terms of number of golf courses, each having over 100 of them. Each of these nations, plus Argentina with 85 courses, has between 25 - 50,000 golfers.

Writing about a beautiful golf course is very demanding and somewhat unfulfilling journalism. No one wants to hear a play-by-play of the writer's game or a mind-boggling hole-by-hole description of an unfamiliar course. Writing about a great golf course is a little like sending a critic to the theatre and telling him he can write only about the stage sets. Perhaps no American golf writer has fielded more golf course writing assignments than Cal Brown, now editor of books and special projects at *Golf Digest,* and come up with better results. Without Brown's many inspired pieces scattered throughout this volume, *Great Golf Courses of the World* would not have

been possible. Among the features from *Golf Digest* we use in much their original form are his excellent pieces on Pine Valley (page 34) and the Monterey Peninsula (page 143). Cal also served as my editor on the complete work.

Many other members of the *Golf Digest* staff made vital contributions to this volume. Among them are John May, senior editor, and Hubert Mizell, now sports writer for the St. Petersburg Times. May, who has written on the battlegrounds of golf for more than 20 years, not only authored several parts of the book, but also assisted with caption writing and research. Mizell is one of the most facile writers I've ever worked with. Had we given him an open-ended airline ticket and a few typewriter ribbons, we could have had all the writing for this volume finished a year earlier. I also received valuable assistance from *Golf Digest* staffers Howard Gill, publisher, Paul Menneg, associate publisher, Nick Seitz, editor, and Jay Simon, managing editor.

Were it not for the efforts of Barbara Kelly, former member of our editorial department and a free-lance editorial researcher of unlimited talent and organizational ability, we might never have been able to pull all the loose ends together. Angela Hester, my own secretary, and Charlene Cruson of our books division also made vital contributions toward editorial coordination.

The help we received outside our own organization was also indispensable. In acknowledgement and appreciation of this, we have set aside a special section on page 270.

Golf is a continually changing scene and until the supply of beautiful open space is crowded from the earth, great new golf courses will emerge. We hope that your interest will justify our revising and updating this volume accordingly.

William H. Davis
President and Editor-in-Chief,
Golf Digest
Norwalk, Conn.
June, 1974

1. WHAT MAKES A GREAT GOLF COURSE

the test of greatness

"What a great golf course!" we have all exclaimed at one time or another, moved either by sheer beauty or captivating challenge.

Everyone carries his own yardstick for a "great" course. Natural beauty is a treat to all, but what a 10-handicapper might consider a challenging 18 holes, Jack Nicklaus might think to be a game of hopscotch.

In these days when the average drive of players on the American professional golf tour is around 255 yards, length becomes an inevitable factor in comparing championship golf courses. It is the major input in the course rating system of the United States Golf Ass'n. However, it is an overemphasized criterion for evaluating courses in terms of their greatness, particularly on a worldwide basis.

If golf were merely a game of distance through the air and accuracy in rolling a ball along the ground into a hole, then clearly the greatest test of golf in the world would be a course like Dubs Dread, 8,010 yards of endurance in Piper, Kan., where the par-3s average 270 yards, the par-4s are 500 yards or more and the greens are large enough to encompass most football fields.

The game is far more than either a test of distance or accuracy. Under competitive circumstances it is as much a mental exercise as it is physical. A great golf course should not only test a man's physical skills of strength, coordination and finesse, it should also test his character—his stamina, patience, daring and resolve.

Nearly 500 years after it was built, the old course at St. Andrews, Scotland, still does these things. Yet it ranges from about only 6,580 to 6,950 yards and has none of the lush greenery so characteristic of modern golf courses.

Telling of his first visit to St. Andrews, Sam Snead once wrote, "The train slowed down past some acreage that was so raggedy and beat up I was surprised to see what looked like fairway among the weeds. Down home we wouldn't plant cow beets on land like that."

Many lesser-known Americans have shared this initial impression and have heaped further indignity on the game's hallowed cradle on a balmy day by scoring better on it than they did back home. Yet, four British Open Championships have been played at St. Andrews in the post-war era. The average winning score has been 282, the lowest being 278 by Kel Nagle of Australia in 1960. It took Jack Nicklaus 72 strokes to beat Doug Sanders in an 18-hole playoff in 1970 after scoring 283.

Lacking length and cosmetic beauty, St. Andrews endures as a symbol of greatness. Its architectural qualities have been influencing golf course design for more than a century. It is understandable that we should find some of the character of St. Andrews at Shinnecock Hills near the tip of Long Island, N.Y. This great linksland course is in view of Long Island Sound, as the Old Course is of the Firth of Forth. Shinnecock was built at the turn of the century when St. Andrews was a model for the growing game.

But what tribute it is to the enduring charms of the Old Course that they should be emulated from the heartland of America to the interior of

Golf's standard of greatness for over 200 years, the Old Course at St. Andrews, Scotland (above), is a unique challenge on barren linksland. A thousand miles from any ocean, the Prairie Dunes Country Club, Hutchinson, Kan. (right) has captured the Scottish flavor with an artistry all its own.

Japan. Any visitor to Prairie Dunes at Hutchinson, Kan., who has been to St. Andrews will immediately draw a comparison between the links-like character of this 6,500-yard course and the Old Course. If the highest form of compliment is straight-out imitation, it has been paid to St. Andrews by the Japanese, who with recompense to the government of the Scottish town, are building an exact replica of the Old Course in Japan.

It is no accident that the great players have experienced their finest moments on the world's best courses. One thinks of Jones at Merion, Hogan and Player at Oakland Hills, and Palmer and Nicklaus at Augusta. It is said that a great golf course brings out the best in a great golfer and, as if to keep us from forgetting it, Sam Snead, three-times Masters champion, is still threatening at Augusta, and at age 61, nearly won the 1974 Los Angeles Open at Riviera, finishing two strokes behind winner Dave Stockton.

Carnoustie in Scotland is another example of a golf course with an affinity for great golfers or vice versa. The last two British Opens played there in 1953 and 1968 were won by Ben Hogan and Gary Player, respectively. In 1953 Hogan set and still holds the record with 282. Player scored 289 in winning 15 years later. No one has broken 280 there.

By comparison, the average winning score at the U.S. Masters since 1950 has been 281, with Nicklaus holding the record at 271. The average winning score at the U.S. Open during the same period has been 282, with Nicklaus at Baltusrol and Lee Trevino at Oak Hill sharing the record at 275. The average winning score at the British Open has been 281, with Tom Weiskopf setting the record with 276 at Troon in 1973.

This is not to say that all that matters is the score, that the test of greatness is solely a test of resistance against the play of top professionals. Gary Player, who on one hand asserts that Carnoustie is the toughest course he has ever played, has said, "It seems to me that this course is almost unfair. You find bunkers in the middle of the fairway, and that's where I was always taught it is safe to hit the ball. Some of the fairway bunkers are so deep that the only way you can escape is to hit it out backwards. On some holes there is no telling in which direction the ball will kick. Difficulty alone does not make a championship course; the element of luck must be minimized."

H. N. Wethered, an English student of course design, takes an opposing view on the subject of luck. He said, "In the old spirit of golf, luck was regarded as part of the legitimate fun of the game. The attraction that counted most was the test of ingenuity in getting around difficulties and in overcoming new and unexpected situations. If the best man did not always win (although he usually did) it merely reflected that life is not infallible."

Jack Nicklaus, who has turned designer in recent years and created an outstanding course near Columbus, Ohio, called Muirfield Village, takes a position in between Player and Wethered. He says, "the element of luck should be minimized, but not eliminated," adding "It's nice to be able to know approximately what the ball is going to do when it lands, but it still ought to bounce. Some of today's fairways and greens are like turf nurseries. You have to make a terrible shot to make a mistake."

Nicklaus believes that golf should be a game with a small margin for error and a large element of fun. Most of the great courses in this volume, particularly those in resort areas, possess fun-producing qualities. Resort golf courses usually cannot be measured in the same way as tournament courses, and we often wonder why they so frequently advertise themselves as "championship courses" when they are designed more for enjoyment than competition.

Cal Brown, *Golf Digest* editor who supervises the biennial selection of America's 100 Greatest Tests of Golf, observes that "most of the great golf courses seem to have an aesthetic appeal in their conformation, a distinction of line or form that satisfies man's yearning for natural beauty. The aesthetic can be overpowering, as it is beside the crashing surf of Pebble Beach or the sandy wasteland of Pine Valley, or subtle, as on the windswept plains of Prairie Dunes or the wooded parkland of Winged Foot."

The test of greatness is more than just the numerical factors of yardage and score. It is a measure of the intangible attributes that comprise the great game of golf and make it as much a source of enjoyment as a form of competition.
—*William H. Davis*

An unsung gem is the links-style course at exclusive Shinnecock Hills designed originally by native Scot Willie Dunn. Toomey and Flynn redesigned it in 1931 with such imagination that, even at only 6,697 yards, it remains a superb, exhilarating test.

BY
HERBERT
WARREN
WIND

the architect makes a golf course great

Dr. Alister Mackenzie, the Scottish physician who turned golf course designer and built such celebrated courses as Cypress Point, Royal Melbourne, and (with Bob Jones) the Augusta National, was often asked why he had changed professions in mid-stream. "One of the reasons," he once explained, "was my firm conviction of the extraordinary influence on health of pleasurable excitement, especially when combined with fresh air and exercise." Most golfers I know would love to follow Dr. Mackenzie's prescription for self-improvement. In some curious way, just about all of us who play the game consider ourselves unusually gifted when it comes to knowing what alterations are required to turn the ordinary holes at our home club (and others) into veritable jewels of the land; if only it were practicable, we would ditch our banal, stifling jobs tomorrow and start building golf courses—marvelous golf courses.

Especially when a man has advanced to middle age, then in particular the life of a golf architect strikes him as ideal. Apart from the healthful aspects which Dr. Mackenzie mentioned, it offers the opportunity to work with interesting people and to make very interesting sums of money. But above all—and this is surely what Dr. Mackenzie meant by "pleasurable excitement"—it provides the perfect outlet for the creative juices that are dammed up inside so many of us. The classic example of a man who made the break is George Crump, a Philadelphia hotelier, who became obsessed in 1912 with the idea of constructing 18 holes in the sandy wastes of southwestern New Jersey. This Gauguin of golf gave up everything else, disappeared into his wilderness for six years, and built one of the world's authentically great courses—Pine Valley.

Golf architecture has been an accepted profession for less than a hundred years, a relatively short time when one remembers that some Scottish historians believe that a rudimentary form of golf was played in their country as long as eight centuries ago. The profession owed its genesis to the introduction of the gutta percha ball midway into the 19th century as a replacement for the old feather-stuffed ball. Golf then became a better and an infinitely more enjoyable game, and as it spread through England in the 1870s and 1880s, and thence all over the world, courses had to be built, and built rapidly, to take care of the thousands of new devotees.

Into the breach stepped the ranking Scottish professionals, men like Willie and Tom Dunn, Old Tom Morris, and Willie Park Jr. Old Tom and the Dunn brothers, it must be stated, did rather disappointing work, considering that they had grown up on linksland courses which nature, a consummate golf architect, had created with her usual taste and authority. For some unfathomable reason, this trio, instead of following nature's prototypes, built greens that were as flat as gun platforms and exalted such artificial features as cross bunkers running the width of fairways and stiff, geometric hazards that smacked more of Sandhurst than of St. Andrews. The Dunns even threw in an occasional stone wall in the belief that such an obstacle added a dash of glamour to a quiet hole. Willie Park Jr. who did the preliminary work on Sunningdale and Worplesdon and laid out many other fine courses, had a much surer touch for devising golf holes that looked natural and played well. In the opinion of Sir Guy Campbell, the renowned golf antiquarian who was himself a splendid course designer, it is Park who deserves to be honored as the first sound, capable golf architect.

Over the years since Park's heyday, golf course design and construction have benefited from almost a century of technological improvements which have accompanied the game's growth and development. However, before turning back into history, it would seem like a very good idea to discuss for a moment the state of golf course design and construction today.

This, of course, should be the Golden Age of Golf Architecture. Never before has the architect had such wonderful earth-moving equipment or such a wide choice of reliable grasses at his disposal, and very rarely before has he had clients who gave him comparable *carte blanche* and almost unlimited funds. While a number of excel-

Alister Mackenzie

On the other hand, it should be brought out that in Willie Park's day and in the periods that followed, it was much easier to build a memorable course. To start with, since there was a relative paucity of first-rate courses, whenever a Sandwich or a Sunningdale or a Merion or a Country Club (in Brookline) did emerge, it gained almost immediate and excited recognition. Furthermore, in the old days an outstanding new course was, as often as not, quickly selected to serve as the venue of important national championships, and there is nothing like hosting big events at regular periods to spread the fame of a course and fix it in the public eye. In this connection, consider two courses Dr. Mackenzie worked on in this country, the Augusta National in Georgia and Pasatiempo in Santa Cruz, California. Since nearly every Mackenzie product has a good deal to recommend it—the Jockey Club layout in Buenos Aires is the one exception I know of—Pasatiempo, one would assume, must be an extremely good course. It is years, though, since I have heard anyone mention it. But the Augusta National—hardly a week passes when it doesn't pop up in the conversation of the average golfer, whether or not he has actually trod its rolling slopes. As the home of the Masters, the only major championship annually played over the same layout, the Augusta National has become the best known course in the world, eclipsing even the Old Course at St. Andrews. Today when a golfer attempts to describe to other golfers a particular type of hole or shot, nine out of 10 times, if he doesn't use a local course, he will invoke the Augusta National to illustrate his point, assured that there can be no clearer frame of reference for his audience.

This is perhaps the proper juncture to turn to a third course Mackenzie built in America—Cypress Point on the Monterey Peninsula. As one of the three courses over which the Bing Crosby tournament is played each winter, Cypress Point,

lent courses have come into being over the past two decades, many observers are of the opinion that we have experienced something a little less luminous than a Golden Age.

The chief trouble would appear to be the very prosperity the leading architects have enjoyed during these boom years. With so many plush clients seeking their services, it is not uncommon for our modern architects to be involved in anywhere from six to 16 new courses simultaneously, and golf course design, like any fine art, simply demands more of a person's time, sweat, thought, and passion than such a high-powered schedule allows. Moreover, when the architect also has a piece of the real estate development that is built around the course, as is frequently the case these days, he is apt to think more about the frame than the picture, and this doesn't help too much.

The natural beauty, excitement and supreme golfing challenge to which every golf architect aspires was captured indelibly by Alister Mackenzie (next page) when he created the 233-yard 16th hole at Cypress Point Club, probably the most famous par-3 in the world. Faint hearts can go for the flat area short and left of the green.

through press and TV coverage, has become well known to the sports public, much in the way that the Augusta National has. However, long before this familiarity arrived, Cypress Point had impinged itself on the consciousness of golfers around the world. One hole did the trick—the 230-yard 16th which presents the golfer with an awesome carry over 200 yards, invariably into a crosswind or headwind, over the foaming waters of the Pacific to a green perched atop a sharp-cliffed headland that is all but an island. The 16th, understandably, became the most photographed golf hole in the world. Over the past 40 years, architects have tried to copy it whenever they had a similar expanse of water to play with, but there is no question but that the original remains entirely in a class by itself. As goes without saying, it is a rare thing for a golf architect to be given such an intensely dramatic piece of land to work with as Mackenzie received at Cypress Point, and certainly no one expects an architect saddled with rather dull inland acreage to come up with a hole that bowls you over like the 16th does, but the point is that present-day architects seldom create even the minor masterpieces that one feels lies within their grasp. They construct sound holes, nice-looking holes, balanced holes, and holes that test a player's shotmaking ability, but what an infrequent experience it is to come across a hole that arrests you completely because it possesses not only a fascinating strategic challenge, but also a sense of adventure—in brief, to come across a great hole.

The reason why the Old Course at St. Andrews reigned for generations as the queen of golf courses—and the reason why Bob Jones once stated that if he were limited to play his golf on only one course, he would without hesitation choose the Old Course—is that it contained (and contains) a very high number of absolutely first-rate holes. Since the Second World War, the Old Course has not been in especially good condition, and, moreover, by modern standards it no longer has sufficient length to be as exacting as it formerly was, but it is still very easy to see how it earned its colossal reputation—particularly if one plays it on a day when a good spanking wind from the east is coming off St. Andrews Bay. Then, with the wind slightly against the golfer and across the fairways from left to right, on the second nine (the better nine) no less than four holes still play as great holes: the 11th or Eden, 164 yards; the 14th or Long Hole On, 527 yards;

the 16th or Corner of the Dyke, 348 yards; and the 17th or Road Hole, a 467-yarder that now is rated as a par-4. The holes share one thing in common: a key hazard, or series of hazards, is so beautifully positioned that it brings all the contiguous terrain to life.

On the 16th, for example, the key hazard is a cluster of three, mounded bunkers called the Principal's Nose which is situated about 225 yards down the fairway. On a still day, or when the wind is with him, a fairly good golfer can carry the Principal's Nose without much trouble, but under less favorable conditions, attempting to do so is a very risky business. Consequently, he must decide whether to play to the right or left of the hazard. The route to the left offers a huge expanse of open fairway, but the golfer who strays too far to the left of the Principal's Nose then faces a very difficult second shot: he must approach the terraced green at an angle that brings two green-side bunkers into play, and close behind the green lies the out-of-bounds territory. As you can see, this makes it a strong temptation to chance the route to the right of the Principal's Nose, for if a golfer succeeds in hitting that narrow stretch of fairway, the green opens receptively towards him and he is left with only a little pitch or pitch-and-run. The rub, of course, is the severe penalty the golfer must pay if, electing this route, he pushes or cuts his drive the slightest fraction, for the heavy moisture-laden Scottish wind, sweeping across the fairway, will toss his drive out-of-bounds as blithely as a ping-pong ball. Accordingly, every time a golfer comes to the 16th tee, he must study the conditions that prevail at that moment and select the sensible route. And yet, you'd be surprised how many top-notch players, for all their experience, still end up in the Principal's Nose. I can remember watching Don Cherry drive smack into the hazard at a crucial moment in the 1955 Walker Cup match, and five years later Arnold Palmer did exactly the same thing in the British Open. The wonderful thing about the 16th, you see, is that, for all its age, it still plays.

One other hole at St. Andrews, the 164-yard 11th, is eminently worth our attention, not only because its strategic concept is quite different from that of the 16th, but also because of the continuous influence this par-3 has exerted on later golf architects. The key hazard on the 11th, or Eden, is a deep pit called the Strath Bunker which noses into the front right-hand edge of the green, a large green sloping severely down from back to front. The greenside wall of the Strath is so high and steep that, when a golfer's ball lies close to its base, even a well-executed explosion may not get the ball up quickly enough to clear the wall and reach the putting surface. (I remember a strangely resourceful maneuver by Charley Stowe, the English amateur, in the Strath in the 1938 Walker Cup match. With the pin set directly behind the Strath, as it generally is on important occasions, both Stowe and his opponent, Charley Kocsis, caught the bunker off the tee, with Stowe's ball nearer the front wall. After Kocsis, playing first, had left his ball in the hazard, Stowe turned his back on the flag and played out laterally over the moderate side wall onto the apron of the green. He got down from there in a chip and a putt, and won the hole with a bogey 4 to Kocsis' double-bogey 5.) Since the fearsome qualities of the Strath are only too visible from the tee, prudence dictates that the golfer play away from it, to the left. The trouble here is that, with the Strath working on his subconscious, the golfer will frequently play his shot too far to the left, pulling it past the opening to the green and depositing it in Hill Bunker, a hazard not as punishing as the Strath but rugged enough so that on one notable occasion it cost a sand-shot artist of Sarazen's ability three precious strokes to recover. In brief, the Strath and the Hill provide a perfect illustration of the mythological Scylla and Charybdis—the rock and the whirlpool which terrorized ancient sailors—adapted to terrorize modern golfers. Many other earlier golf holes presented this challenge of a pair of severe hazards, the one working in conjunction with the other, but the Eden did it most dramatically and rightfully became one of the most copied holes in golf. Charles Blair Macdonald (1846-1928), the first accomplished American golf architect, not only built a version of the Eden at the National Golf Links, in Southampton, Long Island—his first ambitious project —but he invariably made provision for an Eden-type short hole on all his courses.

In 1931, twenty years after the completion of Macdonald's National, the Eden, still a touchstone for the game's scholars, popped up again at Jones' and Mackenzie's Augusta National. Bob Jones had long admired the original and he and his co-designer were hoping they might find terrain that would suit a nice free-style adaptation. They came up with a very fine one—the fourth hole. Their Strath bunker was moved so that it guards the center of the green, their Hill is much gentler than the original, their green has an entirely different shape, and their hole requires a much longer shot from the back tee, but in its practical strategy the fourth at Augusta is still the good old Eden.

The mention of Charles Blair Macdonald presents the logical spot in this study to pause for a moment and pull some threads together. Far more than any other architect, Macdonald stands as the connecting link between the old and the new. On one hand, no one had a deeper reverence for the great British courses, and, on the other, no one in his time was as forward-looking in realizing that, regardless of the natural felicity of the land a golf architect was working with, he had to be ready to assist nature by moving and shaping tons and tons of earth when a hole cried out for a "natural" feature that wasn't there. Macdonald's projects cost unprecedented amounts of money—the Yale Golf Course, constructed in the mid-1920s, came to $450,000, for example—but Macdonald, an adroit businessman and a born promoter, rarely encountered much, if any, difficulty in getting his clients to put up the necessary funds or, in other cases, assembling his own syndicate of investors. In just about every respect—the quality of his courses, the money they required, and the time he took with them—he was the diametric opposite of the turn-of-the-century "architects" who were littering America with quacky quickie courses. This breed was epitomized by Tom

Charles B. Macdonald

21

Sand creates illusions of whitecaps breaking over the green entrance to 16 at Donald Ross' Seminole.

Bendelow who left the composing room of the New York *Herald* to build the Van Cortlandt Park course and then went out to the Middle West where there was a huge demand for golf facilities. It took Bendelow less than a day to lay out a course. He would walk to the spot he'd selected for the first tee and mark it with a stake; then he'd walk a hundred yards farther down the fairway-to-be and plant another stake to mark the point where the club should dig a cross bunker; proceeding another hundred yards, he'd plant another stake—the area where a collection of chocolate-drop mounds and pot bunkers would go; and then he would walk another 25 yards and plant a fourth and final stake to demarcate the center of the green. On each nine, Bendelow gave you four par-4s of this type, two par-3s and one long hole. He charged $25 for the complete job, and the next day was off staking out a "sporty little course" for another starry-eyed group of innocents.

Charley Macdonald brought this sort of nonsense to an end by educating his countrymen in the true principles of golf architecture. The scion of a wealthy Chicago family, Macdonald was sent to Scotland in 1872 to attend St. Salvador and St. Leonard's College in St. Andrews. Those boyhood years in the old gray town molded the man. He took up golf there and became so proficient at it that he had the chance to play with the best amateurs and professionals. Golf became a passion with him, and when it was time for him to return home in 1875 to what was then a golfless United States—remember, it wasn't until 1888 that St. Andrews (in Yonkers, N.Y.), our first permanent golf club, was established—Macdonald was, in this respect, a dreadfully frustrated young man.

At length, in May, 1892, after golf had made its first indentations on the Atlantic seaboard, Macdonald was invited to lay out seven abbreviated holes on the expansive lawn of Senator John B. Farwell's estate in Lake Forest, Ill. Later that year, having whipped up the requisite enthusiasm among his friends to form the Chicago Golf Club, he laid out nine respectable holes on a stock farm, 20 miles west of the city, which the club had purchased. He subsequently added another nine, and then in 1895 persuaded his fellow members that the time was ripe to do things in a really big time way. The club purchased a 200-acre, black soil farm, south of Wheaton, and there Macdonald built eighteen solid holes. He used red top grass for the fairways and bent grass for the greens, he provided for the greens to be watered from a central plant, and he saw to it that the course measured 6,200 yards—then the same length as the Old Course in St. Andrews. The routing of the holes, however, left something to be desired, for a good many of

them trailed along the perimeter of the plot in a clock-wise progression. The members who hooked were at a tremendous disadvantage, for they were constantly hitting the ball off club property and incurring out-of-bounds penalties. (This property is where the out-of-bounds rule originated.) Charley Macdonald, as you have probably guessed, was a fader and not a hooker, and when he mis-hit a shot, it slid conveniently away from the out-of-bounds territory and came to rest in comparatively pleasant, playable rough.

The actual construction of Macdonald's National Golf Links, the first great American course, was not started until 1907, but it might be said that the preparatory work started as early as 1901. In that year a British golf magazine conducted a survey called the Best Hole Discussion in which prominent golfers were asked to select the best holes in their country and to state their reasons for their choice. Intrigued by this symposium, Macdonald made two trips to Britain to study the most popular courses—St. Andrews, Prestwick, North Berwick, Hoylake, Sandwich, Deal, Westward Ho!, Machrihanish, Littlestone and Brancaster, among them — and to collect sketches and surveyors' maps of the most highly esteemed holes. After a period of exploration back home, he found the seaside land he wanted to build on, 205 acres near Peconic Bay three miles from Southampton on Long Island, and set to work clearing it of its dense growth of bayberry, huckleberry

and blackberry bushes. Not one to hurry himself, he took four years to complete the National, carefully utilizing the best natural features of the terrain and patiently re-shaping the other stretches to fit his grand design: the creation of a course that would rank with the finest in the world since (a) it would be based on Americanized versions of such classic holes as the Eden and the Road at St. Andrews, the Alps at Prestwick, and the famous par-3 Redan at North Berwick, and since (b) the "original" holes would likewise be designed in accordance with the soundest principles of golf architecture.

Macdonald hoped that his course would "serve as an incentive to the elevation of the game in America," and indeed it did. Visitors to the National, well-traveled foreign players and American neophytes alike, were equally bowled over by its strategic and scenic beauty, and many American clubs that were planning to build new courses dispatched committees who studied the National and brought back notebooks filled with observationss. When the National was first opened, incidentally, it measured 6,100 yards but by the mid-20s it had been extended to 6,650. Nowadays, because of the lively ball and vastly improved clubs, the course plays rather short for a big hitter, but when there is a little wind prowling around, it is still a fine test for anyone, quite exacting and full of the true breath of golf. (It was finally stretched to 7,020 yards in 1974.) Macdonald went on to build many other first-rate courses (such as Mid-Ocean, Lido, Pip-

23

ing Rock, Yale, and the St. Louis Country Club), but there is no question that the National Golf Links stands as his *chef d'oeuvre*, his monument.

During the first decade of this century, while Macdonald was slowly but surely bringing to life his dream course, there were other noteworthy breakthroughs in golf architecture on both sides of the Atlantic. In England where, as in Scotland before, the best courses had always been linksland courses by the sea, for the first time some excellent inland layouts were constructed. Up to this time the inland courses, built on non-porous meadowland soil, had been an ordeal—muddy in winter and hard as a rock in summer. Around the turn of the century, the daring idea occurred to some of the more thoughtful architects to try to convert the sandy, heathery stretches south and west of London into golfing country. They were laughed at, naturally, but not for long. Grass grew beautifully on these courses; the drainage was superb, even during the rainiest fortnights; the land was easy to contour; and the fir trees, which grew abundantly in the heathery belts, were a tremendous asset functionally as well as esthetically.

Among the splendid inland courses that suddenly sprouted all over the place, the best were the work of men the English referred to as "amateur architects"—a somewhat confusing term inasmuch as golf architecture was their business but which was intended to distinguish these new practitioners from the older hands like the Dunns, Morris, and Park, whose avenue to architecture had been their stature as professional golfers. Three men in particular of this new school were exceptionally gifted: J. F. Abercrombie, who did Worplesdon and Coombe Hill; Herbert Fowler, who did Walton Heath and the Berkshire, the latter with the assistance of Tom Simpson; and H. S. Colt, who did Swinley Forest, Stoke Poges, Sunningdale, and the Eden course at St. Andrews, and who collaborated with Captain Allison and J. S. F. Morrison on Wentworth. In America, quite apart from Macdonald's immense contribution, golf architecture concurrently took some significant strides forward during the first 20 years of the century. Donald Ross, a Scot from Dornoch who arrived in this country in 1899, was undoubtedly responsible for more fine courses than any other designer. All in all, Ross had a hand in close to 600 courses scattered from Duluth to Palm Beach. Many of these, understandably, were "paper

jobs." After Ross had settled at Pinehurst, where he revised the No. 1 course and built the Nos. 2, 3, and 4 courses, it became a common practice of Pinehurst's regular patrons to bring him topographical maps of newly acquired land their home club wanted to build on. Ross would lay out a course on the topo, and the club's greenskeeper or a local engineer would then oversee the construction. It should be emphasized, however, that Ross personally superintended the actual work on a good percentage of the courses which bear his name, and that, as goes without saying, he bestowed tireless first-hand attention on Pinehurst No. 2, Seminole and his other major projects. His trademark was the crown green at the top of an upslope—a throwback to Dornoch —and, though some critics felt he placed his bunkers too close to his greens, he had a nice flair for hazards.

While other proficient professional architects were soon to come to the fore in America—A. W. Tillinghast (Winged Foot, Baltusrol and Five Farms), Toomey and Flynn, and Styles and Van Cleek are a few that quickly come to mind—curiously, during that eventful period from 1900 to

Donald Ross

A. W. Tillinghast

sites, with the golf course set behind them and getting only an occasional whiff of the ocean.) Grant did not go on with architecture, but Neville did. He later assisted George Thomas in the design of Bel Air in Los Angeles.

However, among our authentic amateur architects, two in particular deserve our admiration: George Crump, the creator of Pine Valley, and Hugh Wilson who, interestingly, finished the four holes at Pine Valley that remained uncompleted at Crump's death.

In a way, Pine Valley's reputation as "the most difficult course in the world" has tended to obscure its true glory. Certainly, if you fail to carry the wide, unraked, bush-strewn sandy wastes between the tee and fairway, or if you tangle with the almost impenetrable woods that frame each hole, Pine Valley will destroy you more cruelly than any other course, but this is not what makes Pine Valley great. What does is the cornucopia of imaginative, challenging shots to the green a golfer is presented with after an adequate drive. The four par-3s are masterly and, all in all, it is hard to think of another course that possesses as many absolutely wonderful holes.

As for Hugh Wilson, he was a Philadelphia insurance man who did only one course of his own, Merion. In 1911 before work on Merion started, Wilson, a relatively young Princeton graduate, was selected by the reigning junta at the club to go to Britain and see what he could learn from studying the famous courses. He may have learned even more than Charley Macdonald did. At any rate, Wilson was not at all impressed by holes like the Alps at Prestwick, which despite their august reputation were essentially blind holes and, it followed for Wilson, obsolete. At Merion, the most classic of our parkland courses, there are in fact only three holes on which the green is not visible from the tee. What Wilson had, in addition to a firm grip on the fundamentals of golf course design, was a rare instinct for the little touch, the slight modification, the miniscule variation that would transform a good hole into a memorable one. He knew how to swing a fairway so that placement of the tee shot was more important than sheer power. He knew how to flash his bunkers in the green area so that, besides catching a poor shot, the bunkers enhanced a green's clarity and its definition and so encouraged an aggressive approach shot. (Before putting in a new bunker, it was his practice to have the club's renowned greenskeeper, Joe Valentine, spread a bed sheet

1920 a high number of our most arresting and durable championship courses were built by men for whom golf architecture was merely an avocation. For example, Oakmont, that awesome avatar of penal design, was the personal project of the Fownes family of Pittsburgh who nurtured its evolution hazard by hazard. (Since deepening Oakmont's bunkers was not feasible because of drainage problems, the Fownes had them furrorwed with special sabre-toothed rakes.) Then there was Pebble Beach, co-designed by Jack Neville and Douglas Grant, two California amateur golfers who had never designed a real golf course before. Along the high, cliff-lined headlands above Carmel Bay, these two novices built some of the most magnificent holes in the world —holes that still both exhilarate and terrify even the world's most accomplished golfers and which have yet to be surpassed for scenic grandeur. (Today, of course, the premium land fronting the bay would be marked for luxury home-

over the spot under consideration, and then, re-treating down the fairway, Wilson would ponder the necessary adjustments.) Dogged by ill health, Hugh Wilson died when he was a com-paratively young man, and it was a loss. There are ample grounds—Merion—for believing that, more than any other American architect, he had the spark of genius.

By today's loftiest criteria, how advanced were they in understanding their profession, the early 20th-century golf architects—Macdonald, Ross, Fowler, Abercrombie, Colt, Simpson, Crump, Wilson, and their less distinguished contempo-raries? Very advanced, I believe one must say. Indeed, I think it would be extremely instructive to review, in compressed form, the body of knowledge they had accumulated by this time.

1. These architects knew that a golf course, whatever its playing qualities, also had to be scenically attractive. They knew that both the holes and the setting had to be natural in ap-pearance. A handful of American builders were still fascinated by "billy-goat courses" where their holes climbed and descended steep hills, but the majority were well past that stage. Gently rolling terrain, they appreciated, was the best land for golf. When they remodeled the existing terrain with earth-moving machinery, instead of striving for sharp ridges they contoured for mod-ulated hillocks and hollows.

2. These architects knew that a golf course was only as good as its drainage and one other unglamorous item—its grass. Some American builders persisted in sowing clover fairways be-cause they looked so green, but, mercifully, most of them realized the virtues of blue grass, red top, the fescues and the bents. They believed in fairly stalwart rough—the type called "4-iron rough"—meaning that, unless you were lucky, the "longest" club you could hope to play from an average lie in the rough was the 4-iron. (It is regrettable that this reasonable standard has all

This is the seductive approach to the 390-yard 18th, Bel-Air C.C., Los Angeles, a George Thomas design.

but disappeared today.) They believed in rather wide fairways because the typical American course was an inland layout containing a number of holes lined by trees on both sides, and so it was felt that a golfer had to be given a little more room to move in.

3. These early architects were adept at routing their courses to provide for an interesting variety of holes in a pleasant sequence. Few of them made the mistake of building "loop courses" where the first nine holes paraded to the turn in a straight line and the second nine paraded back in the same boring manner. They knew and practiced the "triangulation theory" whereby, in a series of three holes, the first would run, say, north, the second west, and the third southeast. On a windy day, the golfer then would not be battling dead into the wind or playing with wind directly behind him over a long unbroken succession of holes. They knew that the first hole, ideally, should be a par-4 that was

neither too long or too exacting, so that a golfer could warm up and get the feel of his swing. They knew that a strong finish (like the last five holes at Hoylake, the last three at Carnoustie, and the last two at Pebble Beach) gave a course punch and distinction.

4. These architects knew that a golf hole should be frank and honest—that, in their phrase, it should offer "strict justice." This meant that a golfer should not be beleaguered with chancy or unexpected problems, like a blind shot. (In the old days, incidentally, a blind approach was one where you couldn't see the green at all; nowadays some of our touring pros have coddled themselves to the point where, if they can see only the upper portion of the flagstick, they call it a blind approach.) In the realm of bunkering, the credo of these architects was very sound: "No visible hazard is an unfair hazard." This took some gumption since on several sacrosanct links—most notably the Old Course at St. Andrews—the fairways were pocked with hidden bunkers. (Some of these ancient bunkers had been formed, as the game's antiquarians explained, by sheep huddling in hollows to keep out of the biting wind, but most of them had a less romantic genesis. Because of the conformation of the land on certain holes, a good many drives would end up in the same pronounced fold of land—sometimes a patch of blown sand. In recovering from this difficult lie, the players kept widening and deepening the original divot scrapes, and, at length, dismayed at ever getting grass to grow in that area, the greenskeeper would simply enlarge the man-made bunker into the real thing.)

5. Additionally, these architects appreciated that a golf hole had to be "of a good length." In their day this meant avoiding holes between 200 and 300 yards long; today, when everyone hits the ball farther, this would mean steering away from holes between 250 annd 350 yards long. These architects were aware that a few holes on every course should demand heroic carries off the tee for the low-handicap players, and they learned to make provision for back and front tees. They knew as well that a fine golf hole should present the player with alternate routes

to the green, to suit his capabilities. They knew, too, that on a hole where a long approach was required, the green should be fairly large, and that a small-sized green was proper on a par-5 hole or a short par-4.

6. Finally, they knew that subtlety wears well. In this regard, in contrast with some of our present day, mass-production builders, they strove to fashion holes where the minor features influenced play because the course was fast and slippery. Today, when a golfer is short with an indifferent approach, as often as not the ball will expire close to where it has landed on the lush green of the apron. Not so in the old days. With the ground firmer and the grass trimmed shorter, the ball would keep running, and the folds of the apron would slyly direct it towards a greenside bunker. Anyone can look good on a slow course but it takes a real golfer to handle a racy one.

If these early architects knew so much, one might well ask, then what have been the contributions made in the more recent decades by the men who followed them? In America, the chief one, perhaps, has been the concerted movement away from penal architecture and the concomitant endorsement of strategic architecture. Before discussing this important distinction, one thing should be made clear: just as every first-class novelist understood human nature long before Dr. Freud made the scene, so, too, every first class golf architect, whatever his era, had an intuitive feeling for the fundamentals of strategic design.

What is the essence of strategic design? To begin with, where penal design calls for a golfer to pay an immediate and decisive penalty for making an error, strategic design places far more emphasis on rewarding a golfer for playing a good shot. Let us say, to simplify matters, that we are concerned with a 400-yard par-4 that doglegs moderately to the right. The penal-minded architect undoubtedly would install, to start with, one or two bunkers edging into the fairway on both sides in the drive zone. This would accomplish his first aim: only a straight drive would go unpenalized. In the green area he would probably leave a small opening leading from the fairway to the putting surface but, aside from this, he would see to it that the green was practically surrounded by bunkers—rather severe ones. This would accomplish his second aim: only a straight approach shot, carrying the requisite distance, would go unpenalized. An architect of the strategic school would

proceed far differently. He might place a shallow bunker or some low mounds in the elbow of the dogleg to exact a mild toll from a wayward tee-shot, but, if he were a purist, he would put in no fairway hazards whatsoever. He would be thinking ahead to the green area which would set up the strategic plan of the entire hole. Most likely, on this dogleg-to-the-right we are talking about, he would install a large, redoubtable bunker that would guard the right side of the entrance to the green and which would extend along the right-hand flank of the green. Perhaps, but not necessarily, he might add some mounding or an auxiliary bunker on the back-left of the green or introduce a pitched run-off on that far side. However, the large bunker would be sufficient in itself to establish how the hole should be played from tee to green. Since the golfer who drove down the right-hand side of the fairway could hit the green only by playing a brilliant second shot over the key bunker, the intelligent player would try to place his tee shot on the left side of the fairway. If he succeeded in doing this (and didn't play too far left and find the rough), then he would be rewarded with a perfect opening to the green—a relatively makeable shot. As Sir Guy Campbell once remarked, playing a strategic course is not unlike playing billiards: on each stroke there is always a special maneuver that must be executed correctly to set up the next stroke or strokes.

Strategic design, as you can see, is substantially more generous to the golfer than penal design. On one hand, it essays to punish a golfer in a just proportion to his degree of error. On the other, it stimulates initiative and rewards daring. In this latter case, though, a golfer must have a realistic opinion of his skill and his limitations, for if he bites off more than he can chew, he must pay for it. Every year in the Masters, the gigantic gallery that congregates alongside the 13th, an exemplary strategic hole, is treated to an almost continuous seminar on the topic. A 475-yard par-5 that doglegs to the left about 260 yards out from the tee, the 13th entices the top-rung golfer to try to reach the green in two. He can do so, except when the wind is against him, by putting together two good woods (and sometimes a wood and a long iron), but a definite gamble is involved: an arm of Rae's Creek curls across the fairway just before the green and then breaks in and hugs the right side of the green. The gamble is so exquisitely balanced that the golfer who has driven well is confronted with a tantalizing decision: should he lay up short of the creek on his second and at least make sure of his par, or should he, at the peril of a possible bogey, go for the green in the hopes of bagging a birdie 4? It is hard to think of another par-5 in golf which tests a golfer's judgment and ability quite as vividly or which offers the spectators as much thrilling action.

It was the Augusta National more than any other course that halted the trend toward the bunker-splattered penal-style layout which in our country reached its peak in the 1920s. As we remarked earlier, the big daddy of this type of course was Oakmont. When it was host to our Open championship in 1927 and 1935, Oakmont contained well over 200 bunkers, not to mention 21 ditches, and when this plethora of hazards was supplemented by close-cut greens that were as fast as linoleum, the wonder is not that only one man broke 300 in 1935 but that the entire field did not come marching off the course and stone the clubhouse. One of the reasons why penal design had taken hold to this degree was that, as balls became livelier and clubs were improved, holes naturally tended to play shorter, and often the first response of a green committee was to try to restore a hole's old ruggedness by adding more hazards or toughening up the existing ones.

In any event, in the years just previous to the emergence of the Augusta National in 1931, a reaction against the excessively penal course began to set in. In the United States, Dr. Mackenzie, who had come over from Britain, was one of the leaders of the movement toward strategic design; his green areas featured the well-placed, natural-looking dune-type bunker along with rather Scottish mounding, and a number of golf scholars, Bob Jones included, were impressed by them. In Canada at this same time Stanley Thompson was preaching much the same doctrine and practicing it with marked success in the courses he built at Banff and Jasper Park. But it was the Augusta National—inevitably a glamour course (even before the Masters was inaugurated) because of Jones' involvement as Mackenzie's collaborator—which dramatized for American architects and golfers the superiority of strategic design in much the same way that Macdonald's National Links had dramatized for a previous generation the essentials of serious, scientific, artistic modern architecture. The Augusta National had only 30 or so bunkers and no rough to speak of, but in order to score well on it, an experienced professional had to think his way around the course, placing his tee shots, making certain on his approaches that he favored the more manageable side of the huge and undulating greens, never forcing his shots but never succumbing to passivity. Furthermore, while the course gave the scratch player all he could handle, it didn't overpower the middle- and high-handicap golfers; from the regular tees, they could score as well, and sometimes better, than they did at their home club.

The Augusta National remains the most influential course in America, and the most copied. In recent years, for example, it has been responsible for the national infatuation with the mammoth green, a rather debatable "improvement" for the average course. As veteran golf observers have pointed out, the Augusta-type green is beautifully right at the Augusta National, where the entire scale is Rubenesque, but transplanted elsewhere it is usually beautifully wrong. Currently there is a strong vogue for duplicating the Augusta National's absence of rough and this, too, I would venture, is of questionable merit (although it must be admitted that on roughless holes much less time is spent looking for balls, and with our courses jam-packed today, this is no small consideration). However, in terms of its over-all impact on American golf, the Augusta National has been an almost unqualified blessing. Of all our courses, it continues to present the most unignorable, articulate and effective case for the charms and worth of strategic design. When the day comes, as it soon will, when television coverage of the Masters will include not only the last seven holes but the full 18, the educative value of the Augusta National will be incalculable.

A professional architect customarily receives as his fee 10 per cent of the total cost of the golf course. Since there are many other attendant satisfactions—plus an abundance of clients during the long boom period which golf in particular and the national economy in general have enjoyed in the last 20 years — the profession has been constantly expanding since the Second World War.

While the public has learned a good deal about the men who have been designing our new courses and remodeling our old ones, only two architects have managed to become really well-known "names"—the late Dick Wilson and Robert Trent Jones.

Wilson, a warm, direct, rugged, extremely likeable, temperamentally volatile man, learned the business as a young employee of the firm of Toomey and Flynn, and in this capacity he did, among other things, some of the remodeling on Merion and in the 1930s helped design the revised Shinnecock course on Long Island. He gradually acquired a solid reputation because of the quality of his work but it was not until the 1950s that he truly came into his own. During that period, he was responsible, for instance, for Meadow Brook and Deepdale on Long Island, Cog Hill No. 4 in Chicago and the new Royal Montreal—all of them are wonderful courses— but it was his work in Florida that attracted the most attention. Working out of his headquarters near Delray Beach, where he gradually put together a sizable and talented organization, Wilson built a succession of extraordinarily solid courses including Doral (outside Miami), the PGA courses (in Palm Beach Gardens, now known as JDM), and, most notably, Pine Tree (outside Delray).

I was fortunate enough to be on hand the March afternoon in 1962 when Ben Hogan came up from Palm Beach to see if Pine Tree was as good as he had heard it was. Accompanied by his three playing partners, a gallery of 15 people, and a very anxious Wilson following in an electric car, Hogan, obviously relishing many finesse shots he was required to bring off, was around in 73, one over par, and then told Wilson in so many words that Pine Tree was the best course he had ever played. (Shortly before Wilson's death, Hogan and the architect were starting to discuss building a course Ben had in mind. It is a pity it never came off. But now Hogan is collaborating with Wilson's protege, Joe Lee, on a new course—the first Hogan will have inspired — near Ft. Worth, Tex.) What makes Pine Tree so formidable and fine is the fact that each par you get must be earned. Especially from the back tees, both power and control are demanded in equal measure. When you hit a green in regulation stroke, a sense of pride surges through you—you know you have played one, two, or three (as the case may be) absolutely first-class shots or else you would never be putting for your birdie. For the short-hitter, Pine Tree may be a trifle too severe. By that stage in his career, Wilson, having arrived at the conclusion that a sound golf hole should be proof against the lucky shot, had begun to bunker his greens so trenchantly that unless your approach carried onto the putting surface,

you just couldn't get home. Pine Tree perhaps does insist that the average golfer play over his head, and this no doubt is a fault, but, for myself, it ranks along with Mackenzie Ross' revised Ailsa at Turnberry, and just ahead of Wilson's Meadow Brook, one of the top courses built since the war. Pine Tree, it should be added, is superbly conditioned.

Robert Trent Jones, a native of Rochester, N.Y., prepared himself specifically for golf architecture at Cornell's graduate schools where his curriculum included engineering, surveying, agronomy, and landscape architecture. As a young man he worked with Stanley Thompson (whose partner he later became), survived the depression years by doing public courses for the WPA in upper New York State, went out on his own before the war, and upon its cessation became the busiest architect in the world. Apart from his domestic credits—numbered among them are Peachtree in Atlanta, the Firestone course in Akron, Bellerive in St. Louis, the Dunes in Myrtle Beach, Spyglass Hill and Pauma Valley in California, and Point O'Woods in Michigan —he has done a slew of courses outside the country, among them Sotogrande in Spain, Cotton Bay on Eleuthera, Dorado Beach in Puerto Rico, Fountain Valley on St. Croix, and Mauna Kea in Hawaii, as well as even more recent courses in Colombia, the Philippines, Thailand, Alaska, Morocco, Japan, Sardinia, and the Fiji Islands.

A good part of Jones' reputation also derives from the many assignments he has had remodeling courses on which the U. S. Open has been played. His first job of this type came in 1950 when he was called in by Oakland Hills, near Detroit, to revise the course so that it would present the field in the 1951 Open with a rigorous but honest test. Jones proceeded to fill in all the old fairway-flanking bunkers 200 to 220 yards from the tees, which the pros would have carried with ease, and to replace them with new bunkers some 230 to 260 yards out. He narrowed the fairways drastically and re-fashioned the bunkering around some of the greens. Jones' Oakland Hills stampeded the Open field, who protested it was grossly unfair, and even Hogan, who mastered it with perhaps the greatest golf of his career, called it "a monster." Oakland Hills in 1951 was, for certain, an exceedingly exacting examination in golf, but the truth of the matter was that it was time for our country's most proficient players to face up to sterner demands on their skill in our

A view of the 18th green at the Pine Tree Golf Club, Delray Beach, Fla., shows one of the course's many large, white sand bunkers so well-placed by architect Dick Wilson.

everybody's great test: pine valley

BY CAL BROWN

Tucked away from public view down an anonymous country road near the small town of Clementon in southwestern New Jersey is Pine Valley Golf Club.

This magnificent—some say fiendish—creation, hewn from pine-covered sandhills that eons ago formed the ocean floor, is as good an argument as you will find that backbreaking length is not essential to a great test of golf.

Pine Valley's full length of 6,765 yards (6,442 from the regular tees) does not strike fear into anyone's breast—not until one steps to the first tee. There one glimpses the two principal design features that give Pine Valley its stern, intimidating character—vast, sandy wilderness and thick forest. There is no "rough" at Pine Valley. Instead, desert-like scrub surrounds every fairway and most of the greens, which are immaculately conditioned and appear, in contrast, as islands of green velvet.

One must play to these "islands" from start to finish. Tee shots must carry expanses of up to 175 yards of unkempt dune on most holes to

Desert-like scrub and thick forests surround every fairway and green at Pine Valley. The unfortunate player who fails to arch his second shot far enough to the elevated green of the 367-yard second hole will land on this jagged dunesland.

reach safe ground. The careless, wild or indifferent shot is dealt with severely. Since rakes are forbidden on the course, the sandy soil expanses are pocked with footprints, mounds, holes of burrowing animals, roots and ragged clumps of scrub, heather, Scotch broom and Poverty grass. If you can find your ball in this or in the woods (which Pine Valley caddies are devilishly adept at doing) you play it as it lies, for there is out-of-bounds on only one hole.

The all-male club is strictly private. Its president for more than four decades, John Arthur Brown, has assiduously guarded its sanctity and the comfort of its members owing to the fact that

Pine Valley is widely discussed wherever genuine golfing spirits gather and has more requests for visits than can possibly be accommodated. It is widely regarded as the toughest golf course in the world. This is certainly not true for the fine player who can strike the ball consistently and truly. It may well be the most testing for the average player of, say, seven handicap or more, whose shotmaking is less reliable.

One or two mistakes is all it takes to raise one's score dramatically at Pine Valley. There is a story about one gentleman who needed a bogey 5 on the 18th hole for an 84 to win a substantial bet that he could break 90. He finished with 97. The late British golf writer Bernard Darwin is said to have played the first seven holes in even par. Following a good drive, he proceeded to take 16 strokes on the short eighth hole and returned to the clubhouse.

It may be adventures like these that inspire poets and writers to describe Pine Valley with adjectives like heroic, majestic, monstrous, sublime, deadly, beautiful and one or two uncomplimentary terms of Anglo-Saxon origin. One would be hard put to soften any of these epithets. It also has been called a penal golf course

which is true only in the sense that it so ruthlessly penalizes poorly struck shots.

The truth is that Pine Valley is eminently fair. The landing areas for tee shots are very wide. Alternative routes to the greens are provided on at least nine of the 14 long holes, although a safe routing will not get you to the green in regulation figures. There is little margin for the player who chooses to risk everything, a feature upholding the principle that a risk is not worthy of the name if one can get away with an error, however slight. The course demands that if you accept challenge you must be prepared to execute.

It is no secret that a number of professional players, particularly long hitters, do not rate Pine Valley among the great challenges in golf. One suspects the reason for this is that Pine Valley is not the place for raw power. It is a place where subtlety and a well-positioned tee shot will pay rewards, where brute strength is tolerated only if accompanied by great control and nerve.

"It is only penal if you are not playing well," says George Fazio, the former touring player who now is designing courses himself, and who was once the professional at Pine Valley. "I think it has been proved over the years in com-

At Pine Valley one plays to "islands" of fairway or green, like the 145-yard 10th (at left) with its Satanic pot bunker (right front of green) or the 185-yard 14th (right) where one man once scored 44.

petition, both amateur and professional, that the best player will win at Pine Valley. You must play the course, not necessarily your own game. The player who does not possess all the shots would not thrive there." It is, in short, a golf course for the man who relishes the game above his own individual prowess.

What sets Pine Valley apart from all but a handful of courses is not only its unusual terrain, but also the number of absolutely first-rate holes it throws at you. It probably has more classic holes than any other course in America.

There are but two par-5s and both are superb. The 15th is surely one of the greatest in the world. Some of the best (and longest) players in golf have surveyed its 603-yard length—Nicklaus, Snead, Harney, Souchak, Bayer, Thomson —and none has ever reached it in two, not even from the middle tees which cut its distance to 584 yards. It is that rare, totally honest hole that hides nothing and yet will succumb to nothing short of perfection. The tee shot must carry over a lovely lake to a wide landing area which slopes lazily uphill and around a gentle bend to the right to a tiny green perched like a sentinel in the distance. The closer one approaches the green, the tighter the fairway becomes as woods and sand converge on a narrow neck that is not more than green's width across. The fairway tilts to the right near the green to send any half-hearted approach careening to disaster. The hole yields par with three adequate shots, but even with a drive of 300-plus yards one does not get home in two.

The 585-yard seventh boasts Hell's Half Acre, considered the largest sand trap in the world, an acre and a half of the most unholy-looking territory this side of the Badlands. It stretches across the entire fairway from about 270 to 370 yards out, and men have been known to disappear there for hours. Once across, the golfer must contend with an approach to a peninsula of putting surface that juts out into a huge estuary of sand.

Pine Valley's four par-3s, collectively, are unmatched for variety and splendor. Any one would be a showcase for most courses. Except for No.

5, they provide no safe tee shots except onto the green. The long-iron third hole is surrounded by a sea of sand. The 10th, a 9-iron pitch, features satanic bunkering. The 14th, a middle-iron shot, nestles between forest and lake.

The fifth hole is one of the most dramatic one-shot holes anywhere. One aims over a narrow lake to an open green 226 yards away. The terrain slopes sharply down to the water about 100 yards from the tee, and then the far slope rises to fearsome bunkers 50 yards in front of the green. Forest closes in on all sides. Standing on the tee with a 1-iron or 3-wood can be the loneliest experience imaginable. The hole has no tricks, and even allows a generous margin of error to be short. But one must never be off line.

One of the popular refrains at Pine Valley is that at the fifth, "only God can make a three." The Almighty has company, to be sure, but all of Pine Valley's par-3s have brought good men to their knees. Gene Littler, in a televised match with Byron Nelson, caught one just a little off line at the fifth, watched his ball tumble down the steep ridge at the right of the green, and eventually scrambled for a 7. The 14th was the scene of the most catastrophic shotmaking in Pine Valley's 56-year history. It was there that John Brooks, a low-handicap player, took 44 blows to negotiate its mountainous, jungle-bestrewn, lake-guarded 185 yards, a score that stands as the single-hole record, if you go for that sort of thing.

Pine Valley is not really the demon it is made out to be in these yarns, however. A great course, believes Pinehurst's respected Richard Tufts, should yield to a great round of golf. Scores indicate that Pine Valley is such a course. The record in competition is 67, by club member George Rowbotham, while the four-round mark is 286 (71-69-71-75) by Craig Wood. Nicklaus and Ted Turner, the club's professional before Fazio, have posted 66 in informal rounds when tee and pin positions were at less than maximum severity. But the record shows that no one has ever given Pine Valley's par 70 a battering.

There have been some sensational starts, the most recent made in 1968 by Major Tom Fotheringham, then captain of Great Britain's Royal and Ancient Golfing Society. Forced to start at the short 10th because the course was crowded, the Major put his first shot at Pine Valley straight in the hole. "Of course, you will keep the ball as a memento of this historic ace," a friend sug-

gested afterwards. "Oh dear, no," the Major replied, "I put it in the water at 16."

The best round by a first-time player was 67, by a British naval officer who was warming up for the club's annual Crump Memorial Tournament, named after the late George Crump who created Pine Valley with architectural assistance from English designer H. S. Colt. In the competition next day, he was unable to break 90. The most popular piece of local folklore has J. Wood Platt, a gifted amateur of the Bobby Jones era, opening his round once with 3, 2, 1, 3—two birdies and two eagles—and then repairing to the bar. He failed to emerge to finish the round.

One must play Pine Valley the same way a porcupine courts its mate—very carefully. In a professional tournament, Ed Dudley shot 68 in the first round and followed that with 77 and 85. One player, who scored 79 his first time around, came back the next day with 98. "I was fine until I found out where all the trouble is," he wailed. Bill Campbell, the former national amateur champion and Walker Cup star, tells of his first experience in the Crump tournament. "In one match I scored seven 3s in 10 holes and closed out my match on 13. I thought I really had Pine Valley's number. The next day Bill Hyndman beat me 7 and 5. We walked in from the same place I had won the day before, but if I had finished the round I would have scored in the mid-80s. Pine Valley tests the mind as well as the stroke."

This demand for mental exercise is not the only reason Pine Valley is celebrated. Its quality and character stand as bastions against the "mischievous tendencies" of modern course design that tradition-minded architects warned about years ago. The notion that length and huge greens make for testing golf has spawned a rather dreary assemblage of courses of little distinction, monotonous replicas of one another. If it is true that life rebels at conformity, it is not hard to see why we react with interest and excitement to a golf course that is imaginative, thought-provoking, appealing to the eye and challenging.

A great test of golf should be a little like an honest judge: no bribes accepted. Pine Valley is like that. For all of its lurking danger and uncompromising retribution, it is a course one plays with relish, where pars are collected gratefully and where birdies are small treasures to be hoarded against one's next visit.

2. NORTH AMERICA

america's 100 greatest tests of golf

Which courses are the finest tests of golf in America?

Every two years *Golf Digest* answers this question with the publication of its list of America's 100 Greatest Tests of Golf. This selection involves extensive research and the active participation of 135 amateur and professional golfing experts from every region of the United States.

The newest list of distinguished courses together with the names of the experts who helped select them appears on the following two pages.

The origins of the project go back to 1962 when *Golf Digest* first undertook an exhaustive survey to name America's 200 toughest courses. We had been seriously challenged for the first time to set some standards for "greatness" by Stuart Hammond, president of Hammond Inc., whose specialty is maps. Hammond, an ethusiastic golfer, wanted to produce a map of the best golf courses in the United States. Our list, published in 1966, was based solely on the United States Golf Ass'n Course Rating System, which is primarily based on yardage or distance.

The list of courses was revised in 1967 and again in 1969 when a nationwide panel of golfing experts was asked to cut the list to 100 courses and to superimpose their judgment of America's most testing courses on the USGA rating system.

In 1971 and again in 1973, the panel was asked to further refine the list, adding any new courses that might have been built since 1969, or older courses that previously might have been overlooked. Each of the 135 regional selectors was asked to rate the courses on the basis of the skill of a scratch golfer playing from the tees normally used in formal competition. Each

One of America's greatest tests is Riviera Country Club in Pacific Palisades, Calif. The huge mound guarding the green on the 422-yard fifth is an unusual and imposing barrier, just one of the many unexpected touches created by architect George Thomas.

america's 100 greatest tests of golf

These rankings were done by the editors of *Golf Digest* and a 135-man Selection Panel of professional and amateur golfing experts. The names of the National Selection Board appear below. The names of the regional selectors appear on page 272. The courses are ranked equally in each group and listed alphabetically for convenience only.

NATIONAL SELECTION BOARD
Deane Beman, Bethesda, Md.
P. J. Boatwright, Far Hills, N.J.
Fred Brand Jr., Pittsburgh, Pa.
William Campbell, Huntington, W.Va.
Charles Coe, Oklahoma City, Okla.
John Dawson, Palm Desert, Calif.
Jimmy Demaret, Houston
Joseph C. Dey Jr., New York
Charles Eckstein, Hazel Crest, Ill.
Hord Hardin, St. Louis
William Hyndman III, Huntingdon Valley, Pa.
Robert Kiersky, Delray Beach, Fla.
Byron Nelson, Roanoke, Tex.
Curtis Person Sr., Memphis
John Roberts, Honolulu
Sam Snead, White Sulphur Springs, W.Va.
Richard Tufts, Pinehurst, N.C.

FIRST TEN

	YARDS	PAR	RATING
Augusta Nat'l G.C. Augusta, Ga. (1932)	6,980	72	73.1
Medinah C.C. (#3) Medinah, Ill. (1930)	7,102	71	75.3
Merion G.C. (East) Ardmore, Pa. (1912)	6,498	70	70.2
Oakland Hills C.C. (South) Birmingham, Mich. (1918)	7,088	72	73.7
Oakmont C.C. Oakmont, Pa. (1903)	6,938	72	73.8
Olympic Club (Lake) San Francisco (1924)	6,669	71	73
Pebble Beach G. Links Pebble Beach, Calif. (1919)	6,815	72	75
Pinehurst C.C. (#2) Pinehurst, N.C. (1925)	7,051	72	73
Pine Valley G.C. Clementon, N.J. (1922)	6,765	70	73
Seminole G.C. North Palm Beach, Fla. (1929)	6,898	72	72

SECOND TEN

	YARDS	PAR	RATING
Baltusrol G.C. (Lower) Springfield, N.J. (1922)	7,069	72	73.6
Champions G.C. (Cypress Creek) Houston (1959)	7,166	71	72
Colonial C.C. Fort Worth, Texas (1935)	7,142	70	74
Firestone C.C. (South) Akron, Ohio (1929)	7,180	70	74.4
Harbour Town Links Hilton Head, S.C. (1970)	6,655	71	*
Pine Tree G.C. Delray Beach, Fla. (1962)	7,197	72	74
Riviera C.C. Pacific Palisades, Calif. (1926)	7,022	72	73.5
Shinnecock Hills G.C. Southampton, N.Y. (1931)	6,697	70	72.5
Southern Hills C.C. Tulsa, Okla. (1935)	7,037	71	74
Winged Foot (West) Mamaroneck, N.Y. (1923)	6,956	72	71

	YARDS	PAR	RATING		YARDS	PAR	RATING
Aronimink G.C. Newtown Sq., Pa. (1928)	6,958	70	73.2	C.C. of Birmingham (West) Birmingham, Ala. (1959)	7,000	71	73
Atlanta C.C. Atlanta (1965)	7,053	72	72	C.C. of Detroit Grosse Pt. Farms, Mich. (1914)	6,875	72	72.1
Baltimore C.C. (Five Farms) Baltimore (1921)	6,833	70	72	C.C. of New Seabury (Blue) Mashpee, Mass. (1964)	7,175	72	74
Bethpage G.C. (Black) Farmingdale, N.Y. (1936)	6,873	71	72.7	Crooked Stick G.C. Indianapolis (1964)	7,086	72	73.7
Beverly C.C. Chicago (1907)	6,923	71	73.6	Desert Forest C.C. Carefree, Ariz. (1962)	6,831	72	73.4
Boyne Highlands G.C. Harbor Springs, Mich. (1968)	7,131	72	73.8	Disney World G.C. (Palms) Lake Buena Vista, Fla. (1971)	6,951	72	73
Champions G.C. (Jackrabbit) Houston (1964)	7,121	72	72	Fishers Island C.C. Fishers Island, N.Y. (1916)	6,434	72	71.1
Cherry Hills C.C. Denver (1922)	6,955	71	69.5	Goodyear G.&C.C. (Gold) Phoenix (1965)	7,220	72	74.2
Chicago G.C. Wheaton, Ill. (1892)	6,553	70	71.7	Grandfather G.C. Linville, N.C. (1968)	7,220	72	*
Coldstream C.C. Cincinnati (1960)	7,170	71	72.3	Greenville C.C. (Chanticleer) Greenville, S.C. (1971)	6,815	72	73.8

THIRD TEN

	YARDS	PAR	RATING
Concord G.C. Kiamesha Lake, N.Y. (1963)	7,205	72	76
C.C. of North Carolina Pinehurst, N.C. (1963)	6,973	72	73
Doral C.C. (Blue) Miami, Fla. (1962)	7,028	72	73
The Golf Club New Albany, Ohio (1967)	7,237	72	74.4
Los Angeles C.C. (North) Los Angeles (1911)	6,813	71	73
Jupiter Hills Club Tequesta, Fla. (1970)	7,248	72	75
Oak Hill C.C. (East) Rochester, N.Y. (1926)	6,962	71	73
J D M C.C. (East) (formerly PGA Nat'l) Palm Beach Gardens, Fla. (1962)	7,096	72	74
Point O'Woods G.&C.C. Benton Harbor, Mich. (1958)	6,906	71	73.9
Quaker Ridge G.C. Scarsdale, N.Y. (1916)	6,745	70	72

FOURTH TEN

	YARDS	PAR	RATING
Bay Hill Club Orlando, Fla. (1961)	7,015	72	70.3
Bellerive C.C. Creve Coeur, Mo. (1960)	7,310	71	75.1
Cascades G.C. (Upper) Hot Springs, Va. (1923)	6,895	71	71
Dunes G.&B.C. Myrtle Beach, S.C. (1949)	7,008	72	74
Congressional C.C. Bethesda, Md. (1924)	7,154	72	74
Laurel Valley G.C. Ligonier, Pa. (1960)	7,045	71	74.1
Peachtree G.C. Atlanta (1948)	7,219	72	74.3
Prairie Dunes G.C. Hutchinson, Kan. (1937)	6,522	70	72
Scioto C.C. Columbus, Ohio (1912)	6,822	71	73.4
Spyglass Hill G.C. Pebble Beach, Calif. (1966)	6,810	72	76.1

FIFTH TEN

	YARDS	PAR	RATING
Bob O'Link G.C. Highland Park, Ill. (1916)	6,731	72	72.7
Canterbury G.C. Cleveland (1922)	6,877	72	72.8
Cog Hill G.C. (#4) Lemont, Ill. (1964)	7,224	72	74.7
Innisbrook G.&C.C. (Island) Tarpon Springs, Fla. (1970)	6,965	72	73
Cypress Point Club Pebble Beach, Calif. (1928)	6,464	72	72
Lancaster C.C. Lancaster, Pa. (1920)	6,672	70	71
Mauna Kea G.C. Kamuela, Hawaii (1965)	7,200	72	74
Meadow Brook Club Westbury, N.Y. (1948)	7,101	72	73.8
Saucon Valley C.C. (Grace) Bethlehem, Pa. (1957)	7,044	72	73.5
The Country Club Brookline, Mass. (1927)	6,464	72	72

SECOND FIFTY

	YARDS	PAR	RATING
Hazeltine Nat'l G.C. Chaska, Minn. (1961)	7,151	72	73.9
Hershey C.C. (West) Hershey, Pa. (1930)	6,928	73	74.2
Interlachen C.C. Edina, Minn. (1919)	6,726	73	70.9
International G.C. Bolton, Mass. (1955)	7,255	73	73.5
Inverness Club Toledo, Ohio (1903)	6,815	71	72
Kittansett Club Marion, Mass. (1922)	6,545	71	71.7
La Costa C.C. Rancho La Costa, Calif. (1964)	7,013	72	73
Lakeview C.C. Morgantown, W. Va. (1954)	6,850	72	72
Maidstone G.C. East Hampton, N.Y. (1891)	6,510	72	70
Moselem Springs C.C. Fleetwood, Pa. (1965)	7,003	70	73
Nat'l. Cash Register G.C. (South) Dayton, Ohio (1953)	6,910	71	71.4
North Shore C.C. Glenview, Ill. (1924)	7,009	72	73
Old Warson C.C. Ladue, Mo. (1955)	7,272	71	74.1
Olympia Fields C.C. (North) Ill. (1922)	6,750	71	73.2
Pauma Valley C.C. Pauma Valley, Calif. (1960)	7,003	71	73.5
Plainfield C.C. Plainfield, N.J. (1920)	6,817	72	72.2
Preston Trail G.C. Dallas (1965)	7,113	71	74.1
Princeville G.C. Kauai, Hawaii (1972)	6,948	72	*
Red Fox C.C. Tryon, N.C. (1965)	7,139	72	74.5
Royal Kaanapali G.C. Maui, Hawaii (1962)	7,179	72	75.1
Salem C.C. Peabody, Mass. (1926)	6,796	72	72.1
San Francisco G.C. San Francisco (1915)	6,794	71	*
Sea Island G.C. St. Simons Is., Ga. (1929)	6,692	72	72.1
Stanford Univ. G.C. Stanford, Calif. (1930)	6,782	71	72
Stanwich C.C. Greenwich, Conn. (1963)	7,179	72	74.1
Torrey Pines G.C. (South) La Jolla, Calif. (1957)	7,011	72	73.1
Univ. of N. Mexico G.C. Albuquerque, N.M. (1966)	7,246	72	74.6
Wilmington (Del.) C.C. (South) (1960)	6,912	71	72.7
Winchester C.C. Winchester, Mass. (1902)	6,659	71	71.6
Yale University G.C. New Haven, Conn. (1926)	6,628	70	72.3

Ratings on chart apply to course when played at yardage shown, except where marked by asterisk, indicating that a USGA rating for yardage shown has not been made. The year in parentheses indicates date course was built.

43

course was evaluated as an over-all test of golf and golf shotmaking.

Finally, a national panel of 17 golfing authorities, in collaboration with our editors, considered the results of this poll and made the final ranking of America's 100 Greatest Tests of Golf.

Three of the top 10 courses — Merion, Olympic and Pine Valley — are under 6,800 yards in length, and more than half of the top 50 courses are under 7,000 yards. Golf course architects would do well to note that recognition of a great test of golf depends more on sound and imaginative design than it does on sheer length, particularly in view of rapidly increasing land costs.

The resulting final selection of America's Greatest Tests of Golf is a combination of the best statistical data available and a consensus of expert judgment never before brought to bear on the subject.

Unusual—for Florida—elevations of up to 70 feet are a feature of the Jupiter Hills Club course in Tequesta, Fla. Sand bunkers have been used sparingly by architect George Fazio, but those in evidence have deep lips, as on this 16th hole, a a par-4.

U.S. OPEN COURSES

The United States Open is golf's premier event not only because of the great field of players but also because it is played under conditions that will produce a true champion. Only a golden few courses meet the stringent standards of the United States Golf Ass'n, which annually sponsors and stages this prestigious championship.

The USGA prepares these courses carefully, some even claim sadistically. Fairways are narrowed, rough is deepened and greens are slickened, and sometimes the course does not respond well to the process, as happened at Hazeltine in Minneapolis in 1970. While such new courses gain admittance to the Open fraternity —as will Atlanta Athletic Club in 1976—it is usually temporary, and inevitably the Open returns to the Baltusrols, the Merions and the Oakmonts.

Even the hallowed sites come in for criticism sometimes. Winged Foot, where only two players broke 290 in the 1974 Open was not unexpectedly criticized by several players whose scores soared into the 80s.

"As long as we're satisfied that an Open course is a great test of golf," says P. J. Boatwright, executive director of the USGA, "then we don't worry much about resulting criticism from the players and media. You can get flack from even the finest courses."

Featured in this section are the courses that have hosted the U.S. Open two or more times. Leading the field are Baltusrol and Oakmont with five Opens apiece and Oakland Hills and the ancient Myopia Hunt Club with four apiece. Myopia is no longer in the circle of greatness that the USGA seemingly travels for sites. "It's probably too short by modern standards," Boatwright says. However, in its day, Myopia was a stringent test. In four Opens the best 72-hole score was a fat 314 by Willie Anderson in 1905. The South Hamilton, Mass., course last hosted an Open in 1908 when Freddy McLeod was the winner.

Boatwright says that Merion, which measures a mere 6,498 yards, is one of the few tests under 6,800 yards that would be considered for the Open. "It is unique," he says. "It can test a player's driving ability even at that short length."

A trademark of any Open layout is the rough, especially around the greens, and the putting surfaces themselves. "We want a golfer to be forced into a delicate touch near the green," Boatwright says. "Then, once he's on the green, we want him to think mightily about the putts he'll face. If a green is as fast and firm as we want it, then an average golfer will not be able to handle it at all. The U.S. Open is not for average golfers."
                                                    —*Hubert Mizell*

early open courses

Many clubs whose golf courses contributed greatly to the popularity and prestige of the game in the United States around the turn of the century no longer provide venues for major championships. However, in their day none exceeded their competitive stature. Three of these are the Chicago Golf Club in Wheaton, Ill., the Philadelphia Cricket Club and the Myopia Hunt Club in Hamilton, Mass. Among them they hosted a total of nine of the first 17 U.S. Open Championships.

CHICAGO GOLF CLUB

Charles Blair Macdonald, a Chicagoan who had learned to play and love golf in Scotland where he spent some of his teenage years, organ-

ized the Chicago Golf Club in 1892. He built nine holes at a site four miles south of Wheaton, but soon he and his fellow members felt they needed a new and larger course (the original nine is now part of the Downers Grove Golf Club). A 200-acre farm closer to Wheaton became the site of the new course which Macdonald designed and whose construction he supervised. When completed in 1894, it became the first course in the United States with 18 holes.

In December 1894, Chicago Golf was one of five clubs to organize and sponsor the United States Golf Ass'n. The other founding clubs were The Country Club, Brookline, Mass.; Shinnecock Hills Country Club, Southampton, N.Y.; the New-

The greens at Chicago Golf resemble platforms raised a foot or so above the sand and water hazards as on the par-4 sixth hole (left) and the par-3 10th. They may appear somewhat old-fashioned but present as strong a test of golf as they did in the early U.S. Opens.

Two of the winners at Chicago Golf were English immortal Harry Vardon (left) who won his only U.S. Open crown in 1900 and Johnny McDermott (above), who became in 1911 the first American to win the title.

U.S. OPEN WINNERS

CHICAGO GOLF CLUB,

Year	Winner	Score
1897	Joe Lloyd	162
1900	Harry Vardon	313
1911	John McDermott*	307

*Won playoff with 80 from Mike Brady (82) and George Simpson (85).

MYOPIA HUNT CLUB

Year	Winner	Score
1898	Fred Herd	328
1901	Willie Anderson*	331
1905	Willie Anderson	314
1908	Fred McLeod**	322

*Won playoff with 85 from Alex Smith (86).
**Won playoff with 77 from Willie Smith (83).

PHILADELPHIA CRICKET CLUB

Year	Winner	Score
1907	Alex Ross	302
1910	Alex Smith*	298

*Won playoff with 71 from John McDermott (75) and Macdonald Smith (77).

port (R.I.) Golf Club and the St. Andrews Golf Club, Yonkers, N.Y.

Macdonald laid out the Chicago course as a par-73 at 6,383-yards, long in those days when you had to give a gutta-percha ball a fearsome wallop to send it anywhere near 200 yards. Today the course is 6,553 yards and par has been reduced to 70. Macdonald incorporated into Chicago Golf many features of Scotland's St. Andrews. Most recognizable are the numerous mounds scattered over the fairways. The terrain is gently rolling, and hilly lies are common. Chicago's greens are not as small as one might expect at an older course, and most of the bunkers are set below green level.

Chicago Golf is a sturdy test even today, although it has not hosted a major event since the 1928 Walker Cup Matches. It's USGA course rating is 71.7 and Bobby Jones' 66 in 1928 is still the course record. In a 36-hole U.S. Open qualifying tournament in 1967, the lowest score was four over par.

The first U.S. Open at Chicago Golf in 1897 was won by Joe Lloyd, an English professional. Macdonald went to great lengths to bring this third Open to Chicago (the tournament had been inaugurated in 1895) and no doubt he hoped the western reaches of the United States would produce a winner. This was not to be. Lloyd, who worked at the Essex Country Club, Manchester, Mass., in the summer and at Pau, France, in the winter, scored 162 for two rounds to beat a field of 35.

In 1900, Harry Vardon, the great English professional, stopped his U.S. exhibition tour long enough to win the Open at Chicago Golf. He and his countryman Ted Ray dominated the field, finishing one-two at 313 and 315 (the Open format was changed to 72 holes in 1898). Chicago Golf's third and final appearance as an Open host came in 1911 and it produced a notable champion. Johnny McDermott, a Philadelphian who was then professional at the Atlantic City (N.J.) Country Club, became the first native-born American to win the Open by scoring a 307, tying Mike Brady and George Simpson and then taking the playoff.

PHILADELPHIA CRICKET CLUB

Only nine holes remain of the Philadelphia Cricket Club as it existed when the 1907 and 1910 U.S. Opens were played there. The 18-hole, 5,954-yard, par-73 course situated in the St. Martin's area was known as the Wissahickon Links.

Only two holes remain intact from Philadelphia Cricket's Wissahickon course, where two early U.S. Opens were held. One is the par-4 finishing hole (above) where the original golf shop, the small white structure to the left of the green, has been preserved in mint condition. The large clubhouse was added later.

In 1922 the club opened a new 18-hole course five miles from Wissahickon at Flourtown, but today's members still like to go to the older nine for a romp through the woods and over the streams.

The club actually was founded in 1854 and for years was the center of the city's cricket activities. The original nine holes were not constructed until 1893, but by 1902 nine more had been added. Wissahickon was noted for its natural hazards, nine of the 18 requiring not a single, man-made obstacle of sand or water. The holes stretched over the hills that bordered the Wissahickon Creek valley, and from some points the vista extended for 15 vivid miles. Because of the course's configuration, every hole required a different type of approach shot.

In 1907 Aleck ("Alex") Ross came down from his new job at the Brae Burn Country Club in Boston to win the Open at the Philadelphia Cricket with a 302. Ross was the brother of Donald Ross, the famed golf course architect then at the Pinehurst (N.C.) Country Club. The first hole-in-one ever scored in Open history was made that year by Jack Hobens in the last round on the 147-yard 10th. One of the amateur contenders and a member at Philadelphia was A. W. Tillinghast, who later became a leading golf course architect and was commissioned to design the club's Flourtown course. No one seems to know who laid out the Wissahickon course. Very likely it was a committee of the club's founding members, as was so often the case in those early days.

Willie Anderson, whose four Open Championships between 1901 and 1905 have never been exceeded, was the professional at Philadelphia Cricket in 1910. He tried in Philadelphia's Open that year for a fifth win, but finished 11th. Alex Smith, however, a member of the famous Scot golfing family, won it by defeating his brother Macdonald and John McDermott in a playoff.

MYOPIA HUNT CLUB

The Myopia Hunt Club near Boston sprang from fox hunting, polo, trap shooting, riding plus a healthy interest in lawn tennis. Myopia first surfaced in 1875 when a tennis club by that name was formed in Winchester, Mass. In 1881 fox hunting became popular, and the Myopia Fox Hounds was founded. Finally, on December 16, 1891, the Myopia Hunt Club became official. It was in 1894, however, that the club's first nine golf holes, measuring only 2,050 yards, were laid out by three club members, R. M. Appleton, T. Wattson Merrill and A. P. Gardner.

Myopia Hunt Club's unusual name comes from the fact that the original founders had two things in common—a compelling interest in "sport," particularly hunting, and myopia or what's commonly called nearsightedness. Yes, they all wore glasses. Myopia's first president, Marshall Kittredge Abbott, even wrote that "eyeglasses were a badge of distinction, amounting to a decoration."

In 1896 Herbert C. Leeds, a club member and its best golfer, laid out on another site the nine holes that form the basis for today's course (the first nine holes were eventually abandoned). It was 2,930 yards long and was shortly afterwards altered again. Myopia proved such an outstanding test that despite the fact that it had only nine holes, it was chosen as the site of the 1898 Open. Fred Herd, a Scot professional working in Chicago, went around the nine holes eight times in two days and won with 328. Designer Leeds, incidentally, finished eighth. Another nine had been added at Myopia by 1901 when Willie Anderson won there the first of his four Open titles. He won it there again in 1905 and little Fred McLeod took the last Open held at Myopia in 1908.

Today Myopia is a 6,353-yard, par-72 course with a rating of 71. It is still a site of occasional state and area tournaments; the 1976 Massachusetts State Amateur will be held there. Fairways burrow through thick stands of trees, marching up and down well-defined grades. Fairway mounds are not uncommon and can cause a sidehill lie on a shot right down the middle. The bunkers around the green are low and not so noticeable from the fairways. The small greens call for pin-point approaches.

With each of the nine holes that existed in 1898 still included in the present course, Myopia is the model par excellence of the marriage between a great golfing tradition and sound course-design principles. Surely, despite their spectacles, Myopia's early designers were far-sighted.

—*John P. May*

This is how the Myopia Hunt Club's eighth hole looked in 1900. The Boston area club by then had already played host to one U.S. Open and was to see three more. The last Open held at Myopia was won by Fred McLeod in 1908.

baltusrol

There are two courses at the Baltusrol Golf Club in Springfield, New Jersey, the Upper and Lower. Both were constructed in 1920 under the direction of golf course architect A. W. Tillinghast, a leading practitioner of his trade in the 1920s, whose list of credits includes the Winged Foot courses in Mamaroneck, N.Y.

Baltusrol's history actually dates from 1895, making this eastern club one of the oldest in the nation. That year Louis Keller built a 9-hole course on the rolling Jersey farmland, and he succeeded in securing 30 members willing to pay the $10 annual dues. Soon the course was expanded to 18 holes, and in 1901 Genevieve Hecker won the first USGA tournament held there, the Women's Amateur.

Two U. S. Opens took place at the original course—in 1903 when Willie Anderson won the second of his four Opens, and in 1915 when amateur Jerry Travers took the measure of his professional rivals. In 1904 H. Chandler Egan won the U. S. Amateur and in 1911 Margaret Curtis the Women's Amateur at Baltusrol.

Thus when the members decided to tear up the original course in 1920 to build two championship tests, they displayed a certain measure of dedication to better golf. After all, they already had a course of enough merit to have attracted no less than five USGA championships. Their decision turned out to be a wise one, for since then Baltusrol has hosted six more national championships, including three U.S. Opens. Only one club, the Oakmont (Pa.) Country Club, has entertained as many Opens as Baltusrol's total five.

Both of Baltusrol's courses are worthy tests, and members continually argue over the merits of each. The Upper was first in the limelight in 1936. Heavily wooded, with sharp fairway slopes and undulating greens, the Upper yielded an Open scoring record of 284 to Harry Cooper that year. Harry was unhappy, though, for he had bogeyed three of the last four holes. Sure enough, Tony Manero, not long out of the New York City area caddie ranks, birdied the 439-yard 16th, then parred in for a 67 to win with 282. Despite breaking the Open scoring record, Manero was never again a factor in major tournament play.

The more familiar, gently rolling Lower Course is deceptive, appearing rather open at first glance. But once even the expert golfer starts negotiating it, he finds that unless he positions nearly every tee shot he will come upon trouble. Tee shot target areas are generally flanked by substantial rough and fairway bunkers. Several approaches are blind. Canyon-like sand bunkers guard every green, so approaches must be especially accurate. The large greens are filled with almost imperceptible hollows and crowns that make the shortest putt a tester.

It is not surprising that the Lower Course is listed among "America's 100 Greatest Tests of Golf" by *Golf Digest*.

Two U.S. Opens held at the Lower Course are especially memorable. Its 1954 Open was the first to be televised nationally, and viewers were rewarded with a dramatic finish. Ed Furgol, the golfer with the permanently bent left arm (the result of a childhood accident), came to 18 a stroke ahead. He hooked his drive over tall trees to the left and his way to the green was blocked. But Furgol played down the Upper Course's 18th fairway and managed his par-5. Gene Littler subsequently missed an eight-foot birdie putt on 18 that would have given him a tie.

In 1967 Jack Nicklaus set a new Open scoring record of 275 by crushing Baltusrol with a concluding 65. He won by four strokes. The old record, 276, had been set by Ben Hogan in 1948. An amateur (now a professional), Marty Fleckman, led after the first and third rounds but succumbed to a concluding 80 and finished 18th. Nicklaus pulled ahead with birdies on five of the six holes from three through eight and went out in 31. Then little-known Lee Trevino finished fifth.

Baltusrol's 623-yard 17th is the longest par-5 hole in the history of the U. S. Open. The tee shot threads a narrow tunnel through tall trees. The second must carry a series of bunkers that stretches across the fairway 300 yards from the tee. Big bunkers guard the elevated green, 95 five feet deep and 40 feet wide. The best par-3 is the 194-yard fourth, which calls for a tee shot entirely across water. A rock escarpment drops from the surface of the green to the water.

—*John P. May*

	U.S. OPEN WINNERS			BALTUSROL SCORECARD*					
Year	Winner	Score	Hole	Par	Yards	Hole	Par	Yards
1903*	Willie Anderson	307	1	5	479	10	4	448
1915*	Jerry Travers	297	2	4	379	11	4	436
1936**	Tony Manero	282	3	4	432	12	3	192
1954	Ed Furgol	284	4	3	196	13	4	394
1967	Jack Nicklaus	275	5	4	384	14	4	409
			6	4	462	15	4	427
			7	5	490	16	3	206
			8	4	365	17	5	619
			9	3	206	18	5	545
				36	3,393		36	3,676

*Original course.
**Upper course.
All others Lower course.

Totals: Par 72, Yards 7,069.
*In U.S. Open play, the first and seventh holes are played as par-4s, reducing total par to 70. Total yardage lowered also.

The blue-blooded membership of Baltusrol has watched from the stately clubhouse as generations of great players have split blood of an entirely different hue on the battleground of its famed Lower Course, whose 18th green (above) climaxes one of A. W. Tillinghast's great tests of golf.

oakmont

If a vote were taken on which are the scariest greens in America, the winners surely would be the 18 storied putting surfaces at Oakmont.

These greens invariably have been a decisive factor in the outcome of the 11 past national championships held at Oakmont (Pa.) Country Club.

The last of these, the 1973 U.S. Open, was perhaps the rare exception. Rains drenched the course, turning the diamond-hard greens into cream puffs that were, as Tom Weiskopf remarked, "like shooting darts . . . you threw the ball at the flag, knowing it would stick."

That was Oakmont's fifth Open. Baltusrol Golf Club, Springfield, N.J., is the only other course to host as many. Oakmont also has been the site of two PGA Championships and four U.S. Amateur tournaments. In staging more national championships than any other course in America, Oakmont's list of winners reads like a Hall of Fame roster. Just about all of them, including Gene Sarazen, Bobby Jones, Sam Snead, Tommy Armour, Ben Hogan and Jack Nicklaus, have come away shaking their heads over the problems posed by Oakmont's greens.

The tiny greens and tricky rolls of Merion, the slick, wind-baked surfaces of Pebble Beach pale before the terrors of Oakmont's greens. With few exceptions, they are large. From a distance they appear rather flat and plain, almost innocent. This is a deception. Oakmont's greens are like polished glass and contain more rolls per square foot than Sara Lee. They are dynamite.

"This is a course where good putters worry about their second putt before they hit the first one," observes Lew Worsham, the pro there for the past 27 years.

The full horror of these greens is not merely that they place an undue premium on putting. But rather, after negotiating difficult driving problems or recovering bravely from clutching lies off the fairways, a player must execute near-perfect approach shots to score well. Hogan astutely put his finger on this after winning the 1953 U.S. Open.

"The problem at Oakmont is not just getting on the green. It's getting in the right position on the best side. If you land on the wrong side of the green there is no way to attack the hole," he said.

Depending on where the flagstick is cut, there may be no more than one or two favored landing positions on a green from which players can putt with confidence along a reasonably level line. Putts from any other position might traverse as many as a dozen subtle, darting contours.

In the 1973 Open, weather conditions were uncharacteristically favorable to low scoring, and allowed Johnny Miller to record the greatest single round in U.S. Open history, an incredible 63. Like never before, the Open scoreboard ran blood red with under-par figures. The mightiest names in golf — Jack Nicklaus, Arnold Palmer and Lee Trevino — all beat the previous record at Oakmont by one stroke, tying at 282. Both Weiskopf and John Schlee scored even lower, but Miller fairly scorched the soggy course. He birdied exactly half the holes during his final, superlative round, the principal feature of which was a string of approach shots flung boldly at the flagstick which stuck like tar on hot cement. Even then, only nine men bettered par and Miller was only five under par in winning the tournament.

In the 1927 Open, Oakmont's first, the legendary Tommy Armour stood on the 18th fairway waiting to play his second shot. An Oakmont member emerged from the gallery and taunted, "I've been reading that you're a great iron player. Let's see you hit one now." The Silver Scot's enormous hands encircled a 3-iron, he swung and the ball rocketed homeward. His shot covered the flag and finally stopped 10 feet from the cup. Armour would sink his birdie putt to tie Harry Cooper, and then beat Cooper in the playoff. Turning to the spectator, Armour politely asked, "Will that do?" The man glanced toward the green to check the ball's position, then grudgingly replied, "Yes, but just."

When Nicklaus won the 1962 Open in a playoff with Palmer after they tied Hogan's Oakmont record of 283, it was said that Nicklaus won with his putting. He had only one three-putt green in five rounds; Palmer had 12. Largely overlooked was the fact that Nicklaus established his superiority because he played better approach shots to the favored spots on the greens.

In spite of the almost infinite variety of rolls, Oakmont's greens are eminently fair because they contain no grain. They putt absolutely true.

U.S. OPEN WINNERS			OAKMONT SCORECARD*					
Year	Winner	Score	Hole	Par	Yards	Hole	Par	Yards
1927	Tommy Armour	301	1	5	469	10	4	462
1935	Sam Parks	299	2	4	343	11	4	371
1953	Ben Hogan	283	3	4	425	12	5	603
1962	Jack Nicklaus	283	4	5	549	13	3	185
1973	Johnny Miller	279	5	4	379	14	4	360
			6	3	201	15	4	453
PGA CHAMPIONSHIP WINNERS			7	4	305	16	3	230
1922	Gene Sarazen	4 & 3	8	3	255	17	4	322
	d. E. French		9	5	480	18	4	456
1951	Sam Snead	7 & 6		—	—		—	—
	d. W. Burkemo			37	3,496		35	3,442

Totals: Par 72, Yards 6,938.
*For the U.S. Open and other major championships the first hole is played as a par-4, reducing total par to 71; total yardage reduced to 6,921.

Huge, undulating greens, among the slipperiest in the world, have terrorized generations of golfers at Oakmont. The ninth green (above) is one of the largest in the world at 20,500 square feet. The back portion is used as a putting clock. A competitor hitting there gets a free drop if a practice cup interferes with his line. The four flagsticks on the green indicate championship cup locations.

The problems are to correctly read the contours and then, with the nerve and touch of a jewel thief, to stroke the ball with just the right speed.

This frequently can be exasperating, as for example at the short, par-4 second hole. Its tiny, lightning-fast green slopes so sharply from back to front that William C. Fownes, who designed the course in 1903, once dropped a ball on the back of the green and watched it roll completely off the front. Snead claims this green is so treacherous that when he marked his ball with a dime even the coin slid downhill.

The famous Church Pew bunkers of Oakmont, formed by large grassy ridges interspersed with narrow bands of sand on the third (above) and 15th holes, both long par-4s, have beleaguered golfers for decades.

Fownes, who was good enough to win the U.S. Amateur title in 1910, traveled to Great Britain to study its golf courses so he could build a facsimile in the farmland of western Pennsylvania. He wanted a links-style course, with no trees, strong bunkering and swift, rolling greens. Oakmont has no water holes.

The course has undergone change, though. Gone forever are the famous furrowed bunkers, the deep, V-shaped gouges that drove many strong men to the spacious bar just inside Oakmont's rambling green and white frame clubhouse. No longer will players face the indignity of Englishman Ted Ray who, when he lost a ball in one of Fownes' furrows, was informed by a spectator that he could find it in row seven.

About 50 of Oakmont's 187 bunkers were repositioned in 1962 to bring them into play for the modern power hitters. Trees planted over a decade ago that were not a factor in the 1962 championship are now larger and beginning to come into play. The course played at par-71, 6,921 yards for the 1973 Open.

In the excitement of the 18-hole playoff in 1962, a medal affair, Nicklaus suffered an uncharacteristic mental lapse. He forgot to hole out on the 18th green. Palmer had missed a putt, giving him 74, then picked up Jack's ball and pitched it to him, conceding Nicklaus a 71 and the match.

The crowd swarmed onto the green, engulfing them and sweeping them into the scorers' tent along with marshals, caddies and all. An alert official noticed Nicklaus' oversight, however, and rushed to tell Joe Dey, then executive director of the USGA.

"Jack has not yet holed out his final putt," the official reported.

Dey received this news with disbelief, looked coldly at the messenger for a moment and then strode resolutely to the green with Nicklaus in tow, clearing the gallery as he went. He carefully ascertained the approximate position of Nicklaus' putt, 30 inches from the hole, and placed Jack's ball there. Nicklaus studied the line momentarily, then holed the putt.

If he had not, a technical question might have been raised later, even though it could be construed that Palmer conceded the match when he tossed away Nicklaus' ball.

Which is another way of saying that almost anything can happen on the greens at Oakmont.

— Cal Brown

Merion, in Ardmore, Pa., just outside Philadelphia on the Main Line, is, perhaps, the classic American golf course. It is neither spectacular nor long but has stood the test of time and the game's greatest players as well as any course.

The United States Golf Ass'n has selected Merion's East Course as the venue of 14 competitive events more than any other course. But the sheer volume of major tournaments there is not nearly as impressive as the magnitude of some of the individual achievements.

Merion is where Bobby Jones first competed in a national tournament, when he was only 14; where he won the first of his five U. S. Amateur titles, and where he climaxed his Grand Slam in 1930. Merion is where Ben Hogan attained his most memorable victory, struggling through 90 holes in four days in the Open in 1950, the year after his ghastly automobile crash. And Merion is where, 10 years later in the World Amateur Team Championship, a 20-year-old Jack Nicklaus slapped together perhaps the finest four-round score ever, a shocking 269 that is the course record.

No tournament site in recent years has engendered so much lively controversy as Merion leading up to the 1971 Open. Could Nicklaus approach his record score? How could he have scored 18 shots better than Hogan at Merion? Can this kind of short, imaginatively designed course (6,498 yards, par 70) survive as a championship test?

Well, not only did the 1971 field fail to break the Open record of 275—it failed to beat par. Nicklaus and Trevino, co-holders of that record, tied at par-280, then Trevino shot 68 to Nicklaus' 71 in the playoff. Merion proved again that a championship course today need not be 12 miles long, have greens the size of football fields, and be built to fit between the streets of a real estate development.

Roone Arledge, the president of ABC Sports, which televised play, made the point that while somewhat fewer spectators can be accommodated on an older Open course like Merion, millions are exposed to the event in tradition-soaked surroundings on television. The USGA is not likely to wait 21 years to ask Merion to host another Open.

The greens gave golf's best players torment in 1971, just as they have in every major event at Merion. Hogan's most vivid recollection of the '50 Open is the speed of the parched greens. He told Jim Trinkle, in an interview for an Open program, that the greens in '50 wouldn't hold at all if you were shooting from the rough. They were so slick to putt that he would never sole his putter because he knew the ball would roll if he did. Every four-footer was a moment of truth.

Hogan has done nothing monumental on the 11th hole at Merion, but almost everyone else has. A monument near the tee proclaims that on the 11th, in the 1930 U.S. Amateur, Bobby Jones closed out—perhaps a stronger verb is called for—Eugene Homans 8 and 7 to consummate the Grand Slam. On the 11th in the 1934 Open, Bobby Cruickshank, ecstatic after his second shot on the 370-yard hole bounded off a rock in Baffling Brook and onto the green, heaved his club high in the air, shouted, "Thank God!"—and was struck on the head by the club when it came down.

The 11th, a picturesque little drive-and-pitch hole, falling off into a spectacularly flowered and wooded setting, has concealed fangs. The landing area for the drive is not visible from the tee, is tighter than it appears, and bristles with trees and several of Merion's 140 bunkers—the famed "White Faces of Merion," sparkling in sharp relief against the bright green of the summer grass.

The green to which the pitch must be hit is narrow and shielded on three sides by the brook and its stone embankment, and on the fourth by a deep, sprawling bunker. Anything less than a perfectly struck shot will not hold. This green, like others at Merion, offers pin-placement possibilities in nooks and crannies that would raise goose-bumps on a riverboat gambler.

The phrase "great finishing holes" is one of the most overworked in golf, but there is no better way to characterize the last three holes, "The Quarry Holes," at Merion. The 16th and 18th, as rugged as the 11th is pastoral, are long par-4s that could have been lifted right out of Pine Valley; the second shot on the elevated 16th and the drive on the 18th cross a desolate old quarry, and that last drive must carry 225 yards to the fairway.

Recalling his inspired par on the 18th that got

him into the playoff for the 1950 Open Championship, Hogan says, "You had to go all out with a driver, then hit all you had to the green." Hogan, for his second, hit the most renowned 1-iron in history onto the roller-coaster green.

Those are the outstanding holes on a course that has no forgettable ones. Not that unforgettability is the ultimate measure of a championship course. Some qualified observers, Julius Boros reputedly among them, say Merion is not a championship course because it is too short and has too many easy holes.

Frank Hannigan, of the USGA, raises a persuasive point about the generally-accepted relationship between scoring and course quality. "You might see some great scores here," he said, "but it's still a great course. The number of strokes taken is not necessarily the best test. This course requires every type of golf shot. If the greens are firm and fast, the scores will probably be high. If the greens are soggy, the scores could be very low. But that doesn't demean the course. The thing is, did the best player that week finish first? Just because a course is 7,000 yards long, it's not great."

One thing about it—Merion cannot be lengthened. It will have to live or die on its present merits, because it is built on only 126 acres, about 75 fewer than some modern courses. Virtually every available inch is put to good use. Out-of-bounds comes into play on 10 holes and is usually in somebody's back yard. From the seventh green to the eighth tee it is four paces. The course is laid out along the two arms of a "V" and bordered by stately stone homes, a main thoroughfare that has to be shut down during tournaments, and a trolley track. Only 14,000

fans were admitted to watch the 1971 Open, and one wondered where half of them were going to go to avoid stepping on the other half. In an area no larger than a basketball court, hard by the clubhouse, are the first tee (it comes smack out of the bar), 18th green, practice putting green and 14th tee. And crowds following players from the nearby 13th green to the 14th tee must cross the first tee.

Let us hope that Merion, congestion and all, will go on as both a shrine and a fine test of golf, where what a few cannot see in person, millions can enjoy on TV. Occasionally, slowness to change is refreshing. One takes away from Merion—as surely as he leaves with vivid memories of every hole on the course—fond recollections of an illustrious past. A trolley still runs regularly alongside the course, in full view of golfers. The atmosphere in the small frame clubhouse with its mammoth fireplace remains constantly comfortable. The flagsticks are still topped not by flags but by traditional wicker baskets, a tribute to the Scottish shepherd said to have invented the game on his noon hour when he fashioned a makeshift club and ball and fired at his staff, on top of which he had placed his lunch basket.

Merion preserves its traditions despite almost any inconvenience. Workers at the course originally made the baskets, but later did not have time. Then a basketmaker downtown in Ardmore built them, but died. Then a Philadelphia company made them, but went out of business. A new batch, the first from the latest supplier, arrived at Merion not long ago. Stamped on the bottom of each wicker basket were the words "MADE IN HONG KONG."   —Nick Seitz

U.S. OPEN WINNERS		
Year	Winner	Score
1934	Olin Dutra	293
1950	Ben Hogan*	287-69
1971	Lee Trevino**	280-68

*Won playoff with Lloyd Mangrum, 287-73, and George Fazio, 287-75.
**Won playoff with Jack Nicklaus, 280-71.

MERION (EAST) SCORECARD					
Hole	Par	Yards	Hole	Par	Yards
1	4	355	10	4	312
2	5	535	11	4	370
3	3	183	12	4	375
4	5	600	13	3	129
5	4	426	14	4	414
6	4	420	15	4	378
7	4	350	16	4	430
8	4	360	17	3	224
9	3	179	18	4	458
	36	3,408		34	3,090

Totals: Par 70, Yards 6,498.

Relatively short, but testing holes abound at the fabled Merion Golf Club in Ardmore, Pa., the work of amateur course designer Hugh Wilson. One is the pictured 11th, a 370-yard gem. The approach must avoid the creek that crosses the fairway and skirts the right side of the green.

A common topic of conversation, if not controversy, among the 450 members of the Winged Foot Golf Club in Mamaroneck, N.Y., had been which of its two courses is the best—East or West. That is, until the 1974 U.S. Open when the West Course so thoroughly humbled the world's best golfers. Further comparison has become simply an exercise in pride. Only two players, including winner Hale Irwin, broke 290. Irwin won with a 287.

Both courses are products of golf course architect Albert W. Tillinghast, who created them in 1923 after moving 7,200 tons of rock and cutting down 7,800 trees to make way for the fairways. Both are situated on gently rolling terrain, are well treed, steeply bunkered and feature rolling greens of varying shapes and sizes. Another common attribute is that both are pictures of painstaking grooming, with velvet fairways and soft silk greens.

Among the better golfers at Winged Foot, there is really little doubt as to which is the tougher to score upon. The differences have long been perceptible to the United States Golf Ass'n, which has selected the West Course for three of its men's Open Championships, including 1974, while selecting the East Course for two of its Women's Opens.

Indeed, the East is more scenic, with stronger par-5s and large ponds coming into play on two holes. Yet, at only 250 yards longer from the back tees, the qualities that make the West the tougher test are a fascinating commentary on golf course design. Just as great artists sometimes produce one good painting and another which is brilliant, so it was with Tillinghast. His East is obviously good. His West is less obviously brilliant.

The West Course is a great driving course—and more. It demands controlled length off the tee, then icy-nerved second shots to greens which are elevated and mounded with many steep-faced guardian bunkers.

The first six holes give Winged Foot West a certain pentameter, a challenging change-up that lets you know you're playing a golf course requiring not only power but accuracy and restraint. Perhaps the key to its greatness is the same as any work of art. It seems to get better the more you get to know it. The mark of an ordinary golf course is that as you get to know it, it gets easier. Winged Foot West smoothly converts from a normal par 72 from the championship tees to a U.S. Open par of 70 by converting two par-5s to par-4s.

Perhaps the toughest par-4, when the fairways are narrowed, is the 449-yard 17th. The tee shot must hug the left-hand side of the fairway to avoid three very large bunkers at the right corner of the dogleg. That leaves a long iron to a narrow green, with two huge bunkers on either side.

Winged Foot was securely placed in the history books of the game in 1929, when Bobby Jones won the U.S. Open on its West Course. Jones had what seemed to be a reasonably safe three-stroke lead going into the last round. But his game faltered so badly he had to make a curving 12-foot putt on the 72nd green to tie Al Espinosa. He had shot an embarrassing 79. In the playoff, 36 hole in those days, Jones redeemed himself by beating Espinosa by 23 strokes (141-164).

The second Open held at Winged Foot was won by Billy Casper in 1959. Casper revealed an exciting kind of game by beating Winged Foot and his personal rivals with an amazing display of sand play and putting. He used a total of only 114 strokes on the greens (an average of 28.5 per round).

The East Course, admired by so many of its members, also has helped make golfing history. It was here at the 1957 U.S. Women's Open that Jackie Pung of Hawaii had apparently won by a stroke when officials discovered she had signed a card with an incorrect score for one of the holes. Officials and club members so sympathized with her plight that they raised $3,000 and presented it to her as a gift.

While the West Course was given a small stretching for the 1974 Men's U.S. Open, the East Course had to be shortened somewhat for the 1972 Women's Open. It simply plays too long for the ladies. Here perhaps the toughest par-3 on both courses came into play on the final round—the 200-yard 17th whose narrow elevated green has no bunkers. Susie Berning birdied the hole and won by a single shot at the same score of 299 that officially won in 1957.

—*William H. Davis*

	U.S. OPEN WINNERS	
Year	Winner	Score
1929	Bobby Jones*	294
1959	Billy Casper	282
1974	Hale Irwin	287

*Won 36-hole playoff from Al Espinosa, 141-164.

WINGED FOOT (WEST) SCORECARD*

Hole	Par	Yards	Hole	Par	Yards
1	4	446	10	3	190
2	4	411	11	4	386
3	3	216	12	5	535
4	4	453	13	3	212
5	5	515	14	4	418
6	4	324	15	4	417
7	3	166	16	5	457
8	4	442	17	4	449
9	5	471	18	4	448
	36	3,444		36	3,512

Totals: Par 72, Yards 6,956.

*In U.S. Open play, both the ninth and 16th holes play as par-4s, reducing total par to 70.

At Winged Foot West, long par-4s are a common and demanding characteristic. From the new blue tee of the fourth hole you look 453-460 yards down a dogleg left to the green. At this great course nothing is spectacular, just decorous and beautifully proportioned.

Perched on a gradually rising slope next to Lake Merced and a puff of wind away from the Pacific Ocean, the Lake Course of the private Olympic Club in San Francisco affords precious few level lies. Nearly every one of the canted fairways tunnels through groves of eucalyptus, cypress and cedar trees, making tee shots especially hazardous. The generally damp weather gives the Italian-rye-grass rough ample opportunity to grow. When it's not cut short, getting the ball back into play is difficult.

Although the greens are guarded by deep sand hazards, there is only one fairway trap on the entire course. It is set in the driving area of the 435-yard sixth and reduces the target to a skinny 25 yards. With so many trees providing natural hazards, Sam Whiting, the Olympic architect, obviously saw no reason to create more— so there are no water hazards at all on the Lake Course.

The greens are small, averaging only 5,000 square feet in size, a fact that makes the short game especially important at this course. High, soft approach shots are demanded.

There are two courses at the Olympic Club, an outgrowth of a city club of the same name founded in 1860. The Lake, described here, is the championship test of the two, having hosted two U. S. Opens and a U. S. Amateur. It is listed in the first 10 of "America's 100 Greatest Tests of Golf" by *Golf Digest*. The Lake and the Ocean courses were both built in 1924. While shorter, the Ocean is an enjoyable and tricky layout and, being closer to the water, is subjected to some stiff winds from time to time.

Both Opens held at the Lake were memorable for major upsets in the last round. In 1955 Ben Hogan was seeking a record fifth Open victory and seemed to have it in hand when he finished at 287. The only man with a chance to catch him was an obscure club professional, Jack Fleck, who needed one birdie and four pars on the last five holes to tie. Fleck, who had not before and seldom since contended in a major professional tournament, bogeyed 14 and now needed two birdies. That's exactly what he got, sinking the tying putt from seven feet on 18. Fleck was never behind in the playoff, which he won 69-72.

In 1966 another great golfer, Arnold Palmer, also appeared to have won the Open championship. Palmer had begun the fourth round three shots ahead of Billy Casper in second, and after nine holes was a seemingly insurmountable seven in the van. But Casper charged in with a 32 to Palmer's fading 39 for a tie at 278. In the playoff Palmer again raced to a first-nine lead, 33-35, and once more faltered. Casper won the playoff, 69-73.

Charlie Coe of Oklahoma City, Okla., won the lone U.S. Amateur played at Olympic, beating Tommy Aaron, now a professional, 5 and 4 in the finals.

The longest hole at the Lake Course is the 600-yard 16th. It is a dogleg-left lined nearly all of the way with those big trees. The second shot must avoid a large tree which intrudes into the fairway from the left. The green, the largest on the course, offers only a small opening between two bunkers. In the fourth round of the 1966 Open, Palmer drove into the rough on the left, moved a 3-iron only 75 yards, chipped out with a 9-iron and then whacked a wood into a bunker by the green. Casper hit two down the middle, a third 12 feet from the hole. He birdied and gained two shots on Palmer, who bogeyed.

The 490-yard 17th is a long-playing par-5, uphill all the way and usually into the wind. The fairway slopes to the right, so the second shot is often from a hanging lie. The 18th is an exceedingly short par-4 at 330 yards, but it's contentious. The fairway runs downhill from the tee, then sharply uphill. In major events the rough is allowed to grow in from the side, leaving only a 25-yard-wide landing area for the tee shot. The green is quite small, only 32 feet at its widest point.

In the 1955 Open playoff Hogan, a shot behind and striving for an advantage, swung a driver off the 18th tee. In other rounds he had used a 3-wood for accuracy and it worked. This time he hooked into the deep rough, took three shots to get out, and lost. There perhaps is no great golf course in the world that more viciously penalizes inaccuracy.
—*John P. May*

Tall pines and eucalyptus line most of the fairways at the Olympic Club's Lake Course in San Francisco. Pictured above is the 130-yard eighth, at left the 150-yard 15th, both relatively short par-3s but unforgiving of errors.

OLYMPIC (LAKE) SCORECARD*

Hole	Par	Yards	Hole	Par	Yards
1	5	525	10	4	405
2	4	400	11	4	425
3	3	216	12	4	380
4	4	420	13	3	188
5	4	455	14	4	412
6	4	435	15	3	150
7	4	285	16	5	600
8	3	130	17	5	490
9	4	423	18	4	330
	35	3,289		36	3,380

Totals: Par 71, Yards 6,669.
*U.S. Open yardage 6,719; total par becomes 70 by reducing the 17th hole to par-4.

U.S. OPEN WINNERS

Year	Winner	Score
1955	Jack Fleck*	287
1966	Billy Casper**	278

*Won playoff with Ben Hogan, 69-72.
**Won playoff with Arnold Palmer, 69-73.

Donald Ross and Dr. John R. Williams Sr. are the architects behind the splendid Oak Hill Country Club courses in Rochester, N.Y. Ross, America's nonpareil course architect of the early 1900s, designed both the East and West courses, which were opened for play in 1926 and 1925, respectively. Dr. Williams, an Oak Hill member when the courses were opened, is responsible for the thousands of oaks and other trees that grace the parkland courses.

The East, site of two U.S. Open Championships, is the better known of the two courses and is one of "America's 100 Greatest Tests of Golf" as designated by *Golf Digest.* Ross, a gentle Scotsman who came to the United States as a golf professional in 1899, soon became immersed in architecture and eventually designed some 600 courses. His trademark was a certain subtlety of design that requires finesse at every turn. Ross' natural style seems to manifest itself in the approach shot, into which he built quietly imposing challenges.

Oak Hill East is a relatively level course with wider-than-average fairways—wider than most Open courses, at any rate—and medium greens with no grain or severe undulations. The innumerable trees form the sternest hazards. They line every fairway, loom at dogleg corners, cluster near tees and greens, and, not coincidentally, lend immense beauty to the course.

When Oak Hill opened in the mid-20s, there were only a few trees on the grounds. Then Dr. Williams became chairman of the landscape committee. He took his position seriously, and soon discovered that the most successful tree in western New York State had always been the oak. Thus the strain became the dominant element in Oak Hill's long-range landscaping plan, although Dr. Williams also planted more glamorous types such as tulip trees, Chinese rain trees and Lemoine crab apples.

With Ross' design and Williams' trees, Oak Hill East does not easily brook aggressive shots. A creek affects play on eight holes, and flirting with it can be dangerous. Bold tee shots can drive through some fairways. The entrances to many greens are narrowed by bunkers and mounds, inhibiting run-ons from great distances.

Oak Hill's West course, 300 yards shorter than the East, plays about one to two shots easier than its bigger brother. There is no creek to contend with, and there are fewer trees. It is as enjoyable to play as the East, however, and enough of a test to be the host of many district tournaments.

The first United States Golf Ass'n tournament held at Oak Hill was the 1949 U. S. Amateur, in which Charles Coe buried Rufus King, 11 and 10, in the finals. Oak Hill became better known in 1956 when the U. S. Open was held on the East course. Before play started, Ben Hogan commented that the course was not tough enough for an Open, what with its wide fairways and shallow rough. But the scores belied Hogan's judgment, and Cary Middlecoff won with a one-over-par 281. He had to come out of 18's rough and sink a four-footer for his par in the last round. Hogan, as it happened, missed a 30-inch putt on 17 and finished a shot behind Middlecoff, tied with Julius Boros. Ted Kroll, needing four pars to win, went five over par on the last four.

In 1968 Lee Trevino, making his first major step toward stardom, won the Open at Oak Hill with a record-tying score of 275. In shooting 69-68-69-69 he became the first player in Open history to score all four regulation rounds under 70. Bert Yancey had led after 54 holes with an Open record count of 205, but faded to a 76 and out of contention. Jack Nicklaus finished a distant second at 279, despite a closing 65.

Many golfers consider the East's 440-yard, par-4 sixth the most demanding of Oak Hill's 36 holes. The creek maneuvers down the right side of the dogleg-right fairway, edges across in front of the green and continues along the left side of the putting surface. The drive should be left of center, leaving a lengthy iron to the sloping, bunkered green. The 449-yard 18th demonstrates typical Ross subtlety, with a valley 90-100 yards in front of the green that makes the approach seem deceptively shorter than it is.

—*John P. May*

A bothersome creek wanders along the left side of the fairway on the 440-yard sixth hole at Oak Hill Country Club in Rochester, N.Y., then crosses in front of the green. Groves of trees line nearly all the fairways at this regal Eastern course.

U.S. OPEN WINNERS

Year	Winner	Score
1956	Cary Middlecoff	281
1968	Lee Trevino	275

OAK HILL (EAST) SCORECARD*

Hole	Par	Yards	Hole	Par	Yards
1	4	445	10	4	420
2	4	390	11	3	192
3	3	208	12	4	380
4	5	571	13	5	602
5	3	180	14	4	327
6	4	440	15	3	163
7	4	443	16	4	441
8	4	432	17	5	463
9	4	428	18	4	449
	35	3,537		36	3,437

Totals: Par 71, Yards 6,974.

*U.S. Open yardage 6,962; total par becomes 70 by lowering the 17th hole to a par-4.

inverness

Ranking high on Donald Ross' list of personal triumphs is the Inverness Club in Toledo, Ohio, a three-time site of the U.S. Open and host to the 1973 U.S. Amateur Championship.

It is a beautiful course on rolling terrain of rich, loamy soil, graced by avenues of evergreens and clusters of hardwoods. Two brooks contribute water hazards and 110 sand traps serve to catch erring long drives or to protect the greens. These are true, fast and undulating, making flat putts a rarity. Most of the greens have elevated levels which present sharp rises or high lips to the guardian bunkers and demand adroit approaches.

The original course was built as a nine-hole layout in 1903, but it received its championship character when it was redesigned in 1919, making it strategically difficult but fair.

Inverness has a number of holes that have been extolled over the years in the golfing world. The 433-yard fifth hole is an exacting par-4 with only natural hazards and no sand traps. The tee on high ground presents the golfer with solid trees on the left and a winding brook that threads across the valley. The green lies upon a natural high promontory which falls away into trouble on each side.

Inverness became the scene of the 1920 U. S. Open Championship tournament, which was won by hard-hitting Britisher Ted Ray. During the play Jock Hutchinson established a course record of 69, which stood unbroken until the next Open at Inverness in 1931.

As part of the 1920 Open, Inverness, in a gesture of recognition and respect, initiated a new era of hospitality for golf players by opening for the first time anywhere its clubhouse to the golf professionals. The pros attending this tournament were elated. To show their appreciation they took up a collection and presented a huge cathedral chime clock to Inverness Club on the final day of the tournament. The clock is in the main lobby bearing this tablet:

"God measures men by what they are
Not what they in wealth possess.
This vibrant message chimes afar
The voice of Inverness"

In the succeeding years a number of improvements were made to the Inverness course lead-ing to it again being chosen for Open competition. The greens on Nos. 2, 13, 16 and 17 were placed on a higher golfing plane, and a number of holes were lengthened to give the par-71 course 6,529 yards.

The 1931 Open was the longest and one of the most thrilling tournaments in golf history. Billy Burke and George Von Elm tied at 292 over the regulation 72 holes, tied again after a 36-hole playoff, so a grueling second 36-hole test was required. After 144 holes Burke prevailed by one stroke.

In 1957 Inverness was for the third time the scene of the U.S. Open. The course was lengthened to play at 6,919 yards and refined through replacement of fairway bunkers more nearly defining the limits of the longer drives. Several traps were added to hug the forepart of four greens, the second, eighth, ninth and 12th holes, for added challenge.

High points in the fairways of the fifth and eighth holes were cut down to give clear visibility of pin placements from normal approaching zones. A special tee was added to the long ninth hole to shorten it to 466 yards and play as a par-4, lowering the total par to 70.

In the 1957 tournament at the end of the regular 72 holes of championship play, Dick Mayer and Cary Middlecoff were tied with scores of two over par. In the next day's playoff, Dick Mayer was the winner with 72.

Perhaps the most challenging Inverness hole is the 433-yard fifth. The view from the highly elevated tee is appalling as the golfer looks down on a solid phalanx of long-leaf pines lining the left of a fairway that doglegs right. Scattered hardwoods and a winding brook hem in that side. The elevated green was recently enlarged and has a partially humped, sloping surface that makes three putts a distinct possibility.

The 330-yard 18th presents birdie opportunities, but it can wreck a score. It's the approach that causes heartbreak. The squarish green is fronted by two huge sand bunkers which mount steeply toward a putting surface that does not include a flat-putt pin position. Two more bunkers are sunk to the left, and on the right is a depression that welcomes off-line shots.

—*Carl G. Staelin*

U.S. OPEN WINNERS		
Year	Winner	Score
1920	Ted Ray	295
1931	Billy Burke*	292
1957	Dick Mayer**	282

*Won scheduled 36-hole playoff that went 72 holes, scoring 149-148, from George Von Elm, 149-149.

**Won playoff with Cary Middlecoff, 72-79.

INVERNESS SCORECARD*					
Hole	Par	Yards	Hole	Par	Yards
1	4	393	10	4	368
2	4	389	11	4	380
3	3	168	12	5	521
4	4	467	13	3	167
5	4	433	14	4	450
6	4	383	15	4	463
7	4	334	16	4	412
8	3	212	17	4	452
9	5	493	18	4	330
	35	3,272		36	3,543

Totals: Par 71, Yards 6,815.

*In some major tournaments par is reduced to 70 and yardage increased to as high as 6,919.

Low ridges and bunkers make tee shot placements important at the Inverness Club, Toledo, Ohio, designed by Donald Ross. As on this hole, the 330-yard 18th, distance is not always paramount.

canterbury

Located 10 miles from Cleveland's Public Square in the suburb of Shaker Heights, the Canterbury Golf Club is sited on a bluff that towers 600 feet over Lake Erie. Because of this, it is often buffeted by substantial winds. This is only one of several reasons why Canterbury may be called a Scottish-type course. Like many of its "cousins" in Scotland, Canterbury rests its golfing challenge on strategic values. Not excessively long at 6,877 yards for a major tournament, the Ohio course demands accurate drives and approaches. Canterbury greens are small by modern standards, averaging only 5,500 square feet in area.

Nearly every hole has either an elevated tee or green, and some have both. Course knowledge comes into special play on three holes—numbers 4, 8 and 18 —each of which features a blind approach. You can spot the flagstick, but most of the greens' surfaces are out of sight. Off-line shots are severely punished under tournament conditions, for the rough is bent grass and when it's allowed to grow is very thick.

Canterbury's name sounds English, but oddly enough it derives from the Connecticut birthplace of the man who founded the city of Cleveland, Moses Cleaveland. The club was formed by a coterie of members from Cleveland's University Club in 1921, and the course was opened for play in 1922. Originally designed by Herbert Strong of New York, Canterbury underwent extensive changes under the supervision of the club's first professional, Jack Way, in 1929.

Canterbury was the scene of Walter Hagen's last golf championship, the 1932 Western. The Haig outdueled Olin Dutra in a lashing wind in the final round and won his fifth Western title with a 287. The second Canterbury Western, in 1937, was won by Ralph Guldahl, who tied Horton Smith at 288 and won the playoff by four strokes.

In the U. S. Open of 1940, six players teed off on the final day before their assigned starting times to beat an incoming storm and were subsequently disqualified. One of them, Porky Oliver, scored 287. This would have put him in a playoff with Gene Sarazen and Lawson Little, who went on to win the playoff.

In the 1946 Open Lloyd Mangrum defeated Byron Nelson and Vic Ghezzi by a single shot in a playoff that went 36 holes. They had all scored 284. Nelson's caddie had accidentally kicked his ball in the fourth round to cost his golfer a penalty stroke, without which he would have won.

Bill Campbell won the 1964 U. S. Amateur at Canterbury with a one-up victory over Ed Tutwiler in the finals. Tutwiler had won six of seven previous meetings between the two.

Canterbury's final three holes rate among the best finishers. They require both power and finesse. The giant 16th is a back-breaking 605-yard par-5. The prevailing wind is in the face of golfers as they negotiate a drive through a tree-lined chute onto an uneven fairway that falls away down a fairly steep embankment. The second is to an elevated plateau that resists roll. Long hitters are left with a short iron to a small flat green well below the plateau's height.

The 232-yard 17th is the most demanding par-3 on the course. Both the tee and the green are elevated. The tee shot is over a valley with out-of-bounds to the right. Terrain on both sides of the bunkered green slopes dangerously away, and anything but a near-perfect shot will roll into difficulty. The green itself is terraced.

All uphill, the 438-yard, par-4 No. 18 is considered the course's most difficult hole to par. The drive is to an undulating fairway, with out-of-bounds on the right and trees on the sides of the fairway. The green is not visible from the approaching area, and it often takes a long iron to reach. Sand bunkers surround the reasonably flat green.

In all, Canterbury is an exciting course, one that tests a golfer's imagination, not necessarily his total strength.
—*John P. May*

CANTERBURY SCORECARD*

Hole	Par	Yards	Hole	Par	Yards
1	4	430	10	4	360
2	4	372	11	3	165
3	3	180	12	4	372
4	4	439	13	5	490
5	4	405	14	4	385
6	5	500	15	4	358
7	3	201	16	5	605
8	4	410	17	3	232
9	5	535	18	4	438
	36	3,472		36	3,405

Totals: Par 72, Yards 6,877.

*In tournament play, the 13th hole measures 465 yards, par-4, reducing total yardage to 6,852 and par to 71.

U.S. OPEN WINNERS

Year	Winner	Score
1940	Lawson Little*	287
1946	Lloyd Mangrum**	284

*Won playoff against Gene Sarazen, 70-73.
**Won 36-hole playoff (72-72) against Byron Nelson (72-73) and Vic Ghezzi (72-73).

PGA CHAMPIONSHIP WINNER

1973	Jack Nicklaus	277

The narrow, heavily-wooded fairways which mark Canterbury Golf Club are evidenced even at the par-3 holes like the 201-yard seventh pictured at left.

Heroics performed in 1960 at Denver's Cherry Hills Country Club have assured it a permanent place in golf history. That was the year that Arnold Palmer won the U.S. Open with a 65 in the fourth round. Jack Nicklaus finished two shots behind in second place at 282, still the lowest 72-hole score ever recorded by an amateur in the tournament's history.

Established in 1922, Cherry Hills was designed by golf course architect William S. Flynn who produced a course with no parallel fairways and no two holes alike. Its regular 6,955-yard length from the members' back tees is justified because of the extra distance golfers achieve in the thinner mountain air.

The first and 18th holes are near a clubhouse situated on the highest point of the club. From this site, golfers have a commanding view of a 150-mile stretch of the rugged and nearby Rocky Mountain range. The course slopes away from the first tee into a well-turfed, valley-like meadow. The starting holes are somewhat short, but they are toughened by rough encroaching onto both sides of the fairways.

Two brooks run through the course. The longer of the two makes its presence forcefully known on the back side, where the holes get progressively tougher. Since the 1960 Open, a continuing improvement program has been underway, adding 150 yards to the course. Extensive tree-planting has provided even more hazards. Fairway bunkers are at a minimum, but thoughtfully placed to catch errors off the tee. The greens are small by today's standards, normally fast and full of hard-to-detect rolls.

In that 1960 Open, Palmer began the fourth round seven strokes behind the leader, strong, rugged Mike Souchak. Mike had a two-stroke lead over three others. At lunch before his last round (in those days 36 holes were played on the last day of the Open), Palmer maintained that "it isn't too late for me to get back in there."

Palmer's first nine was sensational. He drove the green on the downhill 346-yard first hole, two-putted for a birdie and followed with five more birdies within the next six holes. He was out in 30, which tied the front-nine scoring record, and came back in 35 for a 65 and a 280 total. All of his rivals fell back. Nicklaus' 71 gave him 282. A 48-year-old Ben Hogan had a chance to catch Palmer but hit into the moat that guards the front of the 17th green and bogeyed, then hit his drive into water on 18. Ben finally shot 73—284 to tie for ninth.

In 1938 Ralph Guldahl had become the fourth to win successive Opens when he won with 284 at Cherry Hills. In the second round luckless Ray Ainsley set an Open record for a single hole when he took 19 strokes on the par-four 16th. Cherry Hills' third major championship was in 1941 when Vic Ghezzi surprised Byron Nelson in the finals of the PGA Championship, 1 up in 38 holes.

The two holes considered Cherry Hills' top-liners are the 470-yard 14th and the 489-yard 18th, both par-4s. On the dogleg-left 14th the tee shot is uphill into a fairway that is bordered by trees and out-of-bounds on the right, deep rough that slopes down into a creek on the left. The creek follows the left side of the fairway all the way to the green. The long second shot must cut a corner of the dogleg to one of the course's smaller greens, rising only slightly from front to back. A deep, U-shaped bunker is to the right.

A large lake faces the tee on 18 and follows the left-hand side of the fairway until a quick rise near the green. The fairway slants from right to left to the water's edge, although it is more level near the lake. The best drive target is to the flatter side of the fairway, even though this is dangerously close to the water. (When Tommy Bolt drove into the water on 18 in the 1960 Open, he flipped his club into the lake.) The second shot is an uphill carry all the way and must fly an entrance to the green narrowed by bunkers left and right.

—*John P. May*

U.S. OPEN WINNERS		
Year	Winner	Score
1938	Ralph Guldahl	284
1960	Arnold Palmer	280

PGA CHAMPIONSHIP WINNER		
1941	Vic Ghezzi	1 up (38)
	d. Byron Nelson	

CHERRY HILLS SCORECARD*

Hole	Par	Yards	Hole	Par	Yards
1	4	355	10	4	434
2	4	415	11	5	556
3	4	325	12	3	203
4	4	433	13	4	384
5	5	541	14	4	470
6	3	170	15	3	194
7	4	394	16	4	400
8	3	230	17	5	529
9	4	433	18	5	489
	35	3,296		37	3,659

Totals: Par 72, Yards 6,955.

*In major tournament play, the 18th hole becomes a par-4, reducing total par to 71; yardage increases to over 7,000.

At 468 yards, the 18th hole at the Cherry Hills Country Club in Denver is as rugged a par-4 hole as you'll find. No two holes are alike at this fascinating course, which has no parallel fairways.

the country club

It is, never let it be forgotten, THE Country Club of Brookline, Mass. To refer to this old line Boston suburban establishment as the Brookline Country Club would be as improper as to call San Francisco "Frisco."

The Country Club has 27 holes, its regular 18 a par-71, 6,505-yard test. Its third nine, the Primrose, is a par-35 of 3,020 yards. For major championships held at this New England club, the ninth, 10th and 12th holes of the regular course are deleted with the first, eighth and ninth of the Primrose replacing them. This produces a course that measures 6,870 yards, with a par of 71, from the back tees of every hole.

All of the holes represent a throwback to days when to score well it was absolutely necessary to be accurate off the tees and to be able to hit small greens with regularity. The narrow fairways, which can be thinned to even more fearsome ribbons by letting the rough intrude on the sides, will not tolerate errant drives.

Thickly branched oaks and maples throng the fairway sides and menace the many dogleg corners. Holes farther away from the clubhouse traverse good-sized hills and awesome depressions. Those nearer the clubhouse are more level.

The bent grass greens are mostly small, averaging no more than 6,000 square feet (about half of those on many modern courses), and offer tiny targets from any respectable distance. This is one course where chipping becomes at least as important as putting, for even the best golfers will miss some greens.

The Country Club was just that, long before it became common for a country club to include a golf course. The club was organized in 1882, and in 1892 six golf holes were laid out, designed by three members, Arthur Hunnewell, Laurence Curtis and Robert Bacon. Twelve holes were added by 1909, and the original course was the site of a U. S. Open, a U. S. Women's Amateur and two U. S. Men's Amateurs. The Primrose Nine was added in 1927. Since then only two holes have been redesigned—the first and the 17th—by Geoffrey Cornish. Four more USGA championships, plus the 1932 and 1973 Walker Cup matches, have been played there.

One of golf's greatest turning points came at The Country Club in 1913 when a 20-year-old ex-caddie, amateur Francis Ouimet of Brookline, defeated Great Britain's two greatest champions in the U.S. Open. Before that golf had been considered a game exclusively for the privileged. When Americans saw that an ordinary citizen like Ouimet could successfully compete against established stars, many took up the game.

It was surprising enough when Ouimet, who once had caddied at The Country Club, finished birdie-par to tie Harry Vardon and Ted Ray, the leading British players of the day. But his dominance of the 18-hole playoff has become golf legend. Ouimet scored 72 to Vardon's 77 and Ray's 78 to become the first amateur to win the Open.

The turning point of both Ouimet's fourth round and the playoff came on the par-four 17th, a dogleg left of 365 yards with a small but deep and treacherous sand bunker at the corner. In the fourth round Ouimet slammed his drive safely to the right of the bunker, stopped his approach 20 feet past the hole on the long, narrow green and made the putt. A par on 18 insured the tie. In the playoff, Ouimet came to 17 a single stroke ahead of Vardon—Ray had faded with a double-bogey six on 15. Francis duplicated his fourth-round drive here, a beauty safely on the fairway. Vardon, knowing he had to birdie to catch his upstart rival, played the left edge too boldly. His ball caught the bunker. Ouimet hit the green, and again made a sizeable putt for a birdie. That was it.

Oddly enough, when Julius Boros won the U. S. Open at The Country Club in 1963 he also birdied 17 (as well as 16), making the only strong finish among contenders. Wind played havoc with scores during the tournament proper as Boros, Jacky Cupit and Arnold Palmer tied at 293, nine over par. But it died in the playoff and the sweet-chipping Boros won handily with a 70 to Cupit's 73 and Palmer's 76. .

Although the 17th, by virtue of its place in history, has received more attention than other holes at The Country Club, there are others just as deserving of recognition. One is the 440-yard third hole, the toughest par on the front side. A deep swale on the right and three fairway traps on the left dictate accuracy off the tee. Six bunkers guard the green, surrounded on three sides by tall trees and water behind.

—*John P. May*

	U.S. OPEN WINNERS	
Year	Winner	Score
1913	Francis Ouimet*	304
1963	Julius Boros**	293

*Won playoff with 72 from Harry Vardon (77) and Ted Ray (78).
**Won playoff with 70 from Jacky Cupit (73) and Arnold Palmer (76).

THE COUNTRY CLUB SCORECARD*

Hole	Par	Yards	Hole	Par	Yards
1	4	435	10	4	315
2	4	295	11	5	510
3	4	440	12	3	135
4	4	340	13	4	405
5	4	425	14	5	535
6	4	315	15	4	420
7	3	200	16	3	175
8	4	385	17	4	365
9	4	420	18	4	390
	35	3,255		36	3,250

Totals: Par 71, Yards 6,505.
*For major tournaments, the yardage increases to 6,870. Three holes from the adjacent Primrose Nine replace the ninth, 10th and 12th holes.

Tight fairways, tiny greens and thickly wooded hills make The Country Club's course at Brookline, Mass., both exciting and frustrating to play. Approach shots are always testing, as on this pictured 390-yard 18th.

oakland hills

The Oakland Hills Country Club tumbles across rolling farmland on both sides of Maple Road, one of the busiest streets in Birmingham, Mich. A large, white frame clubhouse on the south side of the road overlooks Oakland Hills' famous South Course which has been the site of four U.S. Opens and one PGA Championship.

The course was created by Donald Ross, the prolific native Scot who became America's premier golf architect. When Ross looked at the Oakland Hills property in 1916, he is said to have remarked, "The Lord intended this for a golf course."

Ross' course opened in 1918 and was the venue for the 1924 and 1937 U.S. Open Championships. In the 1924 event, English-born Cyril Walker, a darkhorse 118-pounder, lived his greatest day by passing Bobby Jones on the last nine to win by three strokes. High winds pushed his winning total to 297. Ralph Guldahl, the tall, slope-shouldered Texan, won the 1937 event which was the start of Sam Snead's grief in the Open. Guldahl beat Snead by two strokes when some thought Sam had it won in the clubhouse with a 283.

Just prior to the 1951 Open, Robert Trent Jones was called in and asked to modernize the par-70 course. (He also designed an additional 18 holes, the North Course, across the road during the same period.) Jones, who has an uncanny genius for remodeling outdated courses, lengthened some holes on the South Course, added 66 bunkers and narrowed the fairways until they resembled the hour-glass figures of a chorus line. Jones' concept was to develop two target areas, "one on the fairway for the tee shot and one at the green, demanding double accuracy on the play of each par-4 and par-5 hole. No mistake could be made without a just penalty," Jones gleefully said.

The result of this happy collaboration between two generations of master course architects is a golf course so tough and unyielding that it sent shock waves through the star players. After scoring 76 in the opening round at the 1951 Open, Ben Hogan studied his card and grimly proclaimed, "This course is a monster."

Hogan responded heroically. His final round of 67 will be talked about as long as golf endures. It was one of two sub-par rounds shot in

the four days of the tournament—Clayton Haefner closed with 69—and gave Hogan the third of his four Open titles. Years later Hogan would be asked to name the greatest round he ever shot. His reply was measured and precise.

"I have always said the greatest round I ever played was the final day at Oakland Hills in 1951 and I see no reason now to change my mind. I made more outstanding shots in that one round than I ever had in my life. They just didn't give you any room to shoot. You had to be almost perfect with every shot and nobody can really make perfect shots."

Ben smiled.

"But I came pretty close to making them that day," he said.

Though Hogan's "monster" tag has stuck with Oakland Hills, the course was eased for the 1961 U.S. Open and the 1972 PGA. Forty-five of Jones' bunkers were removed and the fairways were widened slightly. It is now much fairer and still tough enough to be ranked in the top 10 on *Golf Digest's* list of America's 100 Greatest Tests of Golf.

Probably on no other course in America are there so many superb par-4 holes. One of them, the 459-yard 18th, drew heavy criticism in the 1972 PGA Championship because officials had moved back the tee markers almost 30 yards. This made it virtually impossible for anyone to reach with less than two perfect shots. The field was 246 over par on this hole through the first three rounds. "On 18 I had two pars and two bogeys, so I figure I was two under par for the tournament," said the eventual winner Gary Player afterwards.

The length, 7,054 yards, and bunkering make Oakland Hills difficult enough, but its slick, elevated undulating greens crown its greatness. The course demands accuracy off the tee, masterly putting and daring.

Few would doubt that Player pulled off one of history's most daring shots in the closing round of the 1972 PGA event. He led the tournament by three shots after the third round, but bogeyed three of the first four holes on Sunday, then missed two short putts on the back nine. Discouraged, he sliced his tee shot on the 16th, a 408-yarder that curls to the right around a lake and a huge weeping willow tree. It was on this

U.S. OPEN WINNERS			SCORECARD*					
Year	Winner	Score	Hole	Par	Yards	Hole	Par	Yards
1924	Cyril Walker	297	1	4	446	10	4	459
1937	Ralph Guldahl	281	2	5	521	11	4	420
1951	Ben Hogan	287	3	3	202	12	5	567
1961	Gene Littler	281	4	4	439	13	3	173
			5	4	442	14	4	468
PGA CHAMPIONSHIP WINNER			6	4	368	15	4	388
1972	Gary Player	281	7	4	408	16	4	408
			8	4	478	17	3	201
			9	3	227	18	4	473
			35		3,531	35		3,557

Totals: Par 70, Yards 7,088.
*In major tournaments, the eighth and 18th holes are shortened, reducing total yardage to 7,054.

When Gary Player struck his second shot in the final round of the 1972 PGA it came from the deep rough behind the willow tree on the far side of the pond on this 408-yard 16th hole, a masterly shot on one of golf's masterly par-4 holes.

These hook-lipped bunkers snarling around the 420-yard 11th hole typify the menace of Oakland Hills.

hole that Walter Hagen, Oakland Hills' first home pro, blew himself out of contention in the 1924 Open by hitting his second shot into the lake.

Player found his ball in soggy rough 150 yards from the green. At that moment, four or five others were closing in; a bogey or worse by Player could be disastrous. He would have to loft his next shot over the willow tree and clear the lake which laps inches away from the putting surface.

"Normally I hit a 7-iron 150 yards, but the flag was up front near the water," Player explained. "I had to gamble. I could not see the flag from where I was and so I aimed for a seat stick be-

tween the branches. I hit a 9-iron as hard and high as I could."

The ball soared high over the tree in the drizzly gray afternoon and plugged into the green four feet from the hole. It was one of the greatest shots under pressure that Player or anyone else had ever struck. Player made the birdie putt and went on to score a winning 281 total.

Afterward, Player proclaimed Oakland Hills and Carnoustie, in Scotland, to be the two toughest courses in the world.

The South Course has also hosted the U.S. Women's Amateur, the Western Open and the Ryder Cup. Its host professionals, since the immortal Hagen, have included Mike Brady, Al Watrous and Mike Souchak.

Oakland Hills is a club rich in tradition and golfing lore, and as a test of golf its South Course is as strong and about as mean as they come.

—*Cal Brown*

OTHER GREAT TOURNAMENT COURSES

Not all great American tournament courses are U.S. Open courses. Some of the courses depicted in this chapter have hosted an Open; several have not. All have entertained major championships and consistently inspired 24-karat competitive golf, which in the final reckoning is the measure of a tournament course.

In a very real way these courses make for a more fascinating study than Open sites because they usually have not prepared for tournament play with the same diligent degree of uniformity. They are left more to stand on their own merits— no wild rough around the greens, no alley-tight fairways, no par-5 holes converted to demonic par-4s on comparatively short notice. This is not to demean the thoughtful preparation of Open courses but simply to point up the enchanting variety in other great tournament courses.

If these other courses have one thing in common, it is their distinctive uncommonness. Each of the 10 has its own personality and character as much as the different children in a large family. Sculpted beautifully and naturally out of endemic terrain, they range from the precipitous seaside cliffs of Pebble Beach to the beflowered hills of Augusta National to the sandy woods of Pinehurst.

Esthetics and tactics are married with marvelous subtlety. The shot values of a hole emanate from its setting, to the extent that the artistic appeal at first blush can distract the less-skilled player from the fearsome challenge a great tournament course constantly presents. It is fine if a tournament course can be adapted to play comfortably for a 90 shooter but that, after all, is not its reason for being. Played from the championship tees it can quickly wreck the composure of the weekend golfer. Then the artistic vistas are as hard to appreciate as a grey photograph of a highway lined with gas stations, hamburger stands and signboards.

The great tournament courses on the pages that follow are fair—but their fairness is relative. They demand great play. Bernard Darwin, the hallowed British golf journalist, wrote some years ago, "Nearly all of the famous holes of the world have been accused of being unfair. The margin of error is in places so small and the risk to be taken so big that there must be occasions on which fate deals harshly. That is what has made the holes famous. The too scrupulously fair course need not be lacking in interest, but in fact it often is. I have lately played a little on a course which must in point of fairness be second to none. It has suited my kind of golf well enough, because I have enough to do trying to hit the ball into the air, and I found the ordinary risks quite great enough. But as I have not seen anyone called on to play a shot that could possibly be called unfair, so also I have not seen one that could be called particularly interesting, still less exciting."

Darwin would agree that the courses in this chapter exude excitement.
—*Nick Seitz*

augusta national

If you detained 100 Americans on 100 avenues in 100 towns and asked each to name one golf course, you can bet that a majority would answer "where they play the Masters" or "where Ike used to visit" or just plain "Augusta National."

Augusta National Golf Club, for all its exclusiveness, is known by Idaho farmers, Manhattan apparel merchants, New Orleans jazz players and the warehouse boys in Chicago. People who don't know a drive from a knuckleball have usually had some occasion to either stumble across the home of the Masters tournament in print or catch a glimpse on television.

In all the world, probably only St. Andrews in Scotland—the cradle of golf—is better known.

Augusta National . . . it conjures a variety of memories: Ben Hogan hitting an 8-iron close to the hole on the small, but difficult 12th hole. Arnold Palmer spinning in joy over dropping a 30-footer. Gene Sarazen's famed double eagle. Jack Nicklaus lapping the field with his record 271 total in 1965. Roberto de Vicenzo losing by a shot when his scorecard was incorrect in 1968. Maybe you even recall the immortal Bobby Jones driving around in a motorized golf car surveying the golfing monument that he built.

After Jones completed his Grand Slam in 1930, the famed Atlantan had no more worlds to conquer and he retired from golfing competition. His interests turned to constructing Augusta National on 365 lush acres of northeast Georgia. The property had been a nursery, owned for 73 years by the family of a Belgian baron, Louis Edouard Mathieu Berckmans.

Prosper Berckmans, the baron's son, became a world renowned horticulturist and developed an extensive product catalog for Fruitlands, as the nursery was known. It listed 1,300 varieties of pears and 900 kinds of apples, among other things. Prosper developed his own lines of fruits, shrubs and flowers and it has been said that America might have hardly a single blossoming azalea bush had it not been for the work of Prosper Berckmans.

Even today, many of the incredible variety of trees, flowers and bushes at Augusta National can be traced to Prosper's nursery. Jones realized the promise of the land and joined several associates in hiring Scottish golf architect Dr. Alister Mackenzie to design what Mackenzie

soon began calling "The World's Wonder Inland Course." Jones personally oversaw the designing of Augusta National, its construction and the organizing of the club.

Two years after the club's opening in 1932, an event was inaugurated and named the "First Annual Invitation Tournament." Top golfers from around the world were invited and it was called a "gathering of the masters." The term "Masters" became the official name of the tournament that was to join the U.S. Open, PGA Championship and British Open as one of the world's Big Four golf happenings.

Although often criticized, the Augusta National Club continues to operate the Masters in a relatively secretive manner. Word never leaks out as to how many tickets are sold for the event and the club answers to nobody when second-guessed over its methods. The Masters is wholly administered by a group of green-blazered members who set up the course, run the ticket operation, conduct news media interviews with players and write their own television contract with the chosen network.

The closing four holes are among the best known group of golfing challenges in the world. Millions see them year after year on television: the par-five 15th with its to-gamble-or-not-to-gamble decision of hitting your second shot across a pond that guards the green; the par-three 16th and its gorgeous carry across a tee-to-green pond; the par-four 17th and its subtle putting surface; the par-four 18th, an uphill grind with an infamous fairway trap and a ticklish putting chore.

None of the other Big Four tournaments remains at the same site. The British Open floats among several top courses in England and Scotland. The U.S. Open moves every summer, as does the PGA Championship. But, at Masters time, it's always the same unmatched scenery and recognized test of golf amid the Georgia pines.

Although almost untouched by TV cameras, the most popular series of holes at Augusta National is what is often referred to as "Amen Corner," the 11th through 13th holes. Thousands of persons lucky enough to hold season ticket rights flock to this crucial spot where the 11th green, entire par-three 12th and a long-distance

MASTERS WINNERS

Year	Winner	Score
1934	Horton Smith	284
1935	Gene Sarazen	282
(won playoff from Craig Wood 144-149)		
1936	Horton Smith	285
1937	Byron Nelson	283
1938	Henry Picard	285
1939	Ralph Guldahl	279
1940	Jimmy Demaret	280
1941	Craig Wood	280
1942	Byron Nelson	280
(won playoff from Ben Hogan 69-70)		
1943-45 no tournaments		
1946	Herman Keiser	282
1947	Jimmy Demaret	281
1948	Claude Harmon	279
1949	Sam Snead	282
1950	Jimmy Demaret	283
1951	Ben Hogan	280
1952	Sam Snead	286
1953	Ben Hogan	274
1954	Sam Snead	289
(won playoff from Ben Hogan 70-71)		
1955	Cary Middlecoff	279
1956	Jack Burke	289
1957	Doug Ford	283
1958	Arnold Palmer	284
1959	Art Wall	284
1960	Arnold Palmer	282
1961	Gary Player	280
1962	Arnold Palmer	280
(won playoff with 68 from Gary Player, 71; Dow Finsterwald, 77)		
1963	Jack Nicklaus	286
1964	Arnold Palmer	276
1965	Jack Nicklaus	271
1966	Jack Nicklaus	288
(won playoff with 70 from Tommy Jacobs, 72; Gay Brewer, 78)		
1967	Gay Brewer	280
1968	Bob Goalby	277
1969	George Archer	281
1970	Billy Casper	279
(won playoff from Gene Littler 69-74)		
1971	Charles Coody	279
1972	Jack Nicklaus	286
1973	Tommy Aaron	283
1974	Gary Player	278

No picture could capture the drama and verdant beauty of Augusta National more sharply than this tableau of Arnold Palmer, caught in the amphitheater of the 190-yard 16th.

AUGUSTA NATIONAL SCORECARD*

Hole	Par	Yards	Hole	Par	Yards
1	4	400	10	4	470
2	5	555	11	4	445
3	4	355	12	3	155
4	3	220	13	5	475
5	4	450	14	4	420
6	3	190	15	5	520
7	4	365	16	3	190
8	5	530	17	4	400
9	4	420	18	4	420
	36	3,485		36	3,495

Totals: Par 72, Yards 6,980.

*Yardage for the 1974 Masters changed to 7,020 by increasing the length of the third and 10th holes.

view of the par-five 13th can be seen from one lofty perch. Sarazen, the golfing great from another era, changed the name of this area a bit, calling it "Hell's Corner." It is where heroes are born and also-rans are made.

The 445-yard 11th hole demands a bruising tee shot from a chute back someplace in the sky-seeking pines. The landing area is small and made risky by the unending presence of water to the left. The approach is usually a long-iron shot that, to be close to the pin, must flirt with the water. Players often chicken out, playing well to the right and then chipping for the hole.

Then comes No. 12, as tough a little hole as there is in the world. It is a confusing and frightening 155-yarder that is fronted diagonally by Rae's Creek. It's as deceptively dangerous as a two-foot coral snake. To the viewing multitudes, it would seem to be an easy shot for the greatest of players, but don't try to convince a Masters contender that the 12th is anything but a difficult hole. As far back as 1937, the 12th and its sister hole, the 475-yard 13th, decided the tournament. Ralph Guldahl was moving along with a four-stroke lead when he double-bogeyed the 12th and bogeyed the 13th while young Byron Nelson went birdie-eagle to take the lead and eventually win the Masters.

Sam Snead was a 1952 victim. Dressed neatly in his yellow shirt, blue trousers and straw hat, the Slammer came to the 12th and began the expected fumbling for the correct club. His caddie suggested a 6-iron. Sam said "no suh," and grabbed a seven. His shot plopped into Rae's Creek. Snead took a drop beside the creek and was hitting a delicate pitch for his third shot. That, too, misfired and died in the streak of rough that separates the green from the water. It appeared that a five, maybe even a triple-bogey six, would erase Snead from the tournament lead. But, just then, Amen Corner turned its face to the smiling side. Snead stroked a wedge nicely from the thickness. It hit onto the green and curled into the cup for an incredible bogey four that saved the day . . . and the Masters title for Sam.

The 13th is a severe dogleg left and the critical decision usually comes on the second shot: whether to lay up and then pitch your third shot over a deep creek to the green or to go for broke, hitting your second for the flagstick. A perfect, slightly-drawn tee shot can leave a man anything from a 4-wood to a 3-iron to reach the green, but there's always the danger of splashing into the water and having your dreams of an eagle three replaced by the horrors of a double-bogey seven.

Courage often can be confused with poor judgment on the last link of Amen Corner. Take the Billy Joe Patton case, for example. Patton, a wealthy North Carolina lumberman and strong amateur golfer, was making a strong run at the Masters title in 1954. He was pumped up, his adrenalin gushing. The dream of being the first amateur to win the event was uppermost in his mind. Patton hit a good drive at 13, but a little right of the desired area. Fellow Southerners, in a whooping drawl, advised him to, "Go fuh it, Billy Joe, go fuh it." Patton turned in the gallery's direction, according to more reserved onlookers, and said, "Ah didn't get into contention by playin' safe. I'm ah goin' fuh it." Billy Joe whacked his approach as the crowd gasped, but it fell a few feet short and trickled back into the creek. Patton took a double-bogey and lost the Masters by one shot.

There are many memorials around the grounds of Augusta National, from Jones' old golfing equipment in the great, white-columned clubhouse to numerous fountains, bridges and plaques commemorating wonderful performances in the Masters. Of all these, the best known is the Gene Sarazen Bridge that leads to the 15th green. It was on that par-5 hole that Sarazen, dressed in his famed knickers, sank a 4-wood shot from 230 yards for a double eagle two that enabled him to tie Craig Wood and eventually win the 1935 event in a playoff.

Another bridge, leading to the green at No. 12, is dedicated to Ben Hogan for his record 274 in 1953, a mark that stood until 1965 when Jack Nicklaus finished an eye-popping 17 under par 271, nine shots in front of the rest of the field. Nelson is remembered with a stone walkway that spans Rae's Creek toward the 13th fairway.

All of this enhances the beauty of the place, especially in springtime when the 51-week tranquility of Augusta National is disrupted for the club's main event. Getting a ticket to the Masters may be roughly equal to gaining a seat at Queen Elizabeth's dinner table, but once you're in, you realize that no golf tournament anyplace does more for the spectator at less cost.

Season tickets, good all four days of the tournament proper, go for $30, a modest sum by modern admission standards. The Masters officials are continually looking for ways to reshape the viewing areas, providing elevated spots from which hundreds of fans can sit in a nest that is great for watching. Concession stands are well-manned and prices reasonable. The clubhouse is off-limits except for club members, their guests, players, news media and other select visitors, but almost everything else is within reach for that season ticket. You can stroll left of the 10th tee and look over the cottage, the lovely little house where President Eisenhower stayed during his frequent visits.

Clifford Roberts, the New York investment banker who has administered the Masters' stern by-laws from the beginning, would never talk "for print" about Ike's golfing ventures until after the World War II commander-in-chief died. Then he let the world in on a very human character, a golf enthusiast whose patience was strained in waiting for fellow players to hit their shots. Eisenhower was always eager to streak up the fairway, moving quickly toward his ball and getting ready for his next shot. Roberts told of Ike's temper, of his ill feelings for a certain tree on a certain fairway that kept getting in the way of his shots. Roberts was often in Ike's foursome while the world was fenced out by security guards.

If you look closely at the Masters audience, you can spot the same faces year after year. If a new one appears, it's usually an offspring that has inherited ticket rights. Before too many trips, each one knows the 18 holes by heart and can recall an anecdote about a famous player for nearly every one.

Augusta National, for a course into its fifth decade, is a relatively wide open layout. Long hitters are allowed to cut loose through most of a round. The difference between a 75 and a 68 at Augusta is usually a man's fortune on the greens. Most of the putting surfaces are gigantic, presenting an inviting target from well out in the fairway. But, upon closer inspection, the greens become terrors for putting. An approach to the wrong side of a green can leave an almost certain three-putt. The grass is short and scary fast. A putt from the high side of the green can easily be overstroked and speed past the hole, across the remainder of a green and even into the rough or a bunker. In addition to the quickness, there are also severe undulations.

Augusta National's famous "Amen Corner," the most crucial turning point on this superb parkland course, is pictured in the foreground of this aerial photo with the 11th hole, a par-4, curling in from the right, the treacherous 12th, a par-3, in the foreground and the tantalizing 13th, a short par-5, curving away to the left. These three holes, plus the 15th, are pictured in greater detail on the next five pages.

In the heat of competition some of the world's best golfers often will play the 445-yard 11th (left) safe by aiming their approaches to the right of the green to avoid the pond.

The 155-yard 12th (above) is the toughest short par-3 in golf. The narrow green is pinched between Rae's Creek and a steep knoll and bunkers. Swirling winds make club selection an exasperating test of judgment.

textbook example of how a cunning architect can
rn a short par-5 into a temptress is the 485-yard
th where trees and creek curling along the entire
t flank of the fairway inhibit the big drive needed
go for the green (above) so enticingly near, yet
osely ringed by the twin perils of water and sand.

To go for it, or lay up short of the pond that fronts the green on the 520-yard 15th is a classic Masters' decision. Here Gene Sarazen scored history's most remembered double-eagle, holing his 4-wood second shot en route to winning the 1935 Masters.

The course rests in a spectacular forest-fringed amphitheatre, covering some 385 acres, and its charm stems from its arboretum-like beauty. The only buildings within the confines of the estate are the small Georgian frame clubhouse, the tree-camouflaged press room, and a few simple white bungalows tucked in the woods near the 10th tee. Once you leave this hub of activity, except for the furnishings of golf you might be in a modern Garden of Eden.

Color highlights the Masters, as would be expected of Georgia in springtime. To the first-timer especially, the kaleidoscopic interplay of forest, flower, shrub, stream, lake, sand, fairway and green, all overlaid by a shifting quilt of vividly-attired crowds, is literally breathtaking. For the first few hours of a first visit, the extravagance of the general scene makes it difficult to give close attention to golf.

One probable surprise for the first-timer will be the contouring and expansiveness of the course. The camera tends to flatten and condense landscape. Augusta National is spectacular in photographs and on TV, but in reality it is much more undulating and spacious than one can appreciate secondhand. Almost every hole is sharply or subtly inclined, and generous swathes of manicured land divide most of the holes, giving a wonderful sense of space and freedom. Hence, despite the large crowds that occupy the popular viewing locations and move along with the big names, there are excellent watching points all along the way.

In terms of scoring, it might take the new recruit a while to comprehend the magnitude of the challenge that Augusta National offers the titans of golf. Jones stressed repeatedly that the course was designed primarily to provide pleasure and satisfaction for the average golfer, and at first glance it looks like just that sort of course. Walking the Masters sidelines for the first time, few middle-handicappers would be struck by terror at the thought of having to defend a couple of dollars over such wide-open and immaculately-groomed territory.

The fairways are not only wide but almost always provide a perfect, clean lie. There are only some 30 bunkers and, by comparison with many modern championship layouts, none look particularly difficult in contour or texture. Unless a player is wildly off-line, he isn't likely to find any serious rough. The greens are very large, and despite their rolling character, many look as though they would run the ball towards the hole if it were centrally located. On a few holes water is a problem, but hardly the hazard that it is at other prominent American courses. The yardage is not unduly long since the average length during the Masters measures about 6,850. In 1974, however, total maximum distance finally stretched to 7,020 yards.

If a newcomer to Augusta National feels a little let down by this immediate impression of ease, he can quickly dispel it by placing himself to look down the line of the player's second shot, or his tee shot at short holes. From there he will see the pin positions as the golfer sees them, and the immense and perhaps unique challenge of Augusta National in its Masters dress will become obvious. Probably no other course in the world can change from kitten to tiger so quickly and easily. This chameleon quality derives directly from the vast experience, golfing skill and loving attention to detail that Jones and Scottish architect Mackenzie applied in conceiving and building the course. The challenge is accomplished almost entirely by cup positioning; the key to Augusta National is the configuration of the greens. Each has been carefully contrived to give four or more flagstick locations which will radically revise the difficulty and playing strategy of the hole. An entirely new challenge can be issued every day, depending on weather conditions and the decisions of the officials.

Over the years the Masters has developed momentous financial and status value in the world of sport, and the result has been to make victory worth more to the professional golfer than a win in any other golfing event with the possible exception of the U.S. Open. Today a Masters victory not only assures a man of a good reward for the rest of his days, but it is an absolute requirement if he wishes to enter the lists of truly great golfers. Hence, what you will see at the Masters is probably the ultimate expression of competitive golf, and at the same time one of the greatest extravaganzas in all sport. Most of the competitors are playing for a fortune, and a small, select handful are playing for immortality.

This might not be exactly what Bobby Jones and Cliff Roberts envisioned when they started the Masters, but it makes for the best of all golfing entertainment.
　　　　　　　　　　　　　　　—*Hubert Mizell*

pinehurst no.2

Of all the famous golf courses in the United States, the least obvious gem is the No. 2 course at Pinehurst (N.C.) Country Club. It is not as dramatic as Pine Valley or Pebble Beach, not as elegant as Augusta National or Merion. Pinehurst No. 2 appears quiet, unassuming, almost drab in comparison with those American classics.

Its individual holes are seldom discussed when golfers list the great golf holes of America. Some who play it for the first time are puzzled at its ranking among the top 10 of America's 100 Greatest Tests of Golf.

Except for the 1951 Ryder Cup, Pinehurst has hosted only two major events—the 1936 PGA Championship won by Denny Shute, and the 1962 U.S. Amateur, won by Labron Harris Jr. But in 1973 it hosted the richest tournament in history —the $500,000 World Open. Most of the pros, however, are familiar with Pinehurst from amateur days. The course is noted for amateur tournaments, including the annual North and South. In earlier days there was a North and South Open, which was dropped after 1951.

Pinehurst is a player's course. Sam Snead puts it at the top of his list of U.S. courses because, "You won't see any pitch-and-putt scramblers winning there. You've got to hit every shot on old No. 2."

There is something about Pinehurst No. 2 that strikes responsive chords in men like Ben Hogan, who won his first professional tournament at the course. Like a Bach fugue, Pinehurst presents recurring themes—mounds guarding the green entrances, wire grass and pine needles lurking off fairways, greens that fall away at the edges—all orchestrated into an intricate and balanced whole. The sequencing of holes of different lengths builds with a harmony and logic achieved only in great art.

This may explain why Pinehurst No. 2 is the crowning masterpiece of the late architect Donald Ross. He believed that sand and golf belong together, and in the sandhills of North Carolina he found his perfect medium. He built many courses in and around Pinehurst and over 500 in the U.S., but it was on No. 2 that he lavished his greatest attention.

The pine needles and cones which covered the sandy soil were to be kept, Ross decided, as a hazard. These, together with the short, clumpy, tough wire grass that would form the rough, would prove sufficient penalty for poorly struck shots. Sand bunkers were used sparingly. Water appears only on one hole, the 16th, where it is more a decoration than a hazard.

"Ross considered the ability to play the longer irons the supreme test of a great player," says Richard Tufts, whose family founded Pinehurst in 1895 and operated the resort until 1971. Consequently, the greens were shaped so that they fade away to the sides and back. This created a much smaller effective target area than you might at first think. In some cases you have only 3,000 square feet, roughly half a green, to land on safely. If your ball lands outside this small area, it will run off the green.

Ross had another reason for the contoured greens and mounded approaches which create hollows similar to the Scottish seaside courses where golf and Ross were born. "This mounding makes possible an infinite variety of nasty short shots that no other form of hazard can call for. Competitors whose second shots have wandered a bit will be disturbed by these innocent appearing slopes and by the shots they will have to invent to recover," said Ross.

Until 1934, all the greens had been sand and quite flat. The surfaces were watered, then swept with old carpets before players putted.

Ross built the fairways wide, recognizing that the margin for error should be greatest on tee shots, but he clearly intended that golfers look beyond the landing area before driving. Most of the greens and hazards are visible from the tee, and position driving is required to avoid approaching greens from treacherous angles.

Johnny Revolta, a great player of an earlier era, once said of Pinehurst No. 2, "You must play it with your head as much as with your hands. It demands good driving and great accuracy of approach shots. The greens are true as the sunrise but require careful study, a keen eye and a sound stroke."

Before he died, Tommy Armour said of Pinehurst No. 2, "The man who doesn't feel emotionally stirred when he golfs at Pinehurst beneath those clear blue skies and with the pine fragrance in his nostrils is one who should be ruled out of golf for life. It's the kind of course that gets into the blood of an old trooper."

It is, and always has been, a player's course.

—Cal Brown

PGA CHAMPIONSHIP WINNER		
Year	Winner	Score
1936	Denny Shute	3 & 2
	d. Jimmy Thomson	

PINEHURST No. 2 SCORECARD*

Hole	Par	Yards	Hole	Par	Yards
1	4	414	10	5	596
2	4	454	11	4	434
3	4	345	12	4	423
4	5	532	13	4	378
5	4	438	14	4	444
6	3	216	15	3	206
7	4	398	16	5	504
8	5	487	17	3	187
9	3	162	18	4	433
	36	3,446		36	3,605

Totals: Par 72, Yards 7,051.
*The eighth hole was played as a par-4; total yardage at 7,007 during the 1973 World Open.

Mounds, a somewhat neglected theme in modern golf course architecture, are a distinctive feature of the pine-bordered fairways and greens' entrances on Donald Ross' classic Pinehurt No. 2, a small sample of which can be seen above on the 378-yard 13th.

It's the greatest stage in golf. Producers, directors and cameramen know the layout almost as well as the world's finest players. The Firestone Country Club's South Course in Akron, Ohio, is the most-watched course in America, thanks to television.

Sports fans have watched two televised PGA Championships, in 1960 and 1966, on the spectacular 7,180-yard course. They've seen the American Golf Classic for a dozen years as a regular stop on the pro tour. Viewers have absorbed the World Series of Golf, a TV spectacular matching the winners of the world's Big Four pro tournaments, from Firestone since 1962. It is also the site of the CBS Classic television series.

Firestone, like any television giant, has suffered its cancellations, too. All-Star Golf, its first video exposure in 1962, never caught on with television viewers and was cancelled.

To those around Akron, the par-70 Firestone course is known as The Monster. It was Arnold Palmer who coined the nickname during the 1960 PGA Championship. Palmer was igniting one of his noted charges when, at the 625-yard 16th hole, he was gobbled up by the course. Arnold plunked his third shot into the pond that guards the green and wound up with a triple-bogey eight. In his interview afterward, Palmer referred to the hole and the course as "this monster" and the name stuck.

Firestone South was built in 1928 by the late Harvey Firestone, the rubber millionaire, mainly for the enjoyment of his thousands of employees. Firestone North, a second course, was constructed in 1969 by Robert Trent Jones to share the golfing traffic created by a current membership of 1,500.

The South Course, the one you always see on TV, was redesigned by Trent Jones prior to the 1960 PGA. He added 50 bunkers, two ponds, two new greens and rebuilt and enlarged the other 16 greens. It is not uncommon to face a 100-foot putt on the massive surfaces. Jones beefed up the total yardage from 6,585 yards to 7,180.

"The key factor at Firestone," says Bobby Nichols, who continues to play the tour in addition to being the club's head professional, "is the demand on approach shots. On most courses, pros can count on wedges or 9-irons to many greens. At Firestone, they find themselves hitting a lot of 3-irons, 4-irons and even fairway woods to par-4 holes. It's so long that you need to let out all the shaft, but there's enough trouble that you have to hold back something. It takes an interesting blend of strength and accuracy to win at Firestone."

Every tournament course has its famous "TV holes," but none are so implanted in the minds of American viewers as the 15th through 18th at Firestone. The 15th is a 230-yard par-3, followed by that 625-yard mankiller of a par-5. The 17th is only 390 yards, but severe bunkering makes it a major challenge. And the 18th is a 465-yard par-4 that is extremely stingy with birdies.

If you search for the man who did the most to make Firestone the most-seen golf course in America, you must pass over the Palmers, Nicklauses, Players and Nichols in favor of Walter Schwimmer. Walter Who? Well, it was Chicago producer Schwimmer who came up with the World Series of Golf format and matched the greatest stars head-to-head for a $50,000 top prize. He focused the eyes of a nation on Firestone South. He gave the course exposure that Akron folks never dreamed of when they started the Rubber City Open back in 1953.

The RCO lasted until 1959, when it was pushed aside while Firestone hosted the PGA Championship the following summer. When Akron reactivated its tour event in 1961, it became the American Golf Classic. Jay Hebert won both the 1960 PGA and the inaugural American Golf Classic the following year. When the PGA Championship returned in 1966, it was California thin man Al Geiberger who mastered the course. Geiberger, like Hebert, had back-to-back victories at Firestone since he won the AGC in 1965.

Perhaps the success of Firestone South as a TV studio-golf course can also be traced to the original cast of the World Series of Golf. Schwimmer's series premiere got off to a running start in 1962 with Jack Nicklaus, the U.S. Open winner; Palmer, who took both the Masters and British Open that year; and Gary Player, champion of the PGA. Nicklaus won the 36-hole show with 66-69—135 and a trend was set for the future.

Firestone is seldom farther away than your channel dial.
—Hubert Mizell

FIRESTONE (SOUTH) SCORECARD

Hole	Par	Yards	Hole	Par	Yards
1	4	400	10	4	405
2	5	500	11	4	365
3	4	450	12	3	180
4	4	465	13	4	460
5	3	230	14	4	410
6	4	465	15	3	230
7	3	225	16	5	625
8	4	450	17	4	390
9	4	465	18	4	465
	35	3,650		35	3,530

Totals: Par 70, Yards 7,180.

PGA CHAMPIONSHIP WINNERS

Year	Winner	Score
1960	Jay Hebert	281
1966	Al Geiberger	280

WORLD SERIES OF GOLF WINNERS

Year	Winner	Score
1962	Jack Nicklaus	135
1963	Jack Nicklaus	140
1964	Tony Lema	138
1965	Gary Player	139
1966	Gene Littler	143
1967	Jack Nicklaus	144
1968	Gary Player	143
1969	Orville Moody	141
1970	Jack Nicklaus	136
1971	Charles Coody	141
1972	Gary Player	142
1973	Tom Weiskopf	137

A distinguishing mark of the Firestone Country Club's South Course is the 16th hole, at 625 yards, one of the longest in the United States. Even after two mighty shots you still have to negotiate that pond in front of the green on this Akron, Ohio, layout masterfully re-designed by Robert Trent Jones.

medinah no.3

When a major tournament is played at the No. 3 Course of the Medinah Country Club, officials feel no obligation to toughen the site appreciably. This championship layout, one of three courses at the suburban Chicago private club, is difficult enough as it stands.

Medinah, designed by Tom Bendelow and later revised, is one of the world's greatest driving courses. Its tournament length of over 7,000 yards requires distance, but tall, mature trees line nearly every fairway and dictate accuracy. Many big hitters keep their drivers in the bag off many of Medinah's tees, preferring to be shorter out of the box than in the dense woods.

These stands of trees, besides delineating the only way to go off the tee, also guard dogleg corners. You might call them "enforcers" in that they do not allow any shortcuts to the green. If a hole is a dogleg, you play it as a dogleg.

Fairway turf is lush under normal conditions, and stops the ball soon after it lands. You earn your distance at Medinah. There are only 64 sand bunkers on the course, but every one is in play. The greens are generally large, with contours and slopes that challenge the best putters.

It seems a shame that only one U. S. Open has been played at Medinah—in 1949 and won by Cary Middlecoff. However, the second will be played there in 1975. Many of the day's best competitors have played in three Western Opens there, in 1939 (winner Byron Nelson, 282), 1962 (Jacky Cupit, 281) and 1966 (Billy Casper, 283).

It was in 1929, though, that Medinah first played host to top-line performers. When Harry Cooper won the Medinah Open with a card that included a 63, club members immediately announced a re-designing program that would scuttle such low scores in the future. Five new holes were hacked through wooded areas previously reserved for club members' residential lots. A Shriners' Open was held there in 1935, Cooper won again—with a 289. And no 63s!

In 1949 when Medinah hosted the Open, Middlecoff was in the third year of his brilliant if relatively brief professional career. Ben Hogan, who had won the Open the year before, had since been injured in an automobile accident and could not play. Middlecoff shot a course-record 67 (a record for the course as it stood then) the second day and entered the fourth round with a one-stroke lead over Buck White. However, Clayton Heafner and Sam Snead gave the golfing dentist his most stubborn fight.

Heafner caught Middlecoff during the round, but the latter went ahead with a par-3 on the famous 225-yard 17th. Heafner bogeyed there, and missed a birdie putt on 18 for the tie. Snead, playing later, needed a 33 on the back nine to tie. But he also bogeyed 17, taking three to get down from just off the edge. Sam wound up in a tie with Heafner for second, a stroke behind Middlecoff.

As can be seen, the 17th at Medinah is one of its most intriguing holes. From the tee, the hole presents a terrifying picture. The green is hunkered down well below the level of the tee. A wide outlet of Lake Kadijah crosses the fairway just in front of the green, making the tee shot almost all carry. Oh, you could be short and not in the water—but you'd wind up in a big sand bunker. A large bunker on the left punishes pulled shots, and it's tough to hold the green from there because it slopes away from the golfer.

Most golfing experts believe that Medinah's No. 13 is one of the toughest par-4s in existence. It is a 458-yard par-4 with pickets of tall trees on both sides of the fairway, which doglegs left about 240 yards from the tee and then swings uphill to a slanting green. It demands the ultimate of strength, nerve and control, a quintessential feature of Medinah.

Longest hole at Medinah is the 598-yard, par-5 dogleg-right seventh. It's so rugged you can get tired thinking about it. The drive is from an elevated tee, and it should hug the left side of the tree-lined fairway. Otherwise the big oaks that block the right side will severely limit the second shot. The next shot is into a narrow valley, with fairway bunkers on the left.

Medinah, which is in the first ten of *Golf Digest*'s "America's 100 Greatest Tests of Golf," has a course rating of 74.8 at its tournament length of 7,102 yards. United States courses with higher ratings can be counted on one hand, and absolutely none is considered a tougher, truer championship track.
—*John P. May*

U.S. OPEN WINNER			MEDINAH No. 3 SCORECARD*					
Year	Winner	Score	Hole	Par	Yards	Hole	Par	Yards
1949	Cary Middlecoff	286	1	4	388	10	5	588
			2	3	192	11	4	406
			3	4	430	12	4	389
			4	4	447	13	5	458
			5	5	519	14	3	172
			6	4	446	15	4	327
			7	5	598	16	4	469
			8	3	204	17	3	225
			9	4	427	18	4	417
				36	3,651		36	3,451

Totals: Par 72, Yards 7,102.
*In tournament play, the 13th hole becomes a par-4, lowering total par to 71.

The formidable character of Medinah No. 3, a suburban Chicago course originally designed by Tom Bendelow, becomes quickly evident at the second hole, a par-3 of 192 yards. Here you must fly the ball all the way to the green or suffer an early round indignity.

champions

Precious few of the world's fine golf courses were molded within the last 40 years, but an exception is Champions Golf Club in Houston. Built in 1957 by former Masters champions Jimmy Demaret and Jack Burke Jr., it has already hosted the U. S. Open, Ryder Cup and several Houston pro tour events.

Houston is the prototype of an American boom town with its population exploding from 400,000 to over a million within 20 years in an area adorned by the Astrodome indoor stadium, marvelous hunks of glass and steel that are home to giants of the oil industry, and the nation's Space Center where flights to the moon are manipulated.

"We wanted a club right in our hometown that would be to Houston what Augusta National is to Georgia, what Pinehurst is to North Carolina and what Pebble Beach is to the California coastline," says Demaret. "Jackie and I have played most of the world's finest courses and we modeled the holes at Champions after the great ones we have seen."

Like most of Texas, the terrain at Champions is basically flat and derives its character from countless trees, placid lakes and serpentine Cypress Creek which becomes a natural hazard on the fourth hole, one of the tougest par-3s on earth.

Ralph Plummer was Champions' architect, but he worked with plenty of recommendations from co-owners Burke and Demaret. Fairways are generally bordered with pines and post oaks and several holes meander around man-made ponds. Flowers are plentiful, filling the air with scents of crepe myrtle, ivy, dogwood, roses, holly, fern, firethorn and azalea.

Champions has two magnificent courses, although the best known is Cypress Creek where Orville Moody won the 1969 U.S. Open by one stroke over Deane Beman, Bob Rosburg and Al Geiberger. The course was also the site of the 1967 Ryder Cup matches when the United States pros defeated their counterparts from Great Britain 23½-8½ in the biennial matches. The Houston International, forerunner of the Houston Open on the pro tour, was also played there.

Jackrabbit, the newer 18-hole Champions layout designed by George Fazio, was constructed more in the British style with narrower fairways than Cypress Creek, smaller greens and more severe bunkering.

The fourth at Cypress Creek is beautiful to the eye, but can be fearsome to anyone but the truest shotmaker. Depending on the placement of tee markers, the hole goes from 193 to 228 yards and the longer it gets, the farther the carry over rocky, old Cypress Creek itself, where a spray shot is almost always unplayable. Even for the weak-hearted who keep their shots far to the right, there can be trouble with a clump of trees that shades a bunker beside the ample green. Anything from a 3-iron to a 4-wood is usually required. The same goes for the picturesque 12th, which plays 230 yards across Bob Hope Lake. The body of water was named for the comedian when he became the first of thousands to plunk tee·shots into the lake. The 12th can be a mental disaster since, if you steer well clear of the lake, you can become imbedded in a treacherous trap to the right of the green.

Jack Nicklaus calls the 14th hole, a 430-yarder, the "one that is consistently toughest to par." If your tee shot drifts left, the approach becomes an eye-popping challenge of great length, carrying across a pond at the front of the green and a putting area so expansive that a four-putt green is anything but rare.

Like Augusta National, where Demaret won three Masters and Burke took one, the greens are huge and multi-terraced. Combined with Champions' length and heavy treeing, this becomes one of the great tests of golfing ability.

—Hubert Mizell

94

CHAMPIONS (CYPRESS CREEK)
SCORECARD*

Hole	Par	Yards	Hole	Par	Yards
1	4	454	10	4	448
2	4	452	11	4	466
3	4	397	12	3	230
4	3	228	13	5	544
5	5	513	14	4	430
6	4	418	15	4	428
7	4	428	16	3	180
8	3	180	17	4	420
9	5	510	18	4	440
	36	3,580		35	3,586

Totals: Par 71, Yards 7,166.
*In U.S. Open play, the fifth hole is changed to a par-4 with reduced yardage. Total yardage becomes approximately 7,100; par, 70.

Water affects play on eight holes at the Cypress Creek Course of the Champions Golf Club in Houston, including the 228-yard fourth. The big course—big bunkers, big greens, big problems—tunnels through thick stands of trees.

jdm country club

(FORMERLY PGA NATIONAL)

In golfing parlance, a "driving course" is one on which the golfer is severely challenged off every non-par-3 tee. Such a description fits only a few courses in the world, and one of them that should definitely be included is the East Course of the JDM Country Club (former home golf course and headquarters of the Professional Golfers' Ass'n) in Palm Beach Gardens, Fla. The new name bears the initials of its founder and owner, multimillionaire John D. MacArthur.

It is the most testing of three courses at this Florida east coast golfing center, although its mates, the North and West, have many of the East's characteristics. All were designed by Dick Wilson, whose list of golf course architectural masterpieces includes many in Florida and the Caribbean islands. The PGA courses were opened for play in 1964, and it was not long after the East was recognized nationally as one of "America's 100 Greatest Tests of Golf" as named by *Golf Digest.*

Every driving area at the East Course is threatened by strategic fairway bunkering, lines of tall pine trees or lateral water hazards, and some by all three. There is an angle woven into every one of the full tee-shot holes, ranging from a slight bend near the green as on the 563-yard, par-5 sixth, to a 90-degree turn midway through the 388-yard, par-4 No. 13. Some turns are forced by bunkering, water or trees, others by direct doglegging of the fairways.

It isn't that the drive is the only problem at the East Course. Once in "safe" territory off the tee, the golfer's second shot has to be skillfully directed. The longer holes demand accurate long irons and fairway woods to targets threatened by the same kind of hazards. The East's greens are all elevated and well-bunkered. They are large and eccentrically shaped, providing many difficult pin positions. Some of them are in necks hard by sand and/or sharply sloped embankments. The greens are relatively level, but with many subtle rolls not easily detected.

Add to all this the constant Florida wind and you have a most challenging stretch of holes.

Still, some marvelous scores have been made at the PGA Country Club. The most remarkable was Sam Snead's 268—20 under par—during the 1972 PGA Seniors Championship. Snead, then 60, played 72 holes without once three-putting a green. On one hole he did use a putter from off the green and did not get down in two, if you want to call that a three-putt.

The record Snead broke was a 271, fashioned by Jack Nicklaus in winning the individual championship at the 1971 World Cup, which pits some 30 two-man teams from nations all over the world in stroke-play competition. Nicklaus and Lee Trevino won this one for the United States. But when the PGA Championship was held at the East Course, also in 1971, Nicklaus could shoot no better than 281, and that was a winner. The course measured at its upper limit of over 7,000 yards for all three competitions.

Probably the toughest driving holes are on the back nine. There are two par-3s (11 and 16), but on every one of the other seven holes the drive is crucial. On the 417-yard 10th there are heavy woods on the left and bunkers on both sides of the fairway. The 510-yard 12th doglegs left around a lake, and there are three bunkers in the fairway to the right. The 388-yard 13th presents a 90-degree right turn with the drive down a tunnel cut between tall pines. A line of four fairway bunkers is arranged to the left of the driving area.

Bunkers cluster on both sides of the target off the tee of the 441-yard 14th, as they do on the 369-yard 15th. A long lake presses in on the left side of the big 588-yard 17th. There are no bunkers to the right that will bother the drive, but the second must touch down in an area outlined by sand. The PGA's 18th is a majestic hole, a 421-yard par-4, with water all along its left side. Naturally, there are bunkers to the right. The second must carry another lake and reach a highly elevated green with three sand bunkers in front and more on each side.

—Hubert Mizell

PGA CHAMPIONSHIP WINNER		
Year	Winner	Score
1971	Jack Nicklaus	281

JDM (EAST) SCORECARD					
Hole	Par	Yards	Hole	Par	Yards
1	5	523	10	4	417
2	4	363	11	3	232
3	3	223	12	5	510
4	4	397	13	4	388
5	4	431	14	4	441
6	5	563	15	4	369
7	3	170	16	3	193
8	4	402	17	5	588
9	4	465	18	4	421
	36	3,537		36	3,559

Totals: Par 72, Yards 7,096.

Stiff winds are nearly always an added challenge at the long East Course, designed by Dick Wilson, formerly called the PGA National Golf Club in Palm Beach Gardens, Fla, and recently re-named JDM Country Club. Breezes tend to blow high shots off line into one of the many water and sand hazards. On this 421-yard 18th hole, the direct approach to the green is from the left of the picture over the corner of the water and the trap.

97

southern hills

Southern Hills Country Club in Tulsa is a time-honored testament to man's aggressive optimism. It was opened in 1935 — smack in the middle of the Great Depression.

A civic and business leader donated the 300-acre property on the contingency that it be developed into a first-rate club. More than a hundred other prominent citizens met and pledged a total of $100,000—half the amount needed for the project. The other half was raised and Perry Maxwell of Ardmore, Okla., was hired as the course architect. The layout he designed has been a source of pride to the entire state ever since. Five United States Golf Ass'n national tournaments and one PGA Championship have been held there.

Anyone who has ever played the course comes away with two indelible impressions—you must drive the ball to preferred fairway positions and be able to escape powdery sand. Rated in the top 20 of *Golf Digest*'s 100 Greatest Tests of Golf, Southern Hills yields only to the most skilled players.

Even they have difficulty breaking the tournament par of 70 (it's 71 for members). The course goes at just under 7,000 yards for major events. Tommy Bolt's winning 283 in the 1958 U.S. Open was three over par, while Dave Stockton was one under at 279 in winning the 1970 PGA Championship.

Driving is so important because all but two of the par-4s and par-5s offer doglegged fairways in one direction or the other. Tee shots must be carefully placed around the corners because of tall trees or husky fairway bunkers. There is essentially only one way to play each of these holes, and if the primary target is missed off the tee the golfer has difficulty regrouping. On the 427-yard, par-four 18th, for instance, which doglegs right and up to an elevated green, the drive must travel 220 yards or so to reach an opening at the corner only 30 yards wide.

During major tournaments the thick, matted bermuda rough is allowed to grow about 2¾ inches deep. Strong golfers have been known to injure wrists and hands trying to recover from the rough. For normal play, it is cut down only slightly, to two inches. The rough grass is always lush because the course's irrigation system reaches it.

Southern Hills' sand is distinctively soft and friable. It is called No. 6 Wash and is from the nearby Arkansas River. A ball will often burrow deeply into the sand. It is not, however, the white silica sand used during the 1958 U.S. Open—that sand was even lighter and resulted in numerous fried-egg lies.

Summertime in Tulsa is hot enough to produce steam in the sand traps. Despite the frequently oppressive heat, Southern Hills' turf is exceptionally well maintained. During any 24-hour period in summer about 200,000 gallons of water may be distributed on the course, and the daily gallonage can go as high as 400,000. The greens often are syringed during the day, sometimes even during tournament play, to keep them in good shape.

The bermuda-grass fairways give fine lies—but they aren't all level even though the course is located on prairie land. There are rises to contend with, especially on the six holes that begin or finish near the clubhouse which is situated atop a large hill. The bent-grass greens are medium size, many sloping severely from back to front, all rife with subtle contours. They putt very truly.

The course necessitates all-round ability and Bolt was exceptional when he won the '58 Open at age 39. At that time he had won 11 tour events but no major ones. Always one of the game's most accurate drivers, he put that talent to special use as he swept to a four-stroke victory, with Gary Player in second place. Tommy hit 58 or 59 (he can't remember which) of the 72 greens in par figures or better. When he needed a good recovery shot he usually made it. Ben Hogan had been the favorite, but early in the tournament hurt his left wrist chopping from the wiry rough and did not contend.

Like Bolt before him, Dave Stockton drove well in winning the 1970 PGA Championship. On the rare times when he didn't, he was able to recover from the rough and bunkers. At one time in the last round the determined Stockton had a seven-stroke lead. He finally won by two strokes over Bob Murphy and Arnold Palmer.

"Southern Hills is one of the best driving tests anywhere," Stockton said later. The USGA obviously agrees. It has again selected the course as a U.S. Open site in 1977.   —*Nick Seitz*

U.S. OPEN WINNER		
Year	Winner	Score
1958	Tommy Bolt	283

PGA CHAMPIONSHIP WINNER		
1970	Dave Stockton	279

SOUTHERN HILLS SCORECARD*

Hole	Par	Yards	Hole	Par	Yards
1	4	459	10	4	401
2	4	447	11	3	167
3	4	410	12	4	440
4	4	375	13	5	551
5	5	625	14	3	209
6	3	182	15	4	413
7	4	382	16	5	545
8	3	218	17	4	369
9	4	387	18	4	450
	35	3,485		36	3,545

Totals: Par 71, Yards 7,030.
*In major tournament play, the 13th hole becomes a par-4, lowering total par to 70; total yardage is reduced to under 7,000.

Two of the reasons that Southern Hills is a great driving course are evident on the 427-yard 18th which doglegs abruptly uphill and to the right (above) where the tee shot must be pin-pointed to avoid tall trees and husky fairway bunkers from whose powdery sand escape is difficult.

harbour town

Although golf historians continually debate what was the first course opened in America, there is significant evidence for one named the South Carolina Golf Club. Its backers claim they were teeing off as early at 1786 on the sophisticated acres of Harleston's Green. Original members supposedly played the ancient Scottish game while dodging grazing cattle, cricket players and romping children trailed by nurses.

In the nearly 200 years since, Harleston's Green has been gobbled up by expanding Charleston. SCGC was left in limbo. New sites were tried, but seldom lasted for long. Then, in 1969, the club was revitalized by the Sea Pines Company at its marvelous new Harbour Town Golf Links, down the coastline from Charleston on Hilton Head Island.

The clientele of Harleston's Green, being strict devotees to the Scottish way, would have loved the golfing challenge of Harbour Town. Although measuring 6,655 yards, exceptionally short by American championship standards, the layout at Hilton Head will try the patience of even the most superior of golfers.

Pete Dye, a rebel among golf course architects, mixed his own special effects with the tradition of British links. He used water, wind and the jagged, swampy shoreline. Sprawling bunkers in dozens of shapes are spotted judiciously and often rimmed with such unlikely materials as sawed-off railroad ties or telephone poles.

Jack Nicklaus, the world's top golfer, began to sharpen his talents as a course builder by whispering in Dye's ear during construction. Many jumped to the conclusions that a man so powerful as Nicklaus would build a course 8,000 yards long with mile-wide fairways and greens large enough to house Buckingham Palace. Nothing doing. Jack admires the British philosophies and Harbour Town was opened with tiny greens, pinched fairways and length that a non-Superman can live with.

All of Harbour Town's par-3s are memorable, but the most famous—and most difficult—hole is a par-4, the marvelously-scenic, horribly-treacherous 18th. Someplace in the 458 yards between tee and green there lies a graveyard. If there's one hole that should have a graveyard, this it is. This closing test resembles the final hole at Pebble Beach with a double carry over water but this one may be even tougher to par.

The drive must be adequately long and placed with slide-rule accuracy to avoid the water and provide any kind of approach shot to the green. Even then, a good player can be faced with a fairway wood to the green and, if he's short, there's plenty of Calibogue Sound to swallow the ball. Even a slight hook will risk finding the murky water. If there's one advantage, it is that you can aim your approach shot at a red-and-white-striped lighthouse that adds charm and character to the setting.

The four par-3 holes are classic examples of imaginative par-3 design. Three of them involve carries over water to shallow greens, thus demanding careful club selection. The other has a deep but very narrow green completely encircled by sand. Overhanging trees next to the green make this a picturesque and exacting hole.

Unlike so many modern courses, Harbour Town's par-3 holes all have reasonable yardages. The longest is the 17th, a 188-yard carry over water. Calibogue Sound's presence behind the green causes wind to be an important factor. Club selection can range from a mid-iron to a driver.

The fourth is a 180-yard shot to a green situated on a peninsula in a lake. The only option besides hitting the green is a weak push to the right but this leaves a difficult chip to the green.

The 14th is the easiest of the par-3s but, even at 152 yards, presents a number of problems. You tee off through a chute of trees and must hit the green as there is water short and to the right and a tiny, pot-hole trap to the left.

Harbour Town immediately became host to a pro tour event, the Heritage Classic, and drew unbridled praise from the likes of Arnold Palmer, Gary Player, Lee Trevino and Tom Weiskopf. It is a course that demands the use of all 14 clubs, a layout for the golfing purist who frowns at the trend of building super-long, super-wide courses. It is unquestionably one of the half dozen finest courses built within the last 40 years. It was recognized, after one year of existence, as one of America's greatest tests of golf and is currently ranked in the top 20 courses by *Golf Digest.* Palmer won the inaugural Heritage Classic in 1969 and was followed to the winner's circle by Bob Goalby in 1970, Hale Irwin in 1971 and 1973, and Johnny Miller in 1972 and 1974.

—*Hubert Mizell*

HERITAGE CLASSIC WINNERS		
Year	Winner	Score
1969	Arnold Palmer	283
1970	Bob Goalby	280
1971	Hale Irwin	279
1972	Johnny Miller	281
1973	Hale Irwin	272

HARBOUR TOWN SCORECARD					
Hole	Par	Yards	Hole	Par	Yard
1	4	380	10	4	453
2	5	492	11	4	418
3	4	383	12	4	405
4	3	180	13	4	358
5	5	521	14	3	152
6	4	403	15	5	562
7	3	167	16	4	378
8	4	433	17	3	188
9	4	324	18	4	458
	36	3,283		35	3,372

Totals: Par 71, Yards 6,655.

Treacherous hazards and magnificent scenery make the Sea Pines Plantation's Harbour Town Golf Links on Hilton Head Island, S.C., almost a Circean lure for adventuresome golfers. The 458-yard 18th (this page) and the 180-yard fourth (overleaf) demonstrate how the course can beguile and betray a golfer.

colonial

Arnold Palmer, that legendary conqueror of golf courses, has always had a difficult time with Colonial Country Club in Fort Worth, Texas. His scores in the National Invitation Tournament have included such nasty numbers as 81, 80, 79 and 78.

"It's not my type of course," Arnold says. "It confines me off the tee. There are only two par-5 holes. I get mad and try to cram the ball into the hole. You can't do that at Colonial. You have to romance it, be content with pars."

If the great Palmer can be so victimized by this 7,172-yard monster, pity the 1,000 members who spend lifetimes trying to make pars on treacherous holes such as the 466-yard fifth, which could be the most difficult par-4 on earth.

It was amid such Colonial ruggedness that Ben Hogan molded his unsurpassed skills as a shotmaker. Hogan is a member at the club built by oilman Marvin Leonard in 1936 and Ben won the National Invitation five times. Having practiced at Colonial, he usually found tournament courses elsewhere easy by comparison. Hogan, since he was no longer playing competitively, moved his business across town to the more exclusive Shady Oaks Country Club, but a cache of his trophies glitters in a special room just off the lobby at Colonial.

Not even Hogan parred that infamous fifth hole with any regularity. It's a hole with heavy trees hugging from each side and the Trinity River there to gobble up balls straying past the ample greenery to the right side. A strong drive of over 250 yards with a gentle fade is required to get within striking distance of the green, even with a long iron or fairway wood. If you play safe—to the left—there is still a ditch along with the trees to make life miserable. Most members simply give in, playing the hole—mentally at least—as a par-5.

A poll of touring professionals usually will produce a high degree of support for Colonial as the most demanding tournament site on the regular American circuit. It usually will get stronger support than even Pebble Beach or Firestone, two other notably difficult courses played annually on the tour.

Colonial became one of the newer courses ever to host the U.S. Open when the 1941 event was played there. It was to become known as the "Duration Open" since winner Craig Wood held the title five years when the tournament was suspended during World War II. Even at that, Wood almost succumbed to Colonial's toughness on the second day and had to be encouraged even to continue the tournament.

Wood, who had won the Masters earlier that year, thought seriously about packing up his clubs and walking in from that fifth hole. It was the Open's second round and a storm blackened the Texas sky. Lightning flashed, the rain poured and play was delayed twice. Wood stood three over par for the tournament, his drive was in the fifth hole's ditch and the corset on his aching back was soaked and heavy. Craig told his playing companion, Tommy Armour, that he was quitting. "No, you're not," barked Armour, "this course is eating everyone alive. Keep swinging. You'll be O K." Wood took Armour's advice, but bogeyed the fifth to go four over par. He then played the next 49 holes in even par and beat Denny Shute by three shots for the title.

Colonial has suffered its share of misfortune. The clubhouse has twice burned down. The course has seen floods that caused Texans to say, "See you at the Invitation if the creeks don't rise." It has survived all this to be recognized as one of the country's great golfing tests. "It's the toughest par-70 in the world," says former tour star Cary Middlecoff. And, former Masters winner Jack Burke, co-owner with Jimmy Demaret of the classy Champions Club in Houston, once remarked, "If you were told to try and shoot par on a golf course, Colonial would be the last one you'd try it on."   —Hubert Mizell

U.S. OPEN WINNER			COLONIAL SCORECARD						
Year	Winner	Score	Hole	Par	Yards	Hole	Par	Yards
1941	Craig Wood	284	1	5	572	10	4	416
			2	4	389	11	5	609
			3	4	480	12	4	430
			4	3	236	13	3	209
			5	4	466	14	4	431
			6	4	400	15	4	442
			7	4	438	16	3	200
			8	3	209	17	4	387
			9	4	405	18	4	434
				35	3,595		35	3,577

Totals: Par 70, Yards 7,172.

A Texas gallery surrounds the water-protected green at the 405-yard, par-4 ninth hole at the Colonial Country Club in Fort Worth. This course, a familiar stop on the PGA tour, is known as one that rewards well-placed drives but severely punishes off-line shots from the tees.

pebble beach

Like many of our greatest courses, Pebble Beach was designed by amateurs. Jack Neville and Douglas Grant, both California amateur champions, laid out the 6,815-yard course in 1919. In 1972 Pebble Beach finally hosted the U. S. Open, which incidentally was the first time in history the blue-blooded event was held on a non-private golf course.

At Pebble, which played with even more difficulty than it does in the Crosby tournament, more good players shot more bad scores than at any time since the 1935 Open at Oakmont. Scores of 80 eventually began to look respectable. No one came close to threatening Billy Casper's course record of 65.

Jack Nicklaus won with a two-over-par score of 290, tying Bobby Jones' record of 13 major titles. The winning score has been exceeded only once (a 293 by Julius Boros in 1963 at Brookline) since 1935.

Frank Beard said that, in the process of missing the 36-hole cut with rounds of 85 and 80, he offered the young man carrying the scoreboard for his group $30 to abandon it. One must understand Beard's frugality to appreciate the depth of his despair at the time.

After Mason Rudolph shot a third-round 86 he noted that, "This course is built right around my game. It touches no part of it."

The pros aren't used to this sort of thing. They see a course this challenging only once a year —in the Open. Half the tracks they play make little more demand on their ingenuity than your neighborhood driving range.

George Archer made the cut but wished he'd blown it and gone with the wind. He shot 87 the last day, heaved his ball into the ocean bordering the 18th hole and mustered a disbelieving grin. "What would happen if we played a course like this every week?" he pondered. "I'd quit playing and get a job watering the greens. I could take off all the time and never be missed."

Nicklaus, who has called Pebble Beach the best thinking man's course in the country and possibly the world, said that ill-luck often supplanted skill in the last round. But his skill, while now and again overwhelmed by the elements, was blatantly obvious in the three-stroke victory for his third Open Championship.

Pebble Beach has held three U. S. Ama-teur Championships, the first in 1929. That was the year Johnny Goodman, then an unknown, came out of Omaha to beat Bobby Jones in the first round. The winner was unheralded Harrison Johnston of Minnesota, who bested a field that included Francis Ouimet, Chick Evans, Lawson Little, Chandler Egan and Cyril Tolley. In 1947 the cast included Dick Chapman, Bud Ward, Smiley Quick, Bob Rosburg and Frank Stranahan, but the winner was Skee Riegel, who walked like a fighter and played like a machine, smoking two packs of cigarettes per round, to beat Johnny Dawson in the finals. In 1961, Nicklaus took the second of his amateur crowns here, beating Dudley Wysong 8 and 6 in the final.

Pebble Beach opens like a lamb, with four easy, very ordinary holes. The fifth is a short, quick thrust up through a sliver of light between the trees and then, suddenly, you are upon the ocean riding two terrifying shots along the crest of a massive bluff to the sixth green. To the right, waiting below, thrashing surf and rocks.

The sixth hole, a 515-yard par-5 that Byron Nelson thinks is the toughest hole on the course, begins a stretch of five of the most spectacular holes in golf, three of them on a narrow, craggy spit that overhangs the ocean. The seventh is a tiny, 120-yard downhill pitch that looks almost like a miniature golf hole. But when the wind blows, it can require a solid 4-iron into the gale. The eighth is a marvel, one of the great two-shotters in the world. After a blind tee shot to a plateau, you must hit 180 yards or more over a sheer cliff, across a chasm that resembles a shark's maw and to a green that is pitched into a depression and completely surrounded by bunkers.

The ninth stretches 450 yards along the ocean, its right margin eaten away by surf. When the wind is up, the biggest hitters cannot get home even with two wood shots. During the 1963 Crosby, Dale Douglass took 19 blows here after landing on the steep bank, an even worse place to be than the rocky beach below. The 10th is another long par-4 whose green is also pitched above that treacherous cliff.

There are many who believe the inland stretch from 11 through 16 is inferior and not at all in keeping with the hair-raising ocean holes. This is only partially true. Certainly 11 and 12 are

U.S. OPEN WINNER			PEBBLE BEACH SCORECARD					
Year	Winner	Score	Hole	Par	Yards	Hole	Par	Yards
1972	Jack Nicklaus	290	1	4	385	10	4	436
			2	5	507	11	4	380
			3	4	368	12	3	205
			4	4	325	13	4	400
			5	3	180	14	5	555
			6	5	515	15	4	406
			7	3	120	16	4	400
			8	4	425	17	3	218
			9	4	450	18	5	540
				36	3,275		36	3,540

Totals: Par 72, Yards 6,815.

One of golf's most widely recognized holes, the 540-yard 18th at Pebble Beach, stretches alongside the rocky shore of Carmel Bay, producing a vision of intimidation rarely equalled among golf's great finishing holes.

It's all or nothing at the tiny (120 yards) seventh hole at Pebble Beach, a downhill shot, normally calling for little more than a half wedge. Capricious winds can change this to a full 3-iron.

routine holes, but 13, a straight-away par-4 of 400 yards, is perhaps the most underrated hole on the course. The second shot must fly true to avoid bunkers and trees guarding the green.

The 14th is a marvelously deft par-5 that curls away from the sea to the right and has been the scene of a few miserable encounters. Here Arnold Palmer, who has never won the Crosby, came a cropper in 1964. In going for the green on his second shot, Palmer hit a tree on the right and went out-of-bounds twice. He made nine on the hole and dropped from contention. The next day a storm knocked the tree down.

The 17th, a par-3 surrounded by sand and ocean, looks more beatable in real life than it appears on television—until you play it. The green sits precariously on the edge of the ocean on this 218-yard hole and any shots hit too long will find the rocky beach and cliffs below. The green is pinched at the waist and hump-backed, forcing players to go for the sector of the green on which the flagstick is cut. In the Open, against a strong wind, Nicklaus hit one of the great shots in history, a 1-iron that hit the flagstick and dropped inches away.

The 18th, a journey that ends happily only after three very strong shots and two good putts, is among the most ballyhooed finishing holes in golf, and quite rightly.

This 540-yard par-5 curls frighteningly along the jagged coastline with the ocean at the left from tee to green. Trees on the right serve to define the best, but riskiest, line from the tee, or stymie the golfer on subsequent shots. Only the bravest and luckiest player would try for the perfection needed to reach the green in two shots, a stirring and fitting climax to one of the world's greatest golf courses.

—*Cal Brown*

RESORT GOLF

A majority of the finest resort golf courses in the United States are clustered in areas peculiarly suited to golf because of favorable geographical and climatic features. The following section of this book is devoted to the most popular golfing resort areas of the nation. The principal purpose is to acquaint the reader with the major golfing facilities in each area and their general ambience or atmosphere. It is impossible, of course, to detail each of the courses. A more complete directory is contained in Part 5, beginning on page 243, which lists the locations and other pertinent data for more than 900 golf courses generally available to visitors.

The first resort area of the country to describe itself as "the golf capital" of the United States was Pinehurst. Located in the remote sandhills of North Carolina, it got its start in golf with the opening of its first nine holes in 1898.

For many years thereafter the typical golf resort included a hotel of lavish architectural proportions located in an out-of-the-way place. The frank aims of such places were to attract the very wealthy of the day and, indeed, they did. Among those still in existence, still serving the public are—the Belleview-Biltmore and Boca Raton hotels in Florida; the Broadmoor Hotel in Colorado; the Sheraton-French Lick Hotel in Indiana; the Arlington Hotel in Hot Springs, Ark.; and the two leading mid-south establishments—The Greenbrier and The Homestead across the Virginia-West Virginia state line from one another. For the most part, these grand old resorts still stand alone with little nearby resort development.

In contrast, most of the nation's important resort golf courses today are in areas which have attracted many golf course developments and they have become part of major resort clusters.

An exception to this modern trend is Callaway Gardens which stands by itself with 63 golf holes in Pine Mountain, Ga. Few recently developed enterprises match its self-contained space and charm.

It is time now to embark on a literary golf trip that will take you to every type of course imaginable—those nestled in mountains, cooled by tropical breezes, in tree-choked parklands and even those insulated from surrounding deserts.

mountain courses

Perhaps the most significant influence on golf in the mountainous areas of the United States has been the growth of skiing. Golf facilities have been created to help attract summer business and provide year-round residents with recreation. At the same time, golf course builders are using better techniques in constructing golf courses in the mountains, using new earth-moving equipment, new grasses and more efficient drainage systems. Some exceptional tests of golfing skill have resulted.

Probably the finest mountain course in the United States is the Upper Cascades, a superb William Flynn design that is one of three golf courses at The Homestead in White Sulphur Springs, W.Va. (A separate chapter on the Homestead and The Greenbrier appear on page 116.)

THE ROCKIES AND THE WEST

The first of the great western ski areas, Sun Valley, boasted the first western ski area golf course. It was designed and built by George Von Elm in the 1950s. The successful experience with golf at Sun Valley inspired other western ski areas such as Vail and Snowmass at Aspen to look to the sport as a means of luring people there during the summer.

The Broadmoor in Colorado Springs, Colo., the best known of the western mountain golf resorts, was built without regard to skiing. It

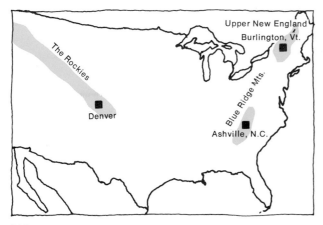

With the Broadmoor Hotel forming a magnificent backdrop, golfers play the 15th hole on the East Course at the Colorado Springs resort. Hilly terrain and numerous large mounds and bunkers produce many an uneven lie on this scenic test.

Dramatic scenery invariably accompanies play at mountain courses such as the Grandfather Golf and Country Club at Linville, N.C. (this page), cutting swaths of green through the pine forests. Next page (upper photo) the white clubhouse at the Concord Hotel, Kiamesha Lake, N.Y., overlooks its famous "monster" course in the Catskills. Below is the picturesque Robert Trent Jones layout at the Woodstock Inn, Vermont. To the right, white birches frame a golfer playing the lovely Equinox course, also in Vermont.

possesses two of the best mountain courses in the United States, both designed by Robert Trent Jones.

THE NORTHERN APPALACHIANS

William Howard Taft, Ulysses S. Grant and Theodore Roosevelt all stayed at the Equinox House in Manchester, in southern Vermont, first established in 1769. The adjoining Equinox Country Club was not added until the late 1920s but it just keeps getting better with age. The name of the designer is lost in the murk of time, but he produced a dandy. Farther north, Massachusetts-born William F. Mitchell created the scenic 18 holes at Stowe, Vt., whose first nine were built in 1950, before any other eastern ski area had golf.

Whereas golf preceded skiing in most of New England, it followed at some popular ski areas such as the Haystack-Mt. Snow area, Stratton, Sugarbush and at Mt. Washington, Me., highest peak in the northeastern states.

Another of the East's popular mountainous areas is the Catskills of New York State, where in recent years golf has become as popular an attraction as kosher cooking. The gem of the Catskills' courses is the "monster" at the Concord Hotel in Kiamesha Lake, designed by Joseph Finger. This gruelling test, normally played at about 6,800 yards, derives its name from the fact that it can stretch to 7,600 yards.

THE SOUTHERN APPALACHIANS

In the Blue Ridge chain of the southern Appalachians running through North Carolina there is a big concentration of resort courses. Around Boone, in the north, the most testing and best maintained is Grandfather Mountain Golf and Country Club. Designed with great care by Ellis Maples, it wanders through a wooded valley at an elevation of 3,800 feet. When stretched to its full length of 6,880 yards, it is a granddaddy of a course.

Near Asheville, N.C., in the southern tier of the mountains, is another cluster of scenic courses, including Beaver Lake, which claims the longest par-5 in the U.S. (690 yards) and Black Mountain, whose 745-yard 17th hole, a par-6, is believed to be the longest in the world.

—*William H. Davis*

poconos

In eastern Pennsylvania, one of the United States' last bastions of peaceful countryside, lie some of the nation's prettiest golf courses. The Pocono Mountains area, in the northeast part of the state and snuggled against the south-running Delaware River, contains more than 35 courses and some 260 resorts of all sizes and descriptions. Between Philadelphia and Harrisburg in the southeast corner is Pennsylvania Dutch Country, rich farming land dotted with fewer but equally attractive courses and resorts.

Many of the resorts in the Poconos were originated by Quakers who populate much of the eastern half of the state. Two with Quaker beginnings are the large and comfortable institutions at Pocono Manor and Buck Hill Falls, both opened in 1901.

Pocono Manor, near Stroudsburg on the way to Scranton, has two 18-hole courses, both par-72s. Buck Hill features 27 golf holes, the regular 18, by William Gordon, a rolling 6,665 yards. Each resort has about 300 guest rooms and, like most of the other Pocono inns, offers many other recreational and entertainment facilities.

There are three other outstanding Pocono resorts — the Shawnee Inn and Country Club, choral director Fred Waring's delightful place right on the Delaware River; the Tamiment Resort and Country Club, pastoral and tranquil; and the newer Le Chateau Country Club, farthest west of the big ones. Shawnee has three nines— Red, White and Blue, apropos to this historical area — fanning out from Waring's unique golf tower. Shawnee's original 18 was designed by A. W. Tillinghast and later remodeled by William Diddle, who also did the third nine. Tamiment's Robert Trent Jones-designed course, which can stretch to 7,110 yards, is packed with spectacular views. From the third tee you can see sections of New York and New Jersey. The Le Chateau course, designed by Geoffrey Cornish of Massachusetts, is a stern test in lakes, hills and woods.

Art Wall Jr., the 1959 Masters champion and the area's most famous golfer, has designed an extremely attractive resort course at Tobyhanna, the Pocono Farms Country Club.

About an hour's drive south from the Poconos is Pennsylvania Dutch Country where the farmers' brightly decorated barns add color to nearly every mile of road.

There are three nicely spaced resorts in Dutch Country, the western-most being the five-course complex at Hershey. Ben Hogan was professional at the original, and still magnificent, Hershey Country Club (West Course) from 1941 through 1951, so the town has a deep running interest in golf. This course, designed by Maurice McCarthy of New York, is rated as one of the nation's 100 greatest tests by *Golf Digest*.

Since then the Hershey company has built four more courses. The most recent is a devilish layout designed by George Fazio, which when it matures might reach that 100-best list itself. All of the courses are beautifully conditioned. One of them, the municipal Parkview Golf Club, has twice been the site of the National Public Links Championship.

One of the nation's largest and most complete vacation spots is the Host Farm Resort in Lancaster, in the heart of Dutch Country.

A few miles out of Philadelphia is the Downingtown Inn in which entertainer Mickey Rooney has a financial interest. The 6,555-yard George Fazio course has the subtle look of a deceiver— it's tougher than it appears at first glance .

While the courses of mountainous eastern Pennsylvania fall short in stature of some of the states' great tests like Merion and Oakmont, they abound in charm and sheer enjoyability.

—*John P. May*

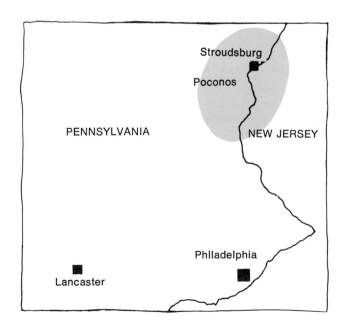

114

Pocono Manor's ski-slope seventh hole (above) is one of Pennsylvania's best-known holes. At right is the Hershey Hotel, centerpiece of one of the state's most noted golfing resorts.

greenbrier/homestead

They sit like two restoration pieces, amid six full-length golf courses in the Appalachian Mountains—The Greenbrier and The Homestead. Encrusted with more wealth and tradition than the annual meeting of the United States Golf Ass'n, these two grand old resorts (dating back to 1776 and 1790, respectively) have stood for many years as a kind of barometer of social and economic success. Many executives have, at one time or another, attended meetings at either The Greenbrier, in White Sulphur Springs, W. Va., or The Homestead, in Hot Springs, Va., although surprisingly few seem to have visited both, even though they are only 40 miles apart by car. If you have been to one, it is said, you're successful, but you're a little more "in" if you've been to both.

Despite the large volume of expense account dollars that circulates at the two resorts, Sam Snead, the host professional at Greenbrier, moans over the loss of "action" on the golf course. "I used to could pick me up a match for a grand or fifteen hundred most any day," he says wistfully, "and now all we got coming down here are these bright young executives in their $90 suits, and they can't figure no way to get more than a $10 Nassau on their expense accounts." A playing lesson with Sam costs $100 and he'll tee it up with anyone who has a bankroll. At age 62, he can still shoot any of The Greenbrier courses, when the ante is right, in under 65.

Snead, who began his golfing career at The Homestead and then moved to The Greenbrier in 1936, is involved in more local folklore than Abe Lincoln in Illinois. He was born in Ashwood, a few miles from Hot Springs, in country so steep, Snead says, "that the dogs only have room to wag their tails up and down."

At The Homestead, each of the three courses has its own identity, clubhouse and golf professional. The Upper Cascades layout, which was built in 1923 by William Flynn, is one of the best courses in the country (ranked by *Golf Digest* in "America's 100 Greatest Tests of Golf"). Located about three miles from the hotel in a setting of pastoral, mountain beauty, it unfolds with a marvelous assortment of shots. Snead believes it is the finest training course he knows. "There isn't any kind of hill you don't have to play from,

or any kind of shot you won't hit there," Sam drawls. "If you could train a youngster to play on that course, he'll play anywhere." Right out the side door of The Homestead is its oldest course, dating from 1892, which winds through the hills behind the hotel. It is easy, pleasant golf with a heavy dose of scenery. John D. Rockefeller used to enjoy pitching dimes into a brook on the first hole and watching the caddies scramble for them. The newest course, laid out in 1962 by Trent Jones, is long and tough and almost never crowded, partly because it is six miles from the hotel and partly because you can't walk it—the distances between tee and green are so long.

At the Greenbrier, all three golf courses fan out from the yellow-awninged Golf and Tennis Club which is just a short walk from the hotel and is the hub of all daytime social and athletic activity. All are well-conditioned, but less demanding layouts than the Cascades courses. The best of them is The Old White, which was built in 1910, and has since been remodeled.

The Greenbrier course, built in 1925, was the scene of Snead's remarkable 59, scored in the third round of the Sam Snead Festival in 1959, the lowest known round of tournament golf in history. In that round, Snead played the last seven holes in 21 strokes, seven under par. The third course, the Lakeside, was added in 1962 and has become well known among lesser golfers for some of its ball-hungry water hazards.

Not far from The Greenbrier, at a private estate called Oakhurst, five Scots began playing

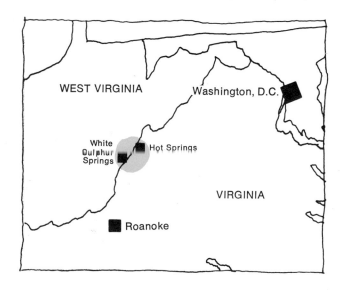

116

Among the pleasures of golf at The Greenbrier are beautifully conditioned fairways, refreshing views of the surrounding blue mountains and then, after finishing a round on the 163-yard 18th (above) of the Old White course, climbing past Sam Snead's golf shop to sip a cool drink on the veranda of the handsome clubhouse in the background.

117

golf with imported sticks and gutta percha balls in 1884, four years before John Reid and his "apple tree gang" were credited with having started golf in America in Yonkers, N.Y.

By appearance and age, The Greenbrier and The Homestead are anachronisms in this day of slick, impersonal, automated resorts. Until recently, they were even hard to reach. You once had to own your own railroad car to get to either White Sulphur Springs or Hot Springs.

But times have changed these spas which grew up around the mineral springs that bubble forth all over the region. Both resorts still maintain therapeutic bath clinics, and at Greenbrier there is a diagnostic clinic for visiting executives who want checkups, where the examinations are fitted around golf starting times. In the early days the resorts were hangouts for southern aristocracy, from Thomas Jefferson to John C. Calhoun to Robert E. Lee. When Henry Clay visited The Greenbrier in 1817, his bill for three days came to $16.51½, including room, board, grog, laundry, a dozen cigars and lodging for three horses and a servant. Today you spend that in tips. Each day.

The style at both places has always been very much ladies and gentlemen. Even today, dozens of uniformed attendants seem to lurk behind the pillars in the oversized, well-stuffed lobbies and hallways. The places became, in time, a favored marketplace for eligible young ladies, most of whom rode side-saddle, sipped colored ice through a glass straw, and looked on the game of golf as a mild form of idiocy.

In the lobbies and expensive shops on the ground floors, you still see old ladies who, in much larger numbers, used to spend a month or two tottering about the hallways and sniffing the rich mountain air. Maybe they remember how it was, maybe they come back to relive some half-remembered romance of their youth, or maybe they just don't know where else to spend the rest of their money. They look slightly confused by all the changes, and disapproving of all the fuss about golf and things. And maybe, like the two resorts whose walls have stood for so long, resembling, as someone once said, a couple of great ocean liners beached among the mountains, they wonder if they are the last of their kind.   —Cal Brown

There are three courses at the aristocratic Homestead in Hot Springs, Va., the oldest of which, the hilly Homestead, is shown here against the backdrop of the resort's 175-foot clock tower.

118

You might call it a gathering of eagles, the way prominent golf architects have risen to the challenge of producing fine courses along a 50-mile strip of flat coastland centered by Myrtle Beach, on South Carolina's Atlantic seaboard. These hard-driving, imaginative men must have by dint of their talent made the Grand Strand, as the area is called, into one of America's most attractive golf resort locations. There are now 29 courses in the area.

There are some things on the architects' side. The weather, for one, features long springs and falls and rather mild winters. Myrtle Beach's busiest golf season is from Feb. 15 through May 1.

The lengthy growing season assures the courses solid and well-grassed turf. Although the terrain is level, there are pine forests to cut through, and the architects have used the numerous trees for many natural hazards as well as beautiful, scenic backdrops.

Golf's most widely known architect, Robert Trent Jones, designed the bellwether of Myrtle Beach's courses, the Dunes Golf and Beach Club. It was in 1948 that the Burroughs family, which at one time owned most of the land along this section of the Carolina coast, donated 270 acres to a small group of far-seeing businessmen, who hired Jones to design the Dunes.

In those early days this club was the social center for the community, its shimmering beaches making it a popular resort area even then. The Dunes was open to the public then, but today is a private club with 150 resident and some 100 non-resident members. But like most of the other 20-plus courses now in play along the beach, the Dunes is open to vacationers who stay at certain motels.

Jones incorporated his favorite golfing features into the Dunes—long tees, big fairway traps to define driving areas, large bunkers surrounding well-elevated and sizeable greens. Every tee shot must be planned to avoid a bunker, or a dogleg corner or a hillock that would interfere with the next shot. The most hair-raising hole at the Dunes is the 534-yard 13th, which doglegs right around water (see photo).

Actually, the Dunes was Myrtle Beach's second course, the first being what is known now as the Pine Lakes International Country Club. It was first constructed in the 1920s, a 27-hole layout designed by Robert White, the first president of the Professional Golfers' Ass'n of America. It went through several ownerships and alterations and today it is a pleasant 18-hole test with narrow fairways, small greens and character.

It took a few years for the Dunes to become established, but once entrepreneurs recognized the resort value of the area other courses began going up in bunches. Such golf course architectural stalwarts as George Cobb, J. Porter Gibson, William Byrd, George Fazio, Russell Breeden, Frank Duane, Gene Hamm, Edmund Ault and Jones' son, Rees, have left their marks in the area.

Among the more ambitious new courses are the Bay Tree Golf Plantation, 54 holes designed by Fazio and Breeden; the four-course Myrtle Beach National Golf Club complex designed by Duane and Arnold Palmer; and the magnificent, new Hilton-Arcadian Shores resort, designed by Rees Jones. —*John P. May*

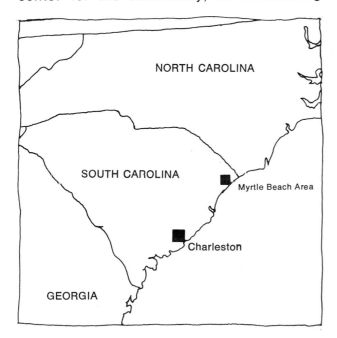

NORTH CAROLINA

SOUTH CAROLINA

Myrtle Beach Area

Charleston

GEORGIA

The 575-yard 13th (next page) at the Dunes Golf and Beach Club is perhaps Robert Trent Jones' most heroic hole. Only one man, Mike Souchak, has ever reached the green in two shots—both drivers.

pinehurst/southern pines

Until the golf course building boom of the 1960s, the undisputed "capital of golf" in the eastern United States was the Pinehurst-Southern Pines area in the sandhills of North Carolina. Including the world-famous No. 2 course at the Pinehurst Country Club as the centerpiece (see page 88), there are more than a dozen golf courses.

Pinehurst is a quaint community, founded in 1895 as a health resort by James W. Tufts. He and his heirs left an indelible New England impress on the area: country cottage architecture, narrow, winding roads and for years a heavily northeastern clientele. The town of Southern Pines, in contrast, a few miles away, became the hub of business activity in the sandhills.

While golf is played almost year-round in the sandhills, spring and fall are the favorite seasons for the sport when temperatures hover in the 60s and 70s. The pine-scented air is bracing and vitally alive. Being in the mid-South, Pinehurst's temperature can climb in the summer, and there is an occasional snow in January and February.

Pinehurst fairways lead golfers through cool tunnels formed by ever-present pine trees. The terrain is gently rolling, providing ample opportunities for the design of interesting courses. Ponds and creeks filled with clear, cold water abound—it's almost a pleasure to see the concentric ripples dilate as your golf ball disappears.

Tufts' heirs operated Pinehurst, Inc., with its five golf courses, until 1971 when it was sold to the giant Diamondhead Corporation for $9 million. The sale included the five courses, five hotels of various sizes and a race track. Diamondhead, developed and controlled by shipping-transportation magnate Malcolm McLean, has modernized Pinehurst's resort accommodations and established there an imposing new Golf Hall of Fame.

High quality amateur competition is often seen, particularly at Pinehurst's No. 2 Course where the North and South Amateur is annually played. After a lapse of nearly 25 years, professional competition has returned with the rich World Open.

Some of the Pinehurst courses are being modified. No. 5, the most recently completed (1961), was the second most difficult until No. 4 was renovated by Robert Trent Jones after the Dia-mondhead sale. Larger bunkers and added yardage has now toughened No. 4. Nos. 1 and 3 are the shortest, a bit over 6,000 yards. Each Pinehurst course includes many of the same strategic challenges favored by Donald Ross, the Scot professional who came to the resort in 1900 and remained there until he died 48 years later.

Immediately after World War II the region's golf facilities consisted of four courses at Pinehurst and one each at the nearby Mid Pines, Pine Needles and Southern Pines clubs. Although seven more courses have been built since, a motorist driving through the peach-growing countryside might not know he was within a few good wood shot's distance of this golfing haven. Signs that announce the existence of most of the courses are unobtrusive and seem to blend in with the green landscape.

All but one of the courses are open to the public. The lone exception is the 27-hole Country Club of North Carolina, recognized as one of the nation's premier courses and designed by Ellis Maples and Willard Byrd. Opened in 1963, this is a residential development which sees quite a bit of play from visitors who know members. Large, comfortable homes in the complex are often rented to groups of golfers for stays of a week or longer. The golf course's second nine, twisting through the colorful pines and strengthened by water hazards, is the showcase. A third nine, while not normally used in championship tournament setups, is an artistic and scenic test with water coming into play interestingly on several holes.

The course at the Pine Needles Lodge and Country Club was designed by Ross and retains its rolling, open character. Pine Needles is owned by Warren and Peggy Kirk Bell and operated on a very informal basis. Golf facilities include covered practice tees, where Mrs. Bell—a former tournament professional—frequently holds golf instruction clinics. All of the guest accommodations are located in comfortable, rustic buildings, well insulated from golf and other activities.

Southern Pines Country Club's original 18 is the second oldest course in the area, having been completed shortly after Pinehurst's first in 1900. It is a relatively hilly semi-private course with a number of interesting doglegs. Another nine has been added.

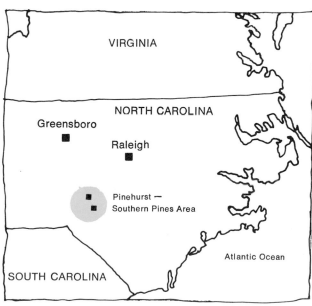

Lush, green grass, deep, blue water and tall, graceful pines encompass the natural setting of the Country Club of North Carolina. The par-3 hole, the 206-yard 16th, plays even tougher than it looks.

The sandhill country of Pinehurst, N.C., is America's original golfing mecca with over two dozen courses. Two of the best are Pine Needles, whose 158-yard third hole is pictured on this page, and Foxfire, whose 175-yard 16th is pictured on the opposite page.

Driving south on Route 1004, about 10 miles west of Pinehurst, the motorist encounters the Foxfire Golf and Country Club, a winding course, designed by Gene Hamm in 1967. This resort has 27 holes, a private airfield for small planes and all the amenities one might expect at a modern, well-planned recreational facility. The course is built on rolling, pine-clad land that once housed a peach farm. There are still fairway-bordering vineyards from which golfers refresh themselves on delicious Scuppernong grapes in the fall. Three spring-fed lakes come into play on seven holes, and the first nine also features a number

of links-type holes. There is also a beach, boat-house and come-to-the-cookout style club along Lake MacKenzie in the heart of the golf course.

The newest course in the area, open in November 1974, is Seven Lakes Country Club, about six miles west of Pinehurst in the small village of West End. It was designed by Peter Tufts, the son of Richard and grandson of Pinehurst's founder. A semi-private course, it is part of a new development called Seven Lakes Resort which will eventually have a par-3 course surrounded by condominiums to go with Tufts' layout. Tufts, not surprisingly an admirer of Donald Ross, has

built traditional themes into the rolling sandhills —mounds around greens, natural rough and small to medium-sized greens an interesting blend of the old and the new.

Indeed, much of the Pinehurst-Southern Pines area has undergone modernization. But, happily, it still bears the imprint of the two most important early figures—founder James Tufts and course designer Donald Ross. Even today everything that is done in the area is inevitably compared with the legacies of these two men.

—*John P. May*

dixie golf islands

Just off the shores of Georgia and South Carolina lie sun-bathed islands, once a hideout for pirates and millionaires. These offer vacationing golfers the same peaceful atmosphere they would normally expect to find on the tropical isles of the Caribbean. Washed by Gulf Stream waters though connected to the mainland by modern causeways, the Dixie Golf Islands string out along the coastline from Charleston, S.C., to near Jacksonville, Fla.

Buccaneers, privateers and slavers once lurked in the protective coves and lagoons now bordered by abundant bermuda-grass fairways. Tall palms and moss-draped oak and pine forests grow from the sandy soil that lines most of the holes. Wild turkey and deer roam the forests, and errant shots are apt to disturb giant sea turtles basking along the shores or alligators which inhabit the numerous inlets.

The area has long been justly famous for one of America's truly fine resorts, The Cloister, with its Sea Island Golf Club whose Plantation and Seaside nines date from 1927. More recently national attention has focused on Hilton Head Island, not only for the high quality of its many championship courses, but also because it is an outstanding example in the trend to golf-oriented communities.

As late as 1968 the only resort developments in this coastal sector were on Hilton Head, St. Simons, Jekyll, Fripp and Wilmington Islands. By 1974 there were not only multiple courses and developments on most of these islands but new resort communities had been completed on Seabrook, Edisto, Skidaway and Amelia Islands plus others slightly inland.

The Cloister at Sea Island was launched as

The stillness of early morning golf beside coastal marshes and beaches typifies Dixie Islands courses. The golfers above are playing the 395-yard seventh hole on George Cobb's plush layout at Sea Palms Golf and Country Club on St. Simons Island, Ga.

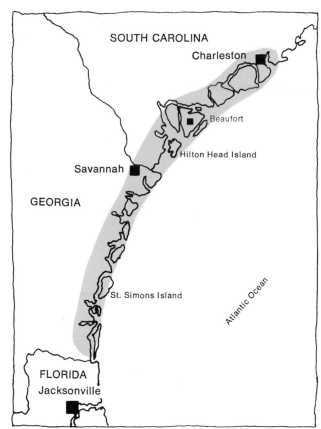

Weaving a tempting risk into the marshland beauty of the 435-yard seventh at Sea Island's Seaside Course was the handiwork of the great British designing team of Colt and Allison.

a resort in 1928 by a local family called Jones. In manner and mood, Sea Island is from another time, a world of quietude and courtliness, ease and elegance, sensibility and service that one finds only rarely nowadays.

Walter Travis put in Sea Island's first nine. He was the first foreigner to win the British Amateur, way back in 1904. Always an individualist, he made heavy use of "chocolate drops"—sharp, grassy hillocks of the type found on many Scottish courses—in designing "Plantation," but died before the course opened. The owners then called in the English architects Colt and Allison to complete the 18, and they built the magnificent "Seaside" nine. Largely man-made on filled marshland, the holes are all of the true "links" type very rare outside Britain, and feature elevated putting surfaces and deep bunkers.

In 1959, the late Dick Wilson put his distinctive style into a third nine, the mellow "Retreat" course. A fourth, by Joe Lee, was put into play in late 1973, giving visitors as intriguing and

challenging a choice of golfing style, strategy and scenic backdrop as you'll come across in 36 holes anywhere in the world.

A completely different flavor will be found just south of St. Simons at the Jekyll Island courses. Originally the private winter playground for the wealthiest families in America, the island was purchased by the State of Georgia in 1947 for $650,000 and is now operated as a state park. The roster of founding families—the Rockefellers, Goulds, Vanderbilts, Marshall Fields, Astors, J. P. Morgans, Pulitzers and J. J. Hills, among others—reportedly controlled one-sixth of the entire world's wealth when they bought the island for $125,000 in 1886.

Nine of the original holes, designed by Travis, remain and still receive a heavy play. Another nine is planned to supplement the two championship 18s built by the state, both designed by Dick Wilson, which fan out from a spacious clubhouse. Golfers will find the motel and golf rates reasonable on Jekyll. —*Howard Gill*

hilton head island

The promised land lies at the end of a lonely road in an unlikely place. One approaches it across the silent South Carolina marshlands, past ghostly plantations reeking of antebellum tradition, toward one of America's most unruly, desolate coastlands.

There, hunkered close against the mainland, is the largest of the Dixie golf islands. In fact it is the largest (save for Long Island) barrier island between Florida and Maine, a 28,000-acre refuge of White Ibis, turtle, alligator, deer, Civil War history and some of the best bank accounts of the upper middle class. Prosperous burghers, merchants and erstwhile practitioners of the martial arts have been drawn to this island retreat, called Hilton Head, by its elegant and peaceful resort environment. The island is a long hop from the blacks and greys of modern city and suburban life; a tasteful amalgam of luxury and rusticity, a mecca of golf, boating, quiet walks along wide beaches, pleasant parties, good service, smiling faces, stunning private homes and plush resort villas: in short, the "good life."

The place literally has been plucked from the clutches of wild animals and even wilder vegetation in the greatest single island-lifting operation of our time; great not so much in size but in manner and style. Substantial areas of land that would make excellent golf courses and home sites are set aside as wildlife sanctuaries. Just by the last hole at Harbour Town Links—which is rapidly becoming one of America's most famous courses—there is an old Negro cemetery on just about the perfect piece of ground to build a luxury villa. The cemetery will never be touched.

The men principally responsible for this rare place are Charles Fraser, a visionary go-getter with a strong sense of style, whose Sea Pines

Marsh grass at the Palmetto Dunes Beach Resort and Golf Club sets the scene for this golfer on Hilton Head Island, S.C.

Placid lagoons flank many of the fairways on the Hilton Head Island, S.C., courses, enhancing their semi-tropical beauty and potential golfing danger. Above is a view of the 16th hole on Sea Pines Plantation's Ocean Course. Below are the 16th and 17th holes at the Port Royal Plantation Barony Course.

Plantation on the southern end of the island has become a sort of template of planned resort development; and Fred Hack, head of Hilton Head's largest development consortium which operates Port Royal Plantation, Hilton Head Golf Club, and owns much of the undeveloped land to the north. Both believe, and have proven, that maximum preservation of the natural environment is a major resort attraction to many who have lived most of their lives in urban conditions.

Since 1959, when the first golf course appeared on Hilton Head, 14 more have been built, for an average of about one course per year. Surrounding each are lovely homes, ranging in price from $40,000 to $300,000, the majority constructed of bleached Cypress which completely blends with and complements the plantation and swamp-forest settings. In the same motif, comfortable fairway villas for vacationers nestle in discreet clusters in the woods. Almost everything that grows on the island seems to be wrapped softly in the ubiquitous epiphytic creeper, Tillandsia, a relative of the pineapple, but better known as Spanish Moss.

Until recently, architect George Cobb of Greenville, S. C., had a monopoly on Hilton Head course-building. He designed the island's first course, the Ocean layout at Sea Pines, and since has created another 18 holes at Sea Pines, two courses for Port Royal, one for Hilton Head Golf Club, a par-3 course for the Adventure Inn, and a nine-hole layout at Spanish Wells.

Cobb, who did the fine par-3 layout at Augusta National, recalls what it was like staking out the center lines for the first Sea Pines course on Hilton Head. "Sometimes when you were walking through the boondocks you thought there was nowhere to go. You'd have a wild boar in front of you, an alligator behind you and snakes on both sides. There were times I wished I could go straight up." Much of the island is still like that.

Other course designers have since produced distinct contrasts to the Cobb style, the most vivid of which is the Harbour Town Links, overlooking Calibogue Sound, created by Pete Dye with Jack Nicklaus' help, for Sea Pines Plantation. (See story on page 100.) It annually hosts the Heritage Classic. Dye's unconventional and highly imaginative little gem is, in many ways, a throwback to more traditional design principles. It has tiny, twisting greens, endless and amorphous bunkers, and trees in places that demand saintly accuracy from the tee. A fourth course opened in 1974 at Sea Pines, designed by Ron Kirby and Gary Player.

Port Royal began in 1963. Its 11,000 acres have spawned to date a 72-room inn, 12 golf cottages and 75 private homes. That spells a great amount of space and privacy and quiet, with man's domain often hardly evident to the Port Royal vacationer, especially once he heads into the Barony and Robbers' Row golf courses.

There are plenty of ghosts, though. Port Royal lies along and behind the island's most seaward bluff, first sighted by Spaniards in 1532, and by Captain William Hilton when he came sailing up in the good ship Adventure a century and a half later, to leave the place his name. Indian artifacts at least 8,000 years old were found beneath the ninth fairway of Robbers' Row, and when you tee off on No. 2 on the Barony you are striking from atop what were once the breastworks of the Yankees 'massive Fort Sherman.

Both courses, designed by Cobb, wander through lovely woodlands of giant live oaks, magnolias and palms, rich in wildlife. Not far from the 10th green was grown the first successful crop of Sea Island cotton.

Two other newer courses are at Palmetto Dunes. One is from the house of Robert Trent Jones, doyen and sometimes bête noire of U. S. golf architect. The Jones layout begins in the forest, breaks out on a series of lagoons, then winds past undulating dunesland to conclude back in the trees. A 265-room condominium inn and convention facility for 1,000 are part of this large development. Palmetto Dunes' newest course is a daring George Fazio design which, though brand new, shows promise of ranking among the south's finest challenges.

—Cal Brown

florida

A 3,351-mile shoreline is Florida's greatest natural asset. Its next most outstanding attraction may well be approximately 1,500 miles of golf fairways, comprising some 465 golf courses.

Despite the combination of golf and sea, Florida amazingly has no true links courses. Golf is mainly a parkland sport with only a few courses providing even an occasional peek at open water. Nonetheless, the tropical peninsula and its warm year-round climate offer a startling variety with some of the finest and most beautiful tests of golf in the world.

Golf Digest's list of America's 100 Greatest Tests of Golf contains six courses in the top 30 from the state of Florida. While three are private (Donald Ross' Seminole in the top 10, Dick Wilson's Pine Tree in the second 10 and George Fazio's Jupiter Hills in the third 10) each of the other three is part of a major golf resort development open to play by visitors. Doral's Blue Course, designed by Dick Wilson, is one of five golf courses of varying degrees of difficulty at the famous Doral resort located not far from the Miami International Airport. Many visitors

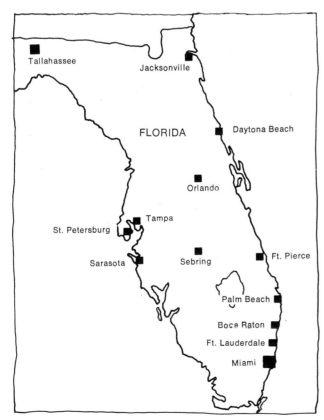

come away thinking Doral's Gold Course, designed in 1970 by Bob Von Hagge and his partner, professional golfer Bruce Devlin, is even more demanding than the famous Blue Course which hosts the annual PGA tour tournament bearing the name of the resort. In the third 10 of America's 100 Greatest Tests of Golf, along with Doral, is the East Course of the JDM Country Club, designed by Dick Wilson, in Palm Beach Gardens. This complex, the former home of the Professional Golfers' Ass'n and called PGA National, boasts three fine golf courses.

There are three nine-hole courses at the Bay Hill Club, near Disney World at Orlando. When you extract two of the best nines, also by Dick Wilson, you come up with a demanding layout of over 7,000 yards that also ranks in the third 10. The development of Bay Hill, located in a picturesque orange grove, is associated with Arnold Palmer who has a minority investment in the project.

Disney World, the incomparable family amusement center, has three fine golf courses of its own, including the Palms Course, a solid 6,951-yarder designed by Joe Lee that is the site of the annual Disney World Open tour event.

Ranking in the same class with Bay Hill and the Disney World courses in the central Florida area are the new Errol Estates and Winter Springs layouts. Both were designed by Joe Lee, who understudied Dick Wilson for many years. Another fine course in the area is Deltona, a rolling and cleverly-conceived David Wallace course.

The Miami metropolitan area has over 100 courses, most of them available to visitors. An exciting new course is the municipal layout on Key Biscayne island, a unique adventure among the mangrove flats designed by Robert Von Hagge. The heavy concentration continues up the Gold Coast to the Palm Beach area. Among the finer courses is Inverrary in Lauderhill, home of the Jackie Gleason tour tournament, which has two excellent Robert Trent Jones courses.

Many of the West Coast courses in Florida are tailored for retirees, but a notable exception is the sensational Innisbrook complex of three courses, all designed by Larry Packard, located near Tarpon Springs, north of Tampa. The Island Course, rated in the fifth 10 by Golf Digest,

If ever a course was appropriately named, it is the Blue Monster at the Doral Country Club in Miami, a Dick Wilson course with almost as much water as grass, as this shot of the 181-yard ninth hole suggests. This resort course is listed among "America's 100 Greatest Tests of Golf."

Sand is much in the scheme of things at these two courses near Orlando, Fla., the Joe Lee-designed Magnolia 18 (above) of the Disney World entertainment center and the Dick Wilson layout at Bay Hill Club (right) in which Arnold Palmer has a proprietary interest. Magnolia's heavily bunkered 174-yard 12th hole and Bay Hill's 238-yard 17th, with water as an added hazard, are pictured.

Another Joe Lee-designed course, the Errol Estates Inn and Country Club at Apopka, Fla. (opposite), is filled with sporty challenges. The 15th, for example, a 530-yard, par-5 calls for a lot of muscle.

is the toughest of the three courses, with heavy woods, ample lakes and tight driving areas.

The Belleview-Biltmore course, adjacent to a grand old hotel in Clearwater, is a sporty test of shotmaking designed by Donald Ross. Farther down the Gulf Coast are fine courses on Marco Island, a David Wallace gem where Gene Sarazen retired, at Palm Aire West (formerly DeSoto Lakes), a typically tough Dick Wilson course, and on Longboat Key, a Bill Mitchell layout, both near Sarasota.

Northern Florida has plenty of golf, too, especially in the east near Jacksonville where the top layouts include Hidden Hills, a Dave Gordon course; Deerwood, designed by George Cobb, and the resort complex at Ponte Vedra Beach whose course was done by Robert Trent Jones. The brightest newcomer in that section is the Pete Dye creation at Amelia Island, a dazzling test of golf cut out of the swamp-like wilderness that is adjacent to the ocean.

—*Hubert Mizell*

A rich blend of old and new golf is found in the Tampa, Fla., area represented by the Innisbrook Resort and Golf Club, Tarpon Springs, opened in 1970, and the Belleview-Biltmore Hotel and Golf Club, Clearwater, founded at the turn of the century. Each resort has three courses. Innisbrook's Island Course, whose 410-yard 18th is pictured above left, is a cunning blend of rolling North Carolina-like terrain and Florida jungle. The Belleview-Biltmore's East Course, whose 410-yard sixth hole, shown above, lies atop a bluff.

137

gulf coast

America's Gulf Coast, along the southerly borders of Florida, Alabama, Mississippi and Texas, offers a delightful array of fine courses from Pensacola to Galveston. The area's growth in golf can be attributed to its balmy weather on a virtual year-round basis. Even in January and February most days are pleasant for golfing in a sweater.

Starting in the eastern sector, you can play a testy 6,871-yard layout designed by William Amick and located on a 1,100-acre resort known as Perdido Bay. Across the bay in Alabama is the Grand Hotel at Point Clear, a luxurious treat even for the most discriminating clientele. Behind the hotel are the three superb nine-hole courses of the Lakewood Golf Club, available to guests of the Grand. Two of the nines were designed by Perry Maxwell, the man who shaped memorable golfing layouts at Southern Hills in Tulsa, Okla., and Prairie Dunes in Hutchinson, Kan. The third nine is the work of Joe Lee.

West of Mobile on Interstate 90 is a community known as St. Andrews-by-the-Sea and it offers a top 6,700-yard course, Ocean Springs designed by Jimmy Thompson and the centerpiece of a large real estate development. In the same area is Gulf Hills, a pine- and oak-studded beauty on the highest ground between New Orleans and Mobile. Also in Ocean Springs is the new Marsh Islands course, designed by Pete Dye along the marshy tidelands.

Biloxi, Miss., long has been a favorite golfing retreat, not to mention its cotton-white beach, and one of the newer challenges is the Sun Course, a tough 7,190-yard monster at the famed Broadwater Beach Hotel. Course architect Earl Stone brought water into play on 14 holes. The old Edgewater Beach course is still operational in Biloxi, now on a daily fee basis. It has the stiff bunkering common with courses 60 years old.

The Diamondhead Golf Course in Bay St. Louis, just east of the Louisiana border in Mississippi, is a contemporary gem built by Bill Atkins. It features massive tees up to 130 yards long and roller-coaster greens. The course stretches over 7,000 yards from the back tees.

West around the Gulf in the Galveston, Texas, area a variety of golf is also offered.

—*Hubert Mizell*

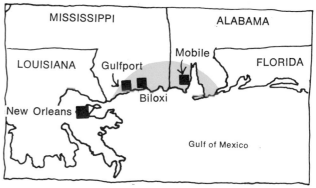

A majestic live oak tree galleries this scene at the Lakewood Golf Club in Point Clear, Ala., where guests at the Grand Hotel play. The generally level fairways are cut through beautiful hardwood forests, a characteristic of Gulf Coast golf.

desert
courses

There is something very special about a sunset in the desert. First It burns orange-yellow like an open-hearth furnace. Then gradually it turns red and purple as it sinks behind distant mountains.

This is also the best time to be on a desert golf course. As shadows lengthen, the grass looks greener—lusher. Almost suddenly it's still and sweater-cool—only you and the evening air and,

perhaps, a lizard or two off there beyond the edge of the fairway.

They grow golf courses in the desert nowadays the way you'd raise radishes in the yard. Grade the sand, toss out some seed, give it some water —a million gallons per day should suffice—and then let that ever-present sun take over.

Top quality desert golf was born in the 1950s in Palm Springs, the California retreat of movie stars, two hours southeast of Los Angeles by car. From there it spread to the gaming capital of Las Vegas and then to hot, dry Arizona in the Phoenix and Tucson areas. The three areas form the travelers' Desert Sun Circle which is really more of a triangle.

Palm Springs has 32 golf courses and among the best are five that have hosted the Bob Hope

140

The Phoenix-Scottsdale area is Barry Goldwater country where solid crewcut citizens run golf tournaments for charity and play on ono or more of over 40 courses. None of them are in the nearby Sun City retirement complex where so-called "senior citizens" wheel around 18 holes in well under four hours. Many of the better courses in this area are associated with elegant resorts such as Camelback, the Arizona Biltmore, a bastion of stateliness with its gold leaf ceilings, and the newer Carefree Inn with its immensely challenging and unusual Desert Forest course, designed by Red Lawrence, northeast of Phoenix.

The gem of the Phoenix-Scottsdale golf scene is the 7,220-yard Gold Course at Goodyear G. and C.C., a Robert Trent Jones course which is ranked in America's 100 Greatest Tests of Golf.

In Las Vegas, golf has become the favorite escape hatch for visitors who need a break from the clickety-clack of slot machines. Just 15 years ago there were two courses here—a municipal layout and the Desert Inn course where Gene Littler won three straight Tournament of Champions titles and a good-sized fortune for singer Frankie Laine who backed him in some over-sized calcutta pools.

Today there are more than a dozen courses in town or close by, most of them little more than 6,000 yards from the back tees and tailored for resort golfers. An exception is the Dunes Emerald Country Club, a 7,240-yard Billy Bell course.

The trend to building golf courses in the desert seems to be growing. Someday even the lizards may be forced into condominiums.

—*Dick Aultman*

Desert Classic, a unique 90-hole tour tournament with a pro-amateur format. They are the fine 7,240-yard La Quinta layout designed by Lawrence Hughes, Bermuda Dunes where architect Billy Bell transformed 6,765 yards of sandhills into lush terrain, Indian Wells, a rugged 7,000-yarder designed by Eddie Susalla and Paul Prom, Eldorado, a very private course of 6,840 yards also designed by Hughes, and Tamarisk, a 7,117 yard Billy Bell course.

Golf may well play an even greater role in the future of the Palm Springs area. Typical is the newly-opened Mission Hills Golf and Country Club, a superb 7,100-yard test designed by Desmond Muirhead that is the site of the richest women's tournament in history, the Colgate-Dinah Shore Winners Circle.

The word "oasis" has taken on a new meaning in the desert of the American southwest where golf courses like the new Desert Island (above) in Palm Springs and the lush Wigwam course (right) in Phoenix offer a welcome contrast to blue-gray mountains and desert scrub.

monterey peninsula

In the Bible it says that God made the world in six days and on the seventh, rested. But I think that on the seventh day he created the Monterey Peninsula. There cannot be another place on earth quite like it, nor another place that has three golf courses of such quality in so small a space.

It is as though every thundering emotion, every subtle line had been withheld from the rest of creation and then dumped in this one place to test our understanding of the superlative. One's response to this angular chunk of land, shaped like the snout of a rhinoceros and jutting into the Pacific about 90 miles south of San Francisco, is instant and elemental. Even on a gray, overcast day or during a winter storm, it is compelling and seductive.

Hills and craggy bluffs tumble into the sea which ebbs and crashes against copper-brown rocks, casting huge white plumes and mist into the air above dozing seals and an occasional solitary beachcomber. Gray-boled and winter-green cypress trees cling to the soil in clumps or in stark individuality, bent and twisted in the wind and spray. Here and there the headland splashes down into uneven, white-faced dunes. Surmounting everything is a sense of quiet, a curious intimation of settled spirit on the raging coast.

Here are three of the world's greatest golf courses, and how could they be otherwise? Their names alone stir juices—Pebble Beach, legendary and rugged with a compelling, elemental force; Cypress Point, shy and mysterious, a splendidly proportioned and artful mistress; and Spyglass Hill, diabolical, controversial and maddening in its newness.

Within 5,200 acres of private land known as the Del Monte Forest, the late Samuel F. B. Morse founded and developed some of the most expensive real estate and one of the most magnificent resorts in the world. The Del Monte property is encircled by a 17-mile drive over which visitors may travel, at $3 per car. No overnight camping is permitted and no plant or animal may be "disturbed, injured or removed." Deer roam freely through the forest and across the golf courses.

The center of it all is the quiet community of Pebble Beach which huddles around the plush Del Monte Lodge overlooking Carmel Bay and the justly famous Pebble Beach Golf Links (see page 106 for story on this course).

There were few more than 400 golf courses in the entire nation when Pebble Beach opened in 1918. Ten years later Cypress Point opened and in 1929 Pebble Beach and Cypress Point served jointly as host to the U.S. Amateur, making its first appearance in the West.

In addition to Pebble Beach, Cypress Point, and the relatively new Spyglass Hill, other courses on the peninsula within the "17-mile drive" include: a nifty par-3 behind the Del Monte Lodge called the Peter Hay Golf Course; Del Monte, a hilly public course; Pacific Grove Golf Course, a short and appealing municipal layout with a dunes flavor along the ocean; and Monterey Peninsula, a private country club with two courses.

Several other golf courses not far from the peninsula are of interest to vacationing golfers. Carmel Valley Golf and Country Club, about four miles southeast of Carmel, is open to guests of the adjoining Quail Lodge, which has a reciprocal guest arrangement with Del Monte Lodge. About two miles east of Carmel is Rancho Canada, a 36-hole public course. Seven miles from Monterey, on the road to Salinas, is Laguna Seca Golf Ranch, a Robert Trent Jones layout.

There are signs of stress on the priceless plot of Monterey Peninsula. One hears grumbling about pollution in Monterey Bay. Someone at Del Monte has allowed a house to be built behind the fifth green at Spyglass Hill which, while architecturally impressive, intrudes on the natural beauty of the hole. But with few such exceptions, there is little to remind one that life is anything but a succession of esthetic fulfillments and magnificent golf holes.

Spyglass Hill is a Robert Trent Jones layout that opened in 1966 and ever since has been the target of strong words from touring pros who are not accustomed to shooting in the 80s.

Spyglass, in its youthful striving for greatness, is too new to be finally judged. Several things

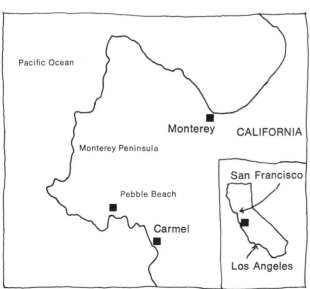

Most experts agree that the Spy-glass Hill golf course is the tough-est of the marvelous family of Pebble Beach layouts. One of this course's handsome holes, if not the most dif-ficult, is the par-three 12th, across a pond to a kidney-shaped green with California pines as a backdrop.

about it are evident, though. It is ruthlessly tough and on windy days almost impossible. In 1970 it was rated 76.1 from the back tees (6,972 yards) but it has never been played in competition over its full length.

The course record is 70, two under par, made by Forest Fezler when still an amateur, who played the ball "as it lies." The best score in competition was also 70, made by Bob Murphy in the 1968 Crosby. But he played from the middle tees (6,609 yards, which carries a rating of 74.1), and was improving his lies.

"People can't believe it's so tough," chortles Spyglass Hill's home professional, Frank Thacker. "The first five holes are more a case of fright than anything else." The first hole sweeps 604 yards through the pines down to the ocean. The next four holes are played on the dunes from one island of grass to the next. The second, though a lay-up hole, is nevertheless an appealing two-shotter that wants a thoughtful golfer and is, for the medium hitter, a fearsome journey past waist-high spikes of pampas grass. The third and fifth are sand-locked par-3s sandwiched around the partially blind par-4 fourth.

These psychological thrillers are among the easier holes. Once the course turns inland, it gets narrower and longer, and your breath and shoulder turn get shorter. Spyglass Hill's greens are huge, and you can three-putt all day long. Putts of 150 feet are possible. A lot of the early criticism of the course centers around the greens which now have been remodeled. The first time the course was used in the Crosby, on the 14th hole, a gem of a par-5 with an angled green perched on the left above a pond, one of the contestants putted off the green and into the water. On the same green, Jack Nicklaus once four-putted from 14 feet.

Is Spyglass Hill tougher than Pebble Beach? Probably. Not too long ago two doctors teed off at Spyglass Hill with three dozen golf balls between them and had to send the caddie in for a new supply after six holes. But though Spyglass is rated a stroke tougher, it lacks the wild, undisciplined spirit of Pebble Beach. Spyglass is a more refined article, with a harder, more sculptured look. Jones was not given the kind of elemental terrain with which to work that is to be found at Pebble and Cypress, yet he has made a great deal with what he was given. One suspects that it is a course whose character is exposed more deeply the more it is played.

"If I were condemned to play only one course for the rest of my life, I would unhesitatingly pick Cypress Point." So says Joe Dey, former executive director of the United States Golf Ass'n and who in 1974 retired as commissioner of the Tournament Players' Division of the PGA. Dey, no mean judge of golf courses, is not alone in this choice. Golfers fortunate enough to play this little masterpiece of a private club more often than not come away feeling that Cypress Point is more fun to play than any other on the peninsula.

Its length alone — 6,464 yards — makes it the easiest of the three Crosby courses. Still, the course record is the same as at Pebble Beach, 65, set by Bill Nary in the 1949 Crosby. Ben Hogan shot the course in 63 during a practice round in 1947 for the unofficial mark.

The course was conceived in 1926 by Marion Hollins, the women's national amateur champion of 1921, and Roger Lapham, who was president of the California Golf Ass'n and a member of the USGA executive committee. They bought property from Del Monte and commissioned Alister Mackenzie to design the course. Mackenzie, a Scot and former doctor in the British Army, later did the Augusta National course in Georgia with Bobby Jones.

Cypress is strictly a golf club, and its members are golfers. There are no pools, tennis courts or other distractions. Non-members are not permitted in the clubhouse, even during the Crosby tournament. For years the pros had to change their shoes outside. Now a separate room has been added for this purpose.

The use of golf cars is discouraged as are other modern frills. The caddies here—many having plied the trade for 40 years—are considered by some visitors the best in the world. When you tee it up at Cypress Point, the game is on.

The first hole is a lazy dogleg to the right and, at 407 yards, long enough to loosen the muscles. Until recently the tee shot had to negotiate an old, dead pine tree that blew down in a storm and had been called "Joe DiMaggio"—it caught everything. The second is a properly menacing par-5 of 544 yards that angles left and thus courts the gambling tee shot. The third is a slender one-shot hole, no more than a middle iron, the fourth a shortish par-4 that carries you deep into the woods and past little bands of deer and a half a dozen beautifully placed bunkers. The fifth, a short par-5 of 490 yards, swoops left abruptly up a hill literally covered with bunkers to a tiny green on top.

By the time you reach the sixth hole you are

caught up in the pure joy of the place. You feel that every shot is just what you always knew golf should be. Soon you are heading toward the distant ocean over the rugged dunes from holes eight through 13. At 15, a mere 139 yards, you play across a narrow gorge where the water boils angrily as its cuts its way into the cliff. The ball must reach the putting surface, for there are trees, sand and clutching ice plant all around. The ice plant—thick, fleshy stuff—is like trying to escape from a vat of marshmallow.

Then comes the 16th which has been called the ultimate test of golfing courage. From the back tees it is 233 yards of carry across the Pacific to a large green on the top of the point. The average golfer must lay up short to the fairway on the left and then pitch to the green. Only on windless days do the pros try for it. The late Porky Oliver made 16 after going in the water four times, and Henry Ransom picked up after 16 attempts to move his ball from the beach up the sheer cliff to the green. Another pro, Hans Merrill, has the all-time record of 19. He made it all with the same ball, going from ice plant to ice plant for nearly half an hour.

The 17th is another heroic hole, a par-4 that runs along the cliff for 375 yards to a green that lurks behind a fat, sprawling cypress tree. The tee, set next to the 16th green on the point, looks into the cliff and you can take as much of the barrier as you like. Jimmy Demaret once played this hole in the wind by hitting two drivers; he aimed the second out over the ocean and let it blow back.

After the excitement of the ocean, the 18th is a soft dissolve swinging gently up through scattered trees to a flagstick silhouetted against the sky next to the clubhouse, of simple Spanish California style that looks so natural it seems to have grown there among the cypress trees.

Opinion about a golf course can be a fragile thing. But taken all as a piece, the Monterey Peninsula and its golf courses are something to behold. There is enough variety to sate the most demanding golfing spirit. It is a special place where the tendons and mind can stretch on equal terms. In fact, if Heaven isn't like Pebble Beach, I won't be going.   —Cal Brown

The 355-yard 13th hole at Cypress Point underscores the compelling natural influences of the Monterey Peninsula—native grasses, ocean, patches of dunesland and silhouetted cypress trees.

san diego

Just off Interstate 5—a main north-south highway—are most of the San Diego area's 60-plus golf courses and 20,000 hotel and motel rooms. The only large metropolitan region in the world with enough courses for its population, San Diego is a great year-round golf center. The problem in a vacation is deciding which to omit.

All but two or three golf courses, including country clubs and resorts, are open to visitors, who may be surprised to find that several of the public courses are every bit as fine as those at the private clubs they're used to. The outstanding example is Torrey Pines, a 36-hole municipal facility in rich, suburban La Jolla to the north, the home of Racquel Welch among other natural wonders. Torrey, designed by Billy Bell, is home to the annual Andy Williams San Diego Open. Arnold Palmer has called it "probably the best public course in the country," and he probably means either 18.

For the tournament, the PGA field staff uses the South Course except for three holes from the North. That amalgamated 18, put together so that players can start from both the first and 10th tees and still be within hailing distance of the clubhouse, is one or two strokes easier than the regular South Course, which is 7,011 yards from the back tees, par 72. The North Course is a maximum of 6,667, also par 72. The ocean views on both courses are worth the greens fee. The views include a large cluster of young people who sun themselves on the beach beneath the seventh hole of the South Course sans clothes, and make the galleries at that spot during the tournament uncommonly large.

When you talk about resorts, though, you have to turn to La Costa, 15 miles north on Interstate 5. Site of the annual Tournament of Champions, the other regular tour event in the area, La Costa must be seen—and heard—to be believed. The first night I was there, I had dinner at a table adjoining that of Clint Eastwood and a group of Hollywood people who spent 90 minutes comparing their nose jobs as they ate.

As a health spa, La Costa is second to none that I know of. You can choose from sauna baths, swirling scented waters, herbal wraps, whirlpools, exercise rooms, massages and much more. Should you wrench yourself out of the spa and find your way to the golf course, you will meet a formidable and scenic challenge. Dick Wilson laid out the 7,200 yards of tight-rolling, tree-lined, well-trapped, heavily-roughed, huge-greened monster that—it is some consolation to remind yourself — gives the pros more trouble than almost any other course on the tour. Long tees afford the average player a break if he doesn't feel constrained to play the course the way the pros do.

The beauty of golfing in and near San Diego is that the variety of terrain as you move from coastline to nearby mountains to nearby desert is so pronounced it is almost impossible to become bored.

Other courses worth staying over an extra day to play include Rancho Bernardo in a winding valley, Balboa Municipal near the zoo and city center and Stardust which formerly played host to the San Diego Open. If your appetite for variety isn't sated, there are always the 60-some other courses in the immediate area, for if you desire golf, San Diego has a wealth of it.

—*Nick Seitz*

148

The par-3 seventh hole typifies the challenge of La Costa in the San Diego area. It's 185 yards from the back tee, and the wind off the nearby Pacific Ocean usually is in your face. The green is jealously protected by water, sand and wiry rough. Dick Wilson designed the course, site of the annual Tournament of Champions, and gave the average player a break with long tees. The seventh can play as short as 130 yards.

As recently as 1967, there were only three full-fledged golf resorts on the Hawaiian Islands: Royal Kaanapali on Maui, Mauna Kea on Hawaii, and Makaha on Oahu. Today there are a dozen. And there are another 35 to 40 private, public or military layouts in Hawaii.

The sudden growth is a result of faster airliners, lower fares, a more affluent society and about as reliable a climate as can be found anywhere. It's golfing weather the year around, the temperature varying between 70 and 85.

It's fair to say that just about everyone wants to visit Hawaii at least once in his lifetime. More are actually doing it each year and more are returning to visit or make residence there.

HAWAII: The Big Island

One could spend an entire vacation right on the island of Hawaii trying to conquer the three fine courses (soon to be five) along the west coast.

A visitor to Rockresort's Mauna Kea Beach Hotel and Golf Club once spent his whole stay trying to find something wrong with the place. The only imperfection he could locate was that the elevator to the beach was much too slow, but even compromised that complaint because seats were provided. The hotel is in the Rockefeller tradition and its architecture might be called modern-open-garden. The golf course is in the Robert Trent Jones tradition and might be called severe-rolling-hogback.

It is long and tough, and the greens demand a master's touch and surveyor's perspective. Many are picture holes, and pro Rags Ragland runs a really top golf operation. It's a place that's difficult to leave, but you'll eventually run out of money. Mauna Kea is not inexpensive.

A few miles to the south is the new (1972) Waikaloa, Boise Cascade's 31,000-acre planned resort community with its first course built at 500 feet above sea level by Robert Trent Jones at Waikaloa Village.

Farther to the south past the resort town of Kailua Kona is the Keauhou Kona Country Club overlooking the big new Kona Surf Hotel at the water's edge and some of the finest deep sea fishing waters in the world. The Billy Bell course is most interesting and fun to play if you don't hit too often into the fairway-bordering black lava

150

flow, which gives you an unplayable lie or a nicked club.

There are airports for inter-island travel on the big island's west coast at both Kamuela (Waimea) and at Kailua-Kona.

MAUI: The Valley Island

The boom in resort golf in the islands probably started with the building of Royal Kaanapali Golf Club and the hosting there of the 1964 Canada Cup, now called the World Cup Matches. The Kaanapali area lies on the west side of Maui near the quaint old whaling town of Lahaina. Even today large schools of whales can be seen traveling the channel betwen Maui and the island of Lanai.

The Kaanapali Golf Course is another in Robert Trent Jones' long list of fine tests. It is built on a gentle slope up from the ocean and provides the player with one gorgeous vista after another. Many modern hotels with views of the golf course abound in the area and there is another executive-length 18-hole course available. An air strip at Kaanapali handles small planes and charters, but the main airport is at Kahului in the center of Maui's northern coast.

Seventeen miles to the south of the town of Kahului on the southern coast of Maui is a huge new resort residential development with a fine course designed by Jack Snyder. Named Wailea, the 6,600-yard course dips and rolls 100- to 300-feet above the sea, overlooking a beach complex.

Sprawling beneath the mountains of Hawaii's Oahu Island are the two scenic courses at the Makaha Inn.

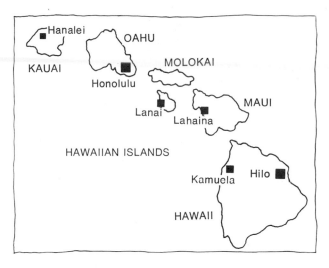

The par-3 third hole on the Ocean nine at Princeville at Hanalei can be played from 135 to 180 yards. The pond in front and the jungle behind pose threats at all distances. This design by Robert Trent Jones Jr.

As do many Hawaiian courses, the Kauai Surf Golf and Country Club on the "big" island of Hawaii provides generous views of the ocean and volcanos that gave birth to this tropical paradise. This is the 150-yard seventh, with the tee 40 feet higher than the green.

MOLOKAI: The Friendly Island

To the west and a little north of Maui lies long and slim Molokai with its still active leper colony on the north coast shut off by cliffs from all entry except by sea.

Louisiana Land & Exploration Company has selected the western tip of Molokai for a large resort complex to be called Kephui. Included will be the island's first golf course, being designed by Frank Duane and Arnold Palmer and scheduled for opening in 1975.

OAHU: The Gathering Place

Two major golf resorts, Makaha on the west coast and Kuilima on the north coast, are both about an hour's drive from Honolulu.

Set in a dramatic valley, Makaha offers complete resort and convention facilities, a 36-hole golf course, and homesites and condominiums. Both of the Billy Bell courses have their own clubhouses. The west course is the resort's private course for guests only and plays to a back-breakingly long 7,252 yards from the tiger tees.

At Kahuku Point near Sunset Beach on the north end of Oahu, sits the beautiful Kuilima Hotel and Golf Course. Architect George Fazio did the course which goes at 7,061 yards from the back, and 6,420 yards from the regular tees. Fairways are spacious which is most welcome because there's usually a pretty good breeze blowing. The course was opened in 1972 and when the 3,000 trees and shrubs mature, the natural beauty of the ocean and mountain backdrop will be even further enhanced.

Another major resort on Oahu opened in 1973. Hawaii Kai, which already had an 18-hole par-3 course, has put in a 7,000-yard Billy Bell course along with a sizeable hotel complex.

KAUAI: The Garden Island

This westernmost of all the large islands boasts the wettest spot on earth. Here the caved-in wall of a volcano produces an upsweep of warm air which causes rain almost continually. Until recently, golf on Kauai has been limited to the fine municipal Wailua Golf Course, laid out by Toyo Shirai, near the Cocoa Palms resort.

But now the Kauai Surf resort at the southern end of the island, has added another nine holes and boasts a 6,808-yard test overlooking Kala-paki Beach.

At the northern end of Kauai near where the movie "South Pacific" was filmed, lies Princeville at Hanalei and its 27-hole Princeville Makai Golf Course. Descriptively named the Ocean, Lake, and Woods nines, they were done by Robert Trent Jones Jr. who says, "If there is a finer place to build a golf course, I haven't seen it. On such great terrain in such a beautiful spot, I was scared stiff I might muff it." He didn't, ample proof of which is that Princeville was promptly named to the list of America's 100 Greatest Tests of Golf.

—Howard R. Gill

NEAR U.S. ISLANDS

Modern air transportation has brought the islands of the Atlantic Ocean, originally settled by Europeans, so close to the United States that they have become an intimate part of the American resort scene. In this volume, we refer to them as the near-U.S. islands.

The golf courses in the islands possess a blend of architectural influences, some British and others American, some old and some very new. No doubt fascinated, if not inspired, by the beauty of the islands, nearly all of the famous golf course designers have left their marks on the islands. In Bermuda Charles Blair Macdonald gave us Mid-Ocean on spectacular ground high above ocean coves; Dick Wilson worked charm into the otherwise flat, dull topography of Grand Bahama Island; on Jamaica, John Harris did Runaway Bay, a rambling beauty of 7,000 yards, an interesting contrast to Ralph Plummer's lovely little Tryall on the same island; Trent Jones' Dorado Beach courses have helped popularize Puerto Rico, while Pete Dye's exciting Cajuiles course has brought golfers for the first time to the shores of the Dominican Republic.

Our near-U.S. island section might well have included courses on other islands, particularly in the Caribbean, where natural beauty is so often overwhelming. There are courses in enchanting places like Trinidad, Barbados, St. Maarten and Tobago, but we believe the following pages take you on a visit to the best in the blue waters off the eastern United States.

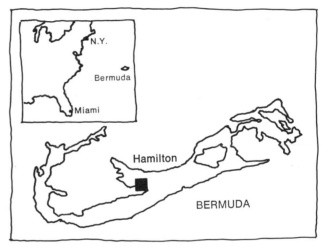

155

bermuda

Bermuda, 21 square miles of British-oriented vacationland, properly promotes golf as a year-round sport. However, the island's eight golf courses are not so crowded from November through March. The reason is that the temperatures sink into the 50s and sometimes even the 40s during the winter months. This tends to keep some of the sun-loving folks away, but those who fly the 774 air miles between New York and Bermuda find the weather then generally delightful for golf.

Both Bermuda and its golf courses are refreshingly "foreign." Speed limit on the narrow, flower-lined roads is 20 mph, and you drive on the left side. You can't rent an automobile because of local regulations, but nearly every visitor rents a motorbike for a pleasant ride. "Free port" shopping is available in Hamilton, the capital. You might run into a retired British brigadier, complete with a bristling mustache and an imperious manner.

Four Bermuda resort hotels operate their own courses. They are Castle Harbour and Belmont, which feature regulation 18-holers; the huge new Princess, with an 18-hole executive layout, and the longer established St. George which has a par-3. There are also two private courses, Mid-Ocean and Riddell's Bay, on which vacationers can play on a selective basis. Then there is the municipal Port Royal, an attractive 18-hole course.

All of the hotel managers can get a guest on any of the non-private courses by means of a telephone call and perhaps a written introduction. You just pay the going greens fee. More planning is required to play the two private clubs.

Everyone who visits Bermuda wants to play Mid-Ocean, the best known and best of the courses. It's a middling 6,519 yards which swirls along high bluffs overlooking the Atlantic. Charles Blair Macdonald, the early American golf pioneer, designed the course and it was revamped in 1953 by Robert Trent Jones.

Castle Harbour borders Mid-Ocean but is nevertheless different than its neighbor. It is downright hilly, with some knockout views throughout its 6,180 yards. The first two holes are especially gorgeous, both of which take you down a steep incline off the tee and wind up with elevated greens. Charles Banks was the original designer of the course; Trent Jones later added some touches.

Port Royal may well be the last full-sized course built on Bermuda. It was completed in 1971, designed by Robert Trent Jones, and there just isn't that much more suitable golf terrain available. Not terribly long at about 6,500 yards, Port Royal is built on a promontory often buffeted by stiff winds. Lovely views and challenging, gentle uphill approaches are the usual order.
—*John P. May*

Here is a panoramic glance down the wildly pitching first hole at the Castle Harbour Golf Club in Bermuda. The neighboring Mid-Ocean Club is visible across the bay. Most Bermuda courses offer sloping fairways and frequently swirling winds.

bahamas

Fresh water is just beneath the surface of most Bahamian islands, a geological fact that leads to excellent golf course conditioning. Fairway grass grows profusely, and you rarely get a bad lie if you keep your shots out of the rough. With water hazards so easy to create from the sub-surface water, golf course architects have used them liberally on most courses.

Although the six full-sized 18-hole courses and the one nine-holer on Grand Bahama Island are essentially level, giant fairway bunkers and tremendously thick stands of pine trees give the golfer the illusion of playing on hillier terrain. There is a profusion of fauna and flora on all of the courses which abound in tropical beauty.

Other islands generally included in the Bahamas are Abaco, Great Harbour Cay, Eleuthera and New Providence, where Nassau is located.

Americans need no passports nor visas to enter these former British colonies, now an independent nation. Rainfall is at its minimum from December through March, the peak of the Bahamas tourist season.

The showplaces on Grand Bahama are the Lucayan and Shannon Clubs and the Emerald and Ruby Courses at the Kings Inn—all around Freeport and all created by that master of sub-tropical flat-land design, Joe Lee. Almost every one of the 72 holes is a separate entity, jungle-wrapped, carpeted wall-to-wall in emerald green, and richly friezed with magnolia, hibiscus, bougainvillea and other flowering trees and shrubs.

Like the late Dick Wilson, his teacher and one-time boss, Lee's trademark is serpentine trapping, plus the imaginative but not overbearing use of water. Surrealistically scalloped bunkers, writhing abreast the driving zones and sternly guarding the fronts of his generous greens, are dominant features of all four courses. But at his latest, Shannon, Lee has opened up the greens, widened the fairways, and set much of his fairway sand out of reach of all but the diabolical shot. On the other hand, he has brought more water beautifully and strategically into play than at the other three courses.

Grand Bahama Hotel, 25 miles from Freeport on the island's western tip, is a self-contained resort village and maintains its own airstrip. Three of the nine new holes added to the excellent original 18 by Mark Mahannah sit right beside the sea.

There are four 18-hole courses on New Providence Island, where Bahamian golf got its start in 1926 with the establishment of the Nassau Golf Club, now called the Sonesta Beach Golf Club and redone by architect Jeff Orcutt in 1961. The Paradise Island Golf Club, across a bridge from the city on an island crowded with resort hotels and gambling casinos, has a Dick Wilson course, with many hazards and big bunkers.

Newest and best course on New Providence is the South Ocean Golf Club, a Joe Lee stunner situated along the ocean, with hotel adjoining.

The private Cotton Bay Club on Eleuthera is a lovely Robert Trent Jones layout, but it is open to guests only from May through mid-December. The quiet Rock Sound Inn is adjacent.

—*John P. May*

It takes steady nerves to combat the 202-yard 13th hole at the Shannon Golf and Club course in Freeport on Grand Bahama Island. A common challenge on Bahamian courses is that shots into the rough often wind up amid white coral rock, beautiful but frustrating.

puerto rico / virgin islands

It is difficult to conceive, but until 1958 golf was virtually nonexistant in Puerto Rico. There were only a few sugar company and military nine-holers. Today golf is very much a part of the Puerto Rico resort picture. The game has spilled over into the neighboring Virgin Islands, a short seaplane hop off the southeastern edge of Puerto Rico. Both locations are, of course, served by commercial airlines, and since they are United States protectorates, no passports are needed for entry by Americans.

San Juan is a lively capital city, and the hotels and resorts there present a wide variety of night club entertainment. Gambling also is featured at a number of well-furnished casinos. The golf resorts are some distance from the metropolis, with limousines making regular runs.

The first major resort on Puerto Rico was the Dorado Beach Hotel, located about an hour from San Juan. It was established in 1958, with plans for two marvelous Robert Trent Jones 18-hole courses sketched in. The last nine was completed in 1966. Both courses have a pleasant combination of seaside and inland holes, water hazards and thick tropical growth, including many brilliantly hued flowering shrubs along the fairways. The area was once a grapefruit plantation, and many of these trees remain. The 13th hole on the East Course is probably the most interesting. A par-5, it doglegs left and the third shot must clear a pond to reach a sharply elevated green. The putting surface is smack against the beach.

The Dorado Beach tourist accommodations are spread out in several buildings, many of them with doors that open directly onto a truly gorgeous beach. Night-time lights play on tremendous breakers rushing over huge, well-worn beachside boulders, a spectacular sight.

In 1971 Laurance Rockefeller, who owns and operates Dorado Beach, opened the Cerromar Beach Hotel and Club not far away from his original enterprise. This resort is directed more toward convention business, but there are individual accommodations. Cerromar Beach also has two Jones courses, one along the ocean and windy, the other inland with attractive mountain views. All four of these courses measure around 6,500 yards from the middle tees.

Some five miles from Dorado Beach is the Dorado Del Mar Hotel and Golf Club, a large resort that recently underwent a change of ownership. Designed by American architect Jim Harrison and opened in 1963, the Del Mar course is built through a former coconut plantation and is deceptively open. There is no undergrowth off the fairways, but those tall palms line each and they have a disconcerting habit of getting into the way of off-line shots.

Puerto Rico's third major resort is the El Conquistador Hotel and Club at Las Croabas, about 30 miles east of San Juan. Designed by Robert Von Hagge, an American, and spectacularly situated on a high bluff overlooking the Caribbean, the 6,626-yard El Conquistador course has the most mountainous contours of any on the island. Blind tee shots from extremely elevated tees are not uncommon. Deeply gouged and sanded bunkers guard greens of a Tifdwarf bermuda hybrid that closely resembles bentgrass. That means they're fast. The modernistic hotel is spectacular, with many levels. You must ride an electric car down a steep incline to reach the lower depths, the beach and the marina.

There is only one 18-hole course in the Virgin Islands, but it is a beauty and one of Trent Jones' best. The Fountain Valley Golf Club in St. Croix is routed through a valley and is laced by water hazards and sundry ravines. It can play up to a testing 6,909 yards. There is no hotel associated with this course, but the island has many attractive hotels. There is a sporty nine-holer at the established Estate Carlton Hotel and Country Club, and another at the newer Reef Golf Club, which has a fine beach. Each measures just over 3,000 yards.

—*John P. May*

This is one of architect Robert Trent Jones' more famous holes, a serpentine par-5, the 13th on the East Course of the Dorado Beach Hotel Club in Puerto Rico. Both Dorado Beach courses are dressed up with broad-leafed trees as well as the more indigenous tropical palms and flowering hibiscus plants.

jamaica

Jamaica's Montego Bay coastline on the northwest corner of the Caribbean island is a fast-developing golf center highly popular with Americans.

Mo Bay, as regulars on the tourist trail call it, has just the right mixture of honky-tonk and elegance, bustle and somnolence, commercial glitter and solitude, bistros and wide beaches to attract everyone from Manhattan jet-setters to Iowa druggists.

Its attractive resorts, wide beaches and varied shopping facilities make Mo Bay the former British colony's tourist center. The capital, Kingston, almost at the other end of the island, is a metropolis of over 100,000 persons and includes the nation's longest golfing history.

The golfing landscape at Mo Bay includes four established courses—Half Moon, Tryall, Ironshore and Runaway Bay. They are attractive, generally well-conditioned and different enough in character to offer pleasant diversion. At least four more courses are on the drawing boards. Within a few years, the northern coast may have as many as 10 golf courses open for play.

The par-71 Tryall course, designed by Ralph Plummer, rolls 6,880 yards along the ocean and through the hills just inland, finishing near a pleasant beach bar. In the evening there are other diversions, the most popular of which are uninhibited pool parties.

The 7,130-yard Half Moon-Rose Hall course is quite a challenge when the wind is up. Half of it then plays against a stiff northeaster, the other half with a glorious following wind. The clubhouse, a pleasant old stone cottage, is a marvelous retreat with fine cuisine.

The courses in Kingston are not directly associated with resorts. One of them is a jewel, the Caymanas Golf and Country Club, designed by Howard Watson of Canada. It nestles in an impressive valley and its 6,280 yards contain many true golf challenges.   —*John P. May*

Stately palms dot Jamaica's Tryall Golf and Beach Club course which slopes from the hills down to the sea.

162

la romana/
dominican republic

Nature, of course, was the original architect. Then came the brown hands of some 300 Dominican laborers, slicing through the underbrush with machetes, planting fairways—yes, blade by blade—and lining them with native coral rock called *dientes del perro,* or "teeth of the dog." Guiding the workers were the red-rough freckled hands of course designer Pete Dye, often sketching tentative hole diagrams in the dirt, erasing, trying again.

Dye didn't create *Campo de Golf Cajuiles* (Ka-wheel-ays) in seven days—and he'll probably still be puttering around with it seven years from now—but he has conceived a thing of almighty beauty. Seven holes skirt or cross the oft-lashing Caribbean. The others, of gentler nature, flow among tall stands of sugar cane and other Dominican flora, including coconut, cashew (*cajuiles*) and citrus trees.

Dye has a special feeling for this course and the people who helped create it. First among these is Alvaro Carta, 45-year-old president of Gulf + Western Americas Corp., which owns the La Romana resort and one of the world's largest sugar refineries nearby.

The mustachioed Carta ranks along with baseball's Alou brothers and Rico Carty as a hero to the some 30,000 citizens of La Romana on the southeast coast of the Dominican Republic. A refugee of Castro's Cuba, Carta, through G + WA, has tremendously upgraded the life of the natives through various philanthropic ventures, including the establishment of a tax-free industrial complex for foreign business. He hopes that the hotel and the course will bring in not only foreign tourist dollars—a runway for private planes splits the course—but also encourage further business investment.

Carta brought Dye to La Romana to build his golf course. Dye took a long look at the jungle and the coral and shook his head.

"Never before had I turned down one job so many times," Dye recalls, "but Alvaro kept calling me back. Finally I figured, 'Well, he's got 300,000 acres, there must be a golf course out there somewhere'."

Dye's first choice of site would have included the local baseball field. "No," said Carta, "that's where the kids play."

Finally Dye found his land, four miles of coastline about 10 minutes by Land Rover from the hotel. He also found the man to help him carve out the course, Bruce Mashburn, a native North Carolinian who learned course building under Donald Ross. During the almost two years before he died of a coronary in September, 1971, "Señor Bruce" became a legendary figure among the people of La Romana. They respected him as a tough boss and loved him for his herculean capacity to party. "The man died at 60," says his successor, Bryan Farris, "but he lived a 260-year life."

Apart from golf, La Romana offers an unforgettable mixture of sights, sounds and smells. There is the ever-present aroma of boiling sugar cane and the blowing of refinery whistles every morning, summoning the townspeople to work and vacationers to play. The hotel and villas, though across from the mill, are secluded in flowers, green lawns, soft-spoken Spanish and excellent dining service. There is a 52-foot schooner for battling wahoo and marlin, and laughing native drivers who rip around rutted roads like A. J. Foyts. There's skeet and trap and tennis and wild rodeo and fat sandwiches under a beachside cabaña.

But above all there is Pete Dye's masterpiece, *Cajuiles,* nicknamed by some "Teeth of the Dog." Inevitably, it will be compared to California's Pebble Beach. Yet one resists the obvious label, "Pebble Beach East." This new course deserves to stand on its own name.—*Dick Aultman*

Architect Pete Dye has created stunning visual and strategic holes at the Cajuiles Golf Club in the Dominican Republic. Examples are the 175-yard 13th (right), the 370-yard 15th (over), reminiscent of Pebble Beach, and the 195-yard seventh (page 168), curving along a gentle beach).

CANADA

Golf actually gained its first formal North American foothold in Canada with the formation in 1873 of the Royal Montreal Club. That was more than a decade before J. M. Fox, a Philadelphian, returned from a Scottish vacation to establish what is generally regarded as the first permanent U.S. course at Foxburg, Pa., in the mid-1880s. Scottish sailors are credited with bringing the game to Canada in the 1840s and 1850s. They put together a couple of three-hole courses in Montreal and Quebec City for use while on shore leave, but these have been lost to antiquity.

Today, Canada's golfing population is estimated at more than 900,000 by the Royal Canadian Golf Association. There are more than 1,100 courses—about 10 per cent of them within a 35-mile radius of midtown Toronto—covering almost every populated area in the land. You can play golf by the midnight sun in summer on rock-strewn fairways and black, oiled sand greens at Annie's Lake in the Silas Mountain range of the Yukon, or at subway stops in Toronto and Montreal. At the underground station in Toronto there not only is a regulation length course, but also a par-3 test with pro shop in the tube.

While Winnipeg lays claim to the title of having the most golf clubs per capita of any city in North America—more than 20 to serve 500,000—Toronto's metropolitan area cannot be far behind. It ranks second in population (2.3 million to Montreal's 2.5 million), and within an approximate radius of 35 miles of its famous twin-towered City Hall, there are 115 golfing facilities, at least 40 open to the general public.

Indian names such as Caughnewaga, Kanawaki, Mississaugua and Niakwa are as commonplace as the British Empire traditionalist prefixes of Royal, as in Royal Montreal, Royal Ottawa and Victoria's beautiful Royal Colwood on Vancouver Island. There's also Jumpin' Jack's Rustico Golf Club on Prince Edward Island.

Among the better-known Canadian course designers are the late Stanley Thompson, whose work included Banff, Jasper and the equally magnificent Cape Breton Highlands course on Nova Scotia terrain not unlike the Monterey Peninsula of California; Howard Watson of Lachute, Quebec; and C. E. Robinson of Clarkson, near Toronto, twice president of the American Society of Golf Course Architects.

Canada's golfing season ranges from a couple of months in the Yukon and Northwest Territories, to year-round play on the west coast of British Columbia. In the populous east, the season may stretch from late March into November, although the better courses are generally open from May 1 to October 31.

In 1974, *Golf Digest* magazine appointed a group of prominent Canadian golfing figures to select Canada's Top 25 Courses. Each course was evaluated as an over-all test of golf and golf shot making, with attention to such factors as physical and mental challenge and aesthetic

169

CANADA'S TOP 25

Golf courses within each group are ranked equally and listed in alphabetical order. Ratings apply to course when played at yardage shown.

TOP FIVE	Yards	Par	Rating
Hamilton G. & C.C.	6,735	72	71.9
Ancaster, Ontario			
London Hunt & C.C.	7,168	72	74.4
London, Ontario			
Royal Colwood G. & C.C.	6,789	70	71.2
Victoria, B.C.			
Royal Montreal G.C. (Blue)	6,840	70	71.6
Ile Bizard, Quebec			
St. Georges G. & C.C.	6,797	71	72.1
Islington, Ontario			

SECOND FIVE	Yards	Par	Rating
Capilano G. & C.C.	6,690	72	71.7
Vancouver, B.C.			
Cherry Hill Club	6,755	72	72
Ridgeway, Ontario			
Ottawa Hunt & G.C.	6,614	73	71.8
Ottawa, Ontario			
Mississauga G. & C.C.	6,720	72	71.9
Mississauga, Ontario			
Toronto G.C.	6,441	70	70.4
Toronto, Ontario			

THIRD FIVE	Yards	Par	Rating
Banff Springs G.C.	6,731	71	71.5
Banff, Alberta			
Brantford G. & C.C.	6,601	71	71.3
Brantford, Ontario			
Cape Breton Highlands	6,475	72	71
Ingonish, Nova Scotia			
Essex G. & C.C.	6,639	72	71.9
Sandwich, Ontario			
Mayfair G. & C.C.	6,632	70	71.1
Edmonton, Alberta			

FOURTH FIVE	Yards	Par	Rating
Ashburn G.C. (New)	7,121	72	74.6
Kinsac, Nova Scotia			
Jasper Park G.C.	6,590	71	71.2
Jasper, Alberta			
Le Club Laval sur-le-lac	6,698	72	70.8
Ville de Laval, Quebec			
Pinegrove C.C.	7,090	72	73.9
St-Luc, Quebec			
Royal Quebec G.C. (Old)	6,650	72	71.5
Boischatel, Quebec			

FIFTH FIVE	Yards	Par	Rating
Riverside C.C.	6,540	72	71
Saskatoon, Saskatchewan			
Scarborough G. & C.C.	6,772	71	72
Scarborough, Ontario			
St. Charles C.C.	6,473	72	70.6
Winnipeg, Manitoba			
Summerlea G. & C.C.	6,690	72	71.7
(Cascades), Dorion, Quebec			
Westmount G. & C.C.	6,729	73	71.9
Kitchener, Ontario			

CANADIAN NATIONAL SELECTION PANEL
Alberta: Amateur—R. Bruce Bailey, Calgary.
British Columbia: Amateur—Peter J. G. Bentley, Vancouver.
  Professional—Stan Leonard, Vancouver.
Manitoba: Amateur—W. Arthur Johnston, Winnipeg.
Nova Scotia: Amateur—Peter Hope, Dartmouth.
  Professional—John Irwin, Sydney.
Ontario: Amateurs—Gary Cowan, Kitchener; Phil Farley, Toronto; Bruce Forbes, Toronto; R. H. Grimm, Rexdale; Nick Weslock, Burlington.
  Professionals—Al Balding, Etobicoke; George Knudson, Willowdale; David Zink, Toronto.
Quebec: Amateur—Dave Shea, Montreal.
  Professional—Pat Fletcher, Ile Bizard.

A helicopter's view of the Royal Montreal Golf Club, a 45-hole spread at Ile Bizard, Quebec. At left, several holes of the Red Course, and at right, the beautiful and more demanding Blue Course, all designed by Dick Wilson.

appeal. The national selection panel consisted of the individuals named under the rankings on the page opposite.

The Hamilton Club dates back to 1919, and no longer has the capability to handle the huge galleries of today's tournaments. But it still is of such fine caliber that you might expect a winning score not too far below the 279 recorded by J. D. Edgar of Atlanta when he beat a fellow

namcd Robert Tyre Jones in 1919; or Tommy Armour's 277 in 1930.

St. George's, built in the 1920s and renovated in the '60s, combines both the finesse game of the past with the power of the present and calls for shots to greens of varying sizes. It may well be the best test of golf in Canada now, although some Canadian golf officials expect maturing landscapes to move London Hunt, with its 74 course rating, and Royal Montreal into one-two positions by the end of this decade. St. George's is long, with relatively tight fairways over rolling terrain.

Mississaugua, a two-level course on an upper plateau and through the valley of the Credit River west of Toronto, was built in 1903 and has endured as a championship test through 70 years—it staged its sixth Canadian Open in 1974. Mississaugua and the Hamilton Club are similar in style to what might be termed "typical" U.S. Open courses, excellent membership layouts with mature development, a record of golfing "character," and the potential to be toughened into championship caliber by the simple expedient of letting the grass grow in a few strategic spots. The greens are small by today's standards, and the emphasis is on a complete repertoire of shots, not merely brute strength. When U.S. pro tournament officials checked out Mississaugua for the 1974 Open, they had no significant changes to recommend.

The setting of the Capilano course in Vancouver makes it possibly the most spectacular of Canada's top tests, but it merits its ranking on its capabilities as a golf course, with a rating of 71 over 6,500 yards. It is, as the British Columbia government's golfing guide notes, "reasonably strenuous," requiring the golfer to play a third of his round down the mountainside, a third across it, and the home stretch uphill. On the way down, at least two holes give you the illusionary effect of teeing off into downtown Vancouver.

Inclusion of Cherry Hill in the "second tier" is a tribute to the work of architect C. E. Robinson, who renovated this one to bring it up to the requirements needed for a national tournament in the 1970s. It was a short, fairly easy, 50-year-old layout, ideal for members, pleasant to play.

By the time Robinson was through adding some bunkers, contouring a couple of fairways, reconstructing a green or two, he had proved once more what Gary Player, among others, has been saying for years: You don't need 7,000 yards to have a golf course. Gay Brewer's winning score in the tournament where, officials feared, par might be annihilated, was nine under par.

There's an ancient story lurking around some customs halls on the northern side of the world's longest undefended international boundary concerning an American tourist who drove across the bridge to Niagara Falls, Ontario, for a Fourth of July weekend, skis strapped to the roof of his

car and the trunk loaded with winter camping gear.

He was astonished to learn that he'd have to go several thousand miles to the northwest and at least a mile-and-a-half up into the Rockies to get what he expected. On the contrary, only a mile or so into those mountains are two of the world's most scenic and excellent resort golf courses, at Banff Springs and Jasper Park.

It's an unfortunate reality that the sports of hunting, fishing, skiing and even mountaineering overshadow golf as a tourist attraction. In actual fact, some of the most magnificent courses in North America are located in Canada.

For the tourist, there is always the problem of getting into many of the private clubs which are listed among *Golf Digest's* 25 top courses in Canada. However, in some cases these private clubs recognize visiting club members and members of foreign golf associations and will grant playing privileges. Following is a rundown of the courses on the list which permit unrestricted public play.

Banff Springs is located 80 miles west of Calgary at the junction of the Bow and Spray Rivers and easily accessible by Trans-Canada highway, train or air from Calgary. The 18-hole, 6,729-yard, par-71, Stanley Thompson-designed course which opened in 1929, stands a mile above sea level. Because of the scenic grandeur and mountainous backdrop, there is a tendency to underclub. The rough is deep and difficult and it is not unusual to see wildlife on the course. The resort hotel is only about 150 yards from the first tee.

Cape Breton Highlands is also known as Keltic Lodge course because of the nearby resort hotel. Located in Cape Breton Highlands National Park near Ingonish Beach, the Stanley Thompson course is set in a combined seaside, valley and mountain location. To play the 6,475-yard, par-72 layout means covering about six miles, with holes bearing such names as Killiecrankie.

Jasper Park course, in the national park 177 miles north of Banff, can be reached by the spectacular Banff-Jasper Icefield Freeway or by train, bus or air from Edmonton. Another Thompson design, the 6,599-yard, par-71 course opened in 1925 and was rebuilt in the mid-1940s. The course ranges over rolling terrain with fairways aligned to various mountain peaks. There are beautiful panoramic views of lake, valley and river. A hotel is situated about 100 yards from the first tee.

Ashburn Golf Club, located at Kinsac Lake in Halifax County, is 20 miles north of downtown Halifax. A Geoffrey Cornish design opened for play in 1970, the par-72 course stretches over 7,121 yards. It is the longest course in Nova Scotia and has been carved out of woodland areas featuring tall stands of trees and breathtaking views of Kinsac and Spruce Lakes.

Some very fine tourist courses are situated in the Laurentians and in the area adjacent to them, northwest of Montreal. One of them is Carling Lake at Brownsburg, Quebec, about 55 miles northwest of Montreal and 70 miles northeast of Ottawa. It is a hilly, well-treed 18-hole course over 6,650 yards with a par of 72. Sheep frequently wander the course in the Scottish tradition and the lake is well-stocked for anglers. It was designed by Howard Watson. And at Monte-

The Hamilton golf course, a stately and marvelous test of golf, is set among mature trees and rolling country much like the 439-yard 18th whose fairway bends toward the bunker and green in background.

bello, Quebec, is Le Chateau Montebello, the former Seigniory Club now operated by Canadian Pacific, with 200 rooms and a beautiful, hilly 6,100-yard, par-70 course that winds through forests and meandering streams.

Other challenging and scenic layouts open to the public in the Province of Quebec include Manoir Richelieu Golf Course, which offers two 18-hole layouts located on the north shore of the St. Lawrence River, 90 miles northeast of Quebec

Banff Springs is the closest one can come in North America to playing golf in the Alps. The Stanley Thompson-designed course and the Chateau Lake Louise (in background) nestle between beautiful Lake Louise (not shown) and the majestic Rockies, providing a combination of breathtaking scenery and old world charm.

City; Le Chantecler in Saint-Adele, 42 miles north of Montreal; Gray Rocks Golf and Winter Club in St. Jovite, a scenic, hilly course 80 miles north of Montreal.

The Atlantic Provinces of Nova Scotia, New Brunswick and Prince Edward Island offer the vacationing golfer some of the most scenic lay-outs to be found anywhere. Among the 18-hole courses the golfer will find available to him in Nova Scotia are The Pines Hotel Golf Course in Digby, located near the southwestern tip of the province; Oakfield Country Club, situated five miles from Halifax International Airport; and Ken-Wo Golf and Country Club in Wolfville, 60 miles from Halifax.

While the remainder of Canada offers hundreds of unique and testing courses open to the public, perhaps none can boast of hosting an event quite as extraordinary as one held at The Yellowknife Golf Club. This nine-hole layout is situated in the Northwest Territory and is the site of the Annual Midnight Tournament. Tee times commence promptly at one minute past midnight and, thanks to the midnight sun, the event continues for two days. —*Ken McKee*

MEXICO

The story of golf in Mexico began in 1905 with a small, 9-hole course in the mining town of San Pedro located near the geographical heart of this big, sprawling country. The course was laid out by Willie Smith, a member of the famous Carnoustie family which included brothers Alex and Macdonald. Willie's credentials for the job apparently were that he had won the U.S. Open in 1899.

Smith was to do other Mexican courses, notably those for the country clubs of Mexico City (1907) and Chapultepec (1921), but these early seeds, authentic as they may have been, could not have fallen on deader ground. A few courses were built by oil and mining companies during World War I days; an awkward goat-course was built in Acapulco by vacationing Englishmen and in the 1930s and 1940s foreign businessmen established courses in Monterrey and Guadalajara, designed by John Bredemus, but the game languished until very recently.

Two things happened to change this. The first was the tourism boom which began in the late 1950s and, under the forceful leadership of former Mexican President Miguel Aleman has become a strong force today. The second was Percy Clifford, Mexico's leading golf course architect.

Clifford, now in his 60s, was born in Mexico City of English parents who imbued him with a strong golfing heritage. He is a fine player who has won six Mexican Amateur championships, three Mexican Open titles and, in 1952, the Central American Amateur Championship. He has either designed or remodeled some 35 Mexican golf courses, nearly half the nation's total of 75. In 1950 he worked with American architect Lawrence Hughes on the Club de Golf Mexico, generally regarded as one of Mexico's top three courses.

The Club de Golf Mexico, a 7,174 yard par-72 test, was the first to be organized by Mexicans. The land for the golf course was bordered by a dormant volcano on one side and a magnificent river valley on the other, looking up to the imposing volcano Popacatepetl, which is covered by eternal snow. The Club de Golf Mexico is the only course in the world that has twice hosted the World Cup matches of the International Golf Association; first in 1958, when it was won by Ireland (Harry Bradshaw and Christy O'Connor), and again in 1967, when it was won by the United States (Arnold Palmer and Jack Nicklaus).

To begin the club, shares were put on the market at 5,000 Mexican Pesos (about $400); now, the price of a membership is over 100,000 Mexican Pesos ($10,000) and it is extremely difficult to obtain.

In a country slow to react to golf, Clifford patiently went about putting in a series of sound golf courses, whose designs were influenced by classical schools of English, Scottish and American course architecture. Among these were the fine Mexico City courses of La Hacienda (1959)

and Bellavista (1960) and the lovely Acapulco resort layout at Pierre Marques (1968).

Clifford did one of the early Mexican resort courses, Avandaro, located about 75 miles from Mexico City at Valle de Bravo where a Mexican "Switzerland" was created in the woodlands and hills. Here amid a rustic environment of chalets with steep, red-Spanish tile roofs is a marvelous little golf course of slightly more than 6,000 yards bordered by century old trees and intersected by a trout-filled river.

A decade ago Mexico's two leading golfing centers, Mexico City and Guadalajara, had seven courses between them; there are now 15, with several more building. The courses in Guadalajara, a city of two million, have a distinct American influence. Hughes, who grew up under Donald Ross and did several courses in Palm Springs,

Calif., did the fine Santa Anita courses there. Joe Finger, the Texan who designed such rugged tests as Concord in New York and the new Colonial in Memphis, designed the Club Atlas course, a 7,225-yard par-72 back-breaker that lives up to its name, part of a huge residential development. In fact, residential-condominium courses are becoming an important part of the new wave of Mexican golf development. Finger is creating a 36-hole complex called Guadelupe Lake near Mexico City and not far away Clifford is doing another, called Valle Escondido.

The character of Mexican golf is changing with the advent of these and the newer resort course developments. The older, private Mexican courses tended to be designed on the penal side, influenced as they were by the early British pros who conceived them. Most of the courses built

Golf in Mexico ranges from the sultry, palm-lined fairways of Acapulco's Pierre Marques course (above) to the garden-like fairyland of the Club Las Hadas in Manzanillo (next page).

before 1970 tended to be flat and wide open because the strategic concept of architecture, where options of varying difficulty are presented to the golfer, does not lend itself to the Mexican temperament which likes to hit the ball fast, loose and far. The newer courses reflect a gradual but certain shifting toward modern design.

Clifford, at Pierre Marques, Robert Trent Jones, at the swank Acapulco resort of Tres Vidas and Ted Robinson, at Acapulco's Princess Hotel, have helped to bring this about. At Tres Vidas, Jones built one course, the West, of moderate transition and another, the East, of a tougher mein. Robinson, on a scaled-down piece of property next to the ocean, created a clever and interesting example of modern strategic golf. The impact of resort golfers, who thirst for new and different challenges, is just beginning. In Manzanillo, Pete Dye has unveiled another of his unusual inventions, a modern fairyland of golf at the plush Las Hadas resort. New resort courses are going in at Puerto Vallarta, Baja, California, Mazatlan, Sonora and Cuernavaca. In the Yucatan, near Merida, a new course called La Ceiba, designed by Mexicans Felix Teran and Jaime Saenz, is going strong, and at Cancun, an island just off the coast near Cozumel, the Mexican government, with a push from Aleman, is creating a second Acapulco which has as its first golf attraction a gem from the house of Robert Trent Jones.

All of this activity is rather uncharacteristic of Mexico where, for 70 years there has never been a public golf course. Even this is changing. There are now 20,000 golfers in Mexico and the stirrings of popular interest in golf are being felt. On the 70th anniversary of Willie Smith's primitive 9-hole course, the nation's first municipal course, Los Colomos, is to be unveiled in Guadalajara. The most interesting chapter in Mexican golf may be just beginning.

—Cal Brown

3. BRITISH ISLES

st. andrews

St. Andrews is not so much a place as a state of mind. It is to golfers what Paris is to lovers and Florence is to artists. In short, this small town on the east coast of Scotland is a mecca and, like the medieval traveler who had not seen Avignon in Papal times, the golfer who has not seen St. Andrews has seen nothing.

When one says "St. Andrews" in the same breath as "golf," he means the Old Course, that one-of-a-kind strip of links which is a devious delight to many and yet, to some, nothing more than an absurd museum piece about which there is little wrong that could not instantly be put right by a team of bulldozer operators.

The British Open—held 21 times on the Old Course—always progresses amid grumbling and the criticism of the course's durable features— the hidden hazards, the crumpled fairways, the gigantic greens — is inevitable. Outmoded by contemporary standards it may be, yet aspects of its design have influenced the thinking of most modern course architects.

One unarguable fact is that the Old Course— together with the three other St. Andrews layouts, the New, Eden and Jubilee—is accessible to all, including foreign visitors. Golf in Scotland has always been the people's game, never exclusive or confined only to the wealthy. There are between 350 and 400 courses in the country, many municipally owned as are the four at St. Andrews. Admission to St. Andrews' courses is by payment of a greens fee, never over one pound (about $2.40); during some years 200,000 rounds are played there.

St. Andrews the town—or, to be accurate, the city, since it received its charter as such in 1140 —is a blend of ancient buildings and modern structures. Most of these are part of the university, founded in 1413, and older than all others in Britain except Oxford and Cambridge.

Golf must have proved as effective a therapy in olden times as it is today. The mental anguish induced by wars, lootings and burnings might be complemented now by anxiety over stock market prices and domestic crises. Optimism, however, is what makes slaves to the game and an hour or two of "head still, left arm straight and slow back" and trying to bash the feathers out of their leather shell must have been a marvelously soothing antidote to the harshness of life.

Psychologically, too, perhaps no other nationality than the Scots could have invented both golf and whiskey. Ever-burdened by a Calvinist conscience which made enjoyment for its own sake a sin, they devoted themselves to golf as a kind of penalty for their transgressions, and to the drink as a consolation and a way of restoring themselves, the better to suffer some more. But why should the national passion have centered on St. Andrews? The answers are natural accident and a sequence of events which led to the establishment of the seat of the game's government in what was, and relatively still is, a quite remote corner of Scotland. The evolution can be precisely dated from May 14, 1754, when 22 gentlemen, being "Admirers of the Ancient and healthful Exercise of the Golf" formed themselves into the "Society of St. Andrews Golfers." Eighty years later the title of The Royal and Ancient Golf Club of St. Andrews (R and A) was granted; the clubhouse, basically as it is now, but later extended, was built in 1840.

The emergence of the links land took rather longer. During the ages the sea withdrew, leaving sandy wastes, which dried out into the dunes, ridges, knolls, and hollows that are the essential character of British seaside courses. Bird droppings help fertilize the seeds blown from the land, and rabbits were attracted by the grasses, creating runs among the heather, whins and broom, which later were widened by animals of prey and then, finally, man the hunter.

When the university was founded at the beginning of the 15th century the Old Course was in existence basically as it is today. It occupied so narrow a strip of ground that until as late as the mid-19th century there was room only for single

ST. ANDREWS (OLD COURSE) SCORECARD

Hole	Par	Yards	Hole	Par	Yards
1	4	374	10	4	338
2	4	411	11	3	170
3	4	405	12	4	312
4	4	470	13	4	427
5	5	567	14	5	560
6	4	414	15	4	413
7	4	364	16	4	380
8	3	163	17	4	466
9	4	359	18	4	358
	36	3,527		36	3,424

Totals: Par 72, Yards 6,951

BRITISH OPEN WINNERS
(Event was over 36 holes through 1891)

Year	Winner	Score	Year	Winner	Score
1873	Tom Kidd	179	1910	James Braid	299
1876	Bob Martin	176	1921	Jock Hutchison	296
	(David Strath tied but			(Won playoff with 150	
	refused to play off)			from R. H. Wethered, 159)	
1879	Jamie Anderson	169	1927	Bobby Jones	285
1882	Bob Ferguson	171	1933	Denny Shute	292
1885	Bob Martin	171	1939	Richard Burton	290
1888	Jack Burns	171	1946	Sam Snead	290
1891	Hugh Kirkaldy	166	1955	Peter Thomson	281
1895	J. H. Taylor	322	1957	Bobby Locke	279
1900	J. H. Taylor	309	1960	Kel Nagle	278
1905	James Braid	318	1964	Tony Lema	279
			1970	Jack Nicklaus	283

If any red-blooded golfer had the chance to pick the one course on which to test his talents, it would probably be Scotland's fabled Old Course at St. Andrews. Here, after all, is the cradle of golf, the place where the legendary Young Tom Morris, Harry Vardon and Bobby Jones displayed their awesome games, the course that every golfer who aspires to international fame must challenge. The 374-yard first hole, pictured above, looks placid enough but a burn fronts the green preventing a run-up approach.

greens, first eleven and then nine. For a full round the same holes had to be played out and back, the off-the-cuff origin of the 18-hole course. Subsequently the greens were extended laterally, producing the seven huge double greens for which St. Andrews is famous.

This widening of the course provided a distinct route for the outward and homeward journeys, disposing of the impression of playing up and down a drainpipe in a cross-fire of golf balls.

To be sure, many of the features of the Old Course are disliked by some today; the tumbling fairways, which seldom give a level lie or stance; the hidden bunkers; and some of the more extreme sloping greens, notably at the short 11th, where in the British Open of 1921 Bobby Jones picked up in disgust, thus withdrawing from play. The affection Jones later developed for the course started as do the best affairs—with a little aversion. Later he actually modeled the fourth

The way we were—we golfers, that is, according to an old print of players at the Royal and Ancient Golf Club in St. Andrews, Scotland. Our favorite is the fellow in the stove pipe hat to the left.

hole at Augusta National after the hole that had prompted his withdrawal.

Compared with Jones' day, and even as recently as the immediate post-war years, the character of the turf has changed greatly. The wear and tear caused by increasingly heavy traffic has led to a greenskeeping policy by which the fairways are more holding than in the past, when the ball would run a country mile, and the putting surface across some of the sharp borrows and contours unnervingly resembled sheet-ice. Even so, there is always more to the Old Course than meets the eye; the variations in tackling it are numberless and invariably depend on the direction and strength of the wind.

One of golf's most notable course architects, Robert Trent Jones, has said that the golfer's first estimate of the Old Course will be that its mysteries are more like a myth and that it is vastly overrated. But he added that "then it begins to soak In that whenever he plays a fine shot he is rewarded; whenever he thinks out his round he scores well."

Jones launched his Grand Slam of 1930 by winning the British Amateur at St. Andrews. Many other Americans have figured prominently in the course's more recent history: Sam Snead winning his only British Open in 1946, Arnold Palmer finishing a stroke short of Kel Nagle in the 1960 Open, Tony Lema with his smashing triumph in the 1964 Open and the missed putt of 2½ feet by Doug Sanders on the 72nd hole which cost him the Open in 1970. Lema had only 27 holes of exposure to the Old Course before he won the Open with his 279 in 1964. That was an astonishing feat, at least in the minds of the Scots. Sanders, after blowing his crucial putt on the home hole six years later, had to face Jack Nicklaus in an 18-hole playoff the next day. Nicklaus beat him by a stroke.

Visitors who wish to play St. Andrews courses should be appraised that hardly a year passes without some form of competition taking up the Old. The R and A's Spring and Autumn Medal meetings, in the first week of May and for much of the first three weeks of September, are best avoided. And there also are certain other fixed times when access is difficult or impossible. It is always closed for the month of March, and on Sunday when, as Old Tom Morris once said to a critic of this custom, "The Old Course needs a rest on the Sabbath, sir, even if you don't."

—*Raymond Jacobs*

OTHER BRITISH OPEN COURSES

There is only one truly major professional golf championship played outside the territorial walls of the United States. Within the kingdom, it's simply called "The Open." To the rest of the world, it's the British Open. But by whatever name, it is an event with incomparable history that is played every summer on tradition-cloaked courses known as Troon, Carnoustie, Royal Lytham and St. Annes, Royal Birkdale, Muirfield, Hoylake and—of course—St. Andrews.

At St. Andrews, you have a prideful shiver over first seeing the site of golf's genesis. It's to the golfer what The Vatican is to the Catholic, what Munich is to a beer drinker and what Mt. Everest is to the adventurer. The Open has been played there 21 times.

Although the British Open has visited 13 courses all told, in recent years it has been confined to a championship rota of seven—with one significant change. The Royal and Ancient has assigned the 1977 Open to the Ailsa course at Turnberry, for the first time. Turnberry, or to be more precise, the Ailsa, is regarded by some knowledgeable people as the finest test of golf in Scotland. Located near Troon, a short drive from the town of Ayr, it was the site of the 1963 Walker Cup matches, an event many visiting Americans still recall with affection. In the consideration of British golf officials Turnberry, with its improved access roads, will prove to be an ideal Open site.

The pervading atmosphere at the Open will vary to some degree with the site, the weather and how well the home forces are doing. Tony Jacklin's emergence as a winner of major titles —he has taken both the British and U.S. Opens —generated a new wave of interest among natives who heretofore had to settle for adopting some foreigner such as Arnold Palmer, Jack Nicklaus, Lee Trevino or British cousin Gary Player of South Africa.

The cycling of seven links courses began in 1952, the year after Max Faulkner won at Portrush in the Open's only visit ever to the country of Ireland. Prior to the change in format, the tournament made many stops in England at historical sites such as Prince's, Deal and Royal St. George's. But it has been Scotland that has so liberally opened its arms to this oldest of the Big Four events. The Scots hosted the Open 70 times in its first 102 years. Four of the seven courses now used are in Scotland—Muirfield, Troon, Carnoustie and St. Andrews—while Royal Birkdale, Royal Lytham and the Royal Liverpool Club at Hoylake are on English soil.

Scotland's famed Prestwick course was the site of the first 12 British Opens beginning with the inaugural, won by Willie Park against a field of seven in 1860. St. Andrews and Musselburgh then began sharing the glory and it was the 34th Open before England first got into the act at Royal St. George's in 1894.

Following is a look, one by one, at the sites for the modern British Open. The scorecards appearing with each course list yardages from the championship tees.

—*Hubert Mizell*

royal birkdale

Royal Birkdale, set close to the sea on Britain's northwest coast in the county of Lancashire, is the youngest course on the Open Championship rota. It staged the Open for the first time in 1954 when Australian Peter Thomson scored the first of his three successive victories.

When Arnold Palmer won his first British Open title at Birkdale in 1961, it became painfully obvious that the Royal Birkdale course and clubhouse were not up to the task of accommodating huge crowds.

The original course had been laid out by Charles Hawtree among the massive sandhills which are a feature of the Lancashire coast. The terrain was so unrelenting between holes that it proved impossible for spectators to move freely about the course without encroaching on the fairway and interfering with play. When Thomson returned to Birkdale for the fifth of his Open triumphs in 1965 drastic changes had been made.

Over a period of three years, members of the club, entirely at their own expense, reshaped the course and clubhouse. Fred Hawtree, son of the man who had designed the original course, was summoned to update his father's work. He advised the moving of six tees to make room for the passage of spectators. He condemned the short 17th hole as a bottleneck and an anti-climax and built a superb new short hole, the present 12th, which had been deleted from his father's first plans for the course due to lack of finance. The demise of the old 17th allowed room to extend the 18th to make it a full two-shotter instead of a rather weak drive-and-pitch finish. Royal Birkdale's four finishing holes now match almost anything in the world for severity. Young Hawtree replaced holes measuring 381, 510, 186, and 450 yards with new ones of 536, 401, 510, and 513 yards. Two of these holes run away from the clubhouse and the 17th and 18th come back in the opposite direction. With the varying wind conditions which play such a large role on all links in Britain, the 15th and 16th are generally played into the wind. All four can be cursed by strong cross-currents.

In addition to four British Open championships, Birkdale has staged a host of British professional and amateur events plus the Carling and Alcan tournaments. It has also seen two Ryder Cup encounters between Great Britain and America, the second being the classic battle in 1969 when, for the first time in the history of the event, the two nations finished three days of matches all square.

Palmer's Open championship at Birkdale has to rate as one of the most popular in the tournament's history. The appealing American had come so close in his first try, at the centenary Open at St. Andrews a year earlier. He finished a stroke behind Kel Nagle in that one, but at Royal Birkdale he dominated the competition to win the first of his back-to-back Opens.

Ironically, Lee Trevino also launched his two-year string of Opens at Birkdale. In 1971, fresh from successive victories in the U.S. and Canadian Opens, Trevino played beautiful golf in the British tournament. He nearly threw it all away with a seven on the 71st hole, but pulled himself together for a finishing par that provided a winning total of 278.

Royal Birkdale has gained a reputation as one of the great venues for major British championships and at the same time an entertaining and elusive challenge to the average golfer. But, lest you become carried away after hitting a particularly good drive on any hole, turn and face in the opposite direction and see if you can even spot the championship tee nestled in the long grass and the sand dunes up to 70 yards farther back. Birkdale uses its great mounds of sand and grass as marvelous spectator viewing areas. The club has extremely large parking lots, too, all of which make Royal Birkdale a wonderful venue for major events such as the British Open.

—Keith Mackie

BRITISH OPEN WINNERS			ROYAL BIRKDALE SCORECARD					
Year	Winner	Score	Hole	Par	Yards	Hole	Par	Yards
1954	Peter Thomson	283	1	5	493	10	4	393
1961	Arnold Palmer	284	2	4	427	11	4	412
1965	Peter Thomson	285	3	4	416	12	3	190
1971	Lee Trevino	278	4	3	212	13	5	517
			5	4	358	14	3	202
			6	4	473	15	5	536
			7	3	158	16	4	401
			8	4	459	17	5	510
			9	4	410	18	5	518
				35	3,406		38	3,679

Totals: Par 73, Yards 7,085

The large mounds at Royal Birkdale Golf Club in Southport, England, provide a natural amphitheater for spectators, one reason it is a frequent venue for the British Open.

royal lytham, st. annes

Royal Lytham and St. Annes is a links out of sight of the sea. It is almost entirely surrounded by houses and none too elegant at that — and must slowly grab you since it is rarely love at first sight. The visiting golfer quickly learns to respect this largely flat terrain, appreciate its subtleties and admire the excellence of its large, true and undulating greens.

Lytham has hosted all the major British golfing championships, but the most famous of them all is still the Open of 1926 when Bobby Jones won the title for the first time.

There can be few dedicated to golf who have not heard of his incredible bunker shot at the 17th hole in the final round. Tied at this point with his playing partner Al Watrous, and with Walter Hagen nine holes behind and well placed to catch both men, Jones hit his tee shot at the 423-yard 17th into a bunker surrounded by deep rough on the left of the fairway. From here his route to the green 180 yards away was over a further series of deep bunkers and knee-high grass. Yet his superb recovery shot finished on the green, inside Watrous, who three-putted. Jones made a safe four, beat Watrous by two shots and Hagen dropped into third place. The club with which Jones struck that historic shot was later presented by him to the members of Royal Lytham, who, in turn, marked the Bobby Jones bunker with a plaque.

It was at Lytham in 1963 that Bob Charles of New Zealand became the first left-handed winner of the British Open, having to go through the agony of a 36-hole playoff against American Phil Rodgers before clinching the title. In those days the final two rounds of the championship were played on one day, so this meant 72 holes in two days for Charles and Rodgers.

The course was even more deeply carved into British minds in 1969 when England's Tony Jacklin won the Open after 18 years of foreign domination, and in 1974 when Gary Player led every round to win his third Open Championship by a decisive four-stroke margin. It was the first Open played with the larger American-size ball.

If there were ever a doubt about Lytham's qualifications as a great test, it was dispelled in 1974. Like most of Britain's western links courses, the winds seldom abate and for the first two days they gustily separated the experienced professionals from the young superstars. But even as the winds subsided, the ground never gave way; the fifth place finisher was 10 strokes off Gary Player's winning score of 282.

These links demand intense concentration and especially true shots. It is a difficult test due greatly to the fact that there are no easy holes, no breathing space between the extremely tight 205-yard first hole, and the 386-yard 18th, which is so ruthlessly bunkered. There are also severe bumps and dips along the final stretch of holes. Three of the four closing holes are dog-legged, with deep bunkers and very thick, high rough waiting to catch a ball which misses either side of the fairway. Above all, Lytham is a test of straight drives and strong nerves. The relatively short 18th hole epitomizes this with its menacing shrubs to the right and a staggered formation of bunkers to the left that leaves only about 35 square yards of safe landing area. As golf writer Pat Ward-Thomas so aptly observed, "Not much of a target for a driver when the ambition of a lifetime is within sight."

Unlike some championship courses where several mediocre holes are completely overshadowed by the great ones that surround them, Lytham is generally considered to be a course with 18 good holes, none particularly dominating or falling below the standard of the others. Founded in 1886, the club offers excellent Dormy House accommodation (a kind of private hotel owned by the club) opposite the clubhouse and within 50 yards of the first tee.

—Keith Mackie

BRITISH OPEN WINNERS		
Year	Winner	Score
1926	Bobby Jones	291
1952	Bobby Locke	287
1958	Peter Thomson	278
1963	Bob Charles	277
1969	Tony Jacklin	280
1974	Gary Player	282

ROYAL LYTHAM AND ST. ANNES
SCORECARD

Hole	Par	Yards	Hole	Par	Yards
1	3	206	10	4	334
2	4	436	11	5	542
3	4	458	12	3	201
4	4	393	13	4	339
5	3	212	14	4	445
6	5	486	15	4	468
7	5	551	16	4	356
8	4	394	17	4	453
9	3	162	18	4	386
	35	3,298		36	3,524

Totals: Par 71, Yards 6,822.

Golfers and their caddies walk toward the 18th green at the Royal Lytham and St. Annes Golf Club in England, one of the great finishing holes in the world. Its greatness owes nothing to length, but rather to a series of treacherous bunkers placed in and around the driving area. The hole measures only 386 yards.

189

Carnoustie, although somewhat ignored as a British championship venue due to its lack of fringe amenities such as hotel accommodations, is a superb and massive links, a complete test of golf that provided two of the most exciting results in the ancient tournament.

When Ben Hogan, following his body-smashing car accident, won the 1953 Open with a course record 68 in the final round, he pulled away from the pack. Frank Stranahan, Dai Rees, Peter Thomson and Antonio Cerda tied for second, the only time four men tied for the runner-up spot in the British Open. Hogan, scoring 282, derived immense satisfaction from that championship. He had never played in the British Open before, the course was set up in extremely difficult fashion and Ben had to contend with a nagging cold most of the week. He improved his score each round, walking off the home hole with the 68 that produced his last major championship.

The Open did not return to Carnoustie until 1968, when Gary Player held off the challenge of Jack Nicklaus to win with a 289. The year previous, at Hoylake, Robert deVicenzo had the low score of 278, and the year following, at St. Annes, Tony Jacklin returned a 280. Small wonder, then, that Player termed Carnoustie the toughest course he had played. Player was speaking, of course, of Carnoustie as it was set up for the Open.

Local golfers cried with anguish when their own Macdonald Smith crashed in the 1931 Open. Until the last three holes, Smith was swinging toward victory. However, he finished 5-6-5, six shots more than he had taken for the same three holes in the previous round, and lost by three strokes to Tommy Armour.

When Henry Cotton won in 1937, his last round at Carnoustie was considered the best he ever played. Reg and Charles Whitcombe were both ahead of Cotton after three rounds but in desperately difficult weather, both came home in 76 while Cotton produced a miraculous 71.

For the average golfer, it is a relief to discover that Carnoustie becomes more difficult the better player you are. All bunkers, and there are relatively few, are strategically placed to trap long shots. Short and straight efforts will keep your score respectable, but the long shot must be extremely accurate. Wind and a particularly tough brand of spiny grass in the rough are major problems, but these are nothing compared with the spasms of anxiety you will suffer as a result of the Barry Burn and Jockie's Burn, two of the most perplexing waterways in golf. As you stand on the first tee, perhaps the Burns 60 yards ahead may not be intimidating, but it is likely that you will have advanced shivers by the time you come to the 18th where the Burn sweeps indecently close to the green.

You can't count on the wind being with or against you on more than two consecutive tees and each hole is picturesquely named, often foretelling of difficulties ahead. For championships, Carnoustie is stretched to 7,252 yards. The longest hole is the sixth at 565 yards and there even the big hitter hesitates to be spectacular. There is a double dogleg and a narrow entrance to the green that is guarded by the end of Jockie's Burn.

To describe the course as difficult could be misleading. Although Carnoustie golf is much too subtle ever to be easy, on a still day most golfers will get by if they keep down the middle. The trouble is that you seldom get a still day. Carnoustie's first 10 holes were laid out by Alan Robertson, the St. Andrews professional, in 1842; in 1872 Old Tom Morris extended the course to 18 holes.

The Carnoustie finish is famous, with holes named "Barry Burn," "Island" and "Home." The looping Burn almost, but not quite, makes an island of the 17th green and is at least 20 feet wide where it guards the final green on one of Great Britain's most massive links tests.

—*Keith Mackie*

BRITISH OPEN WINNERS		
Year	Winner	Score
1931	Tommy Armour	296
1937	Henry Cotton	290
1953	Ben Hogan	282
1968	Gary Player	289

CARNOUSTIE SCORECARD*					
Hole	Par	Yards	Hole	Par	Yards
1	4	406	10	4	446
2	4	468	11	4	370
3	4	343	12	4	473
4	4	429	13	3	168
5	4	389	14	5	485
6	5	565	15	4	460
7	4	386	16	3	243
8	3	163	17	4	458
9	4	475	18	5	525
	36	3,624		36	3,628

Totals: Par 72, Yards 7,252

*In Medal, or non-tournament play, the 12th hole is played as a par-5 and the 18th as a par-4.

Carnoustie has a special appeal for Scots and, being the site of Ben Hogan's dramatic victory in the 1953 British Open, it has also been well-publicized in America. The "Barry Burn" (above) curls menacingly through the home holes, flanking the left side of the 453-yard 18th whose green is located in the upper right, in front of the rebuilt clubhouse.

troon

Gene Sarazen scored a disastrous 85 and missed qualifying for the British Open when it was first played at Troon in 1923. His great rival, Walter Hagen, made the pre-qualifying cut by one stroke despite an 82 in gale-force winds. Hagen rebounded but still lost the championship by one stroke to 23-year-old British professional Arthur Havers.

Only three times in the next half century did the Open return to the toughness of Troon. The wind still rages from the Irish Sea across this linksland strip, the sand dunes are still mountainous, the sand bunkers incredibly deep and the rough unbelievably impenetrable.

In all that time, very little has changed at Troon. Certainly it is a new generation of seagulls which swoops low over the crisp turf. Birds of a different character now cough jet fuel from engines of airliners which deposit Transatlantic passengers at adjoining Prestwick airport after thundering perhaps 100 feet above the 10th green. Havers and Hagen had no such distractions in 1923. Willie Fernie laid out the course in 1909, and James Braid later added some modifications.

A new wing has also been added to the clubhouse. But apart from these changes, golf at Troon is much the same as it was 50 years ago. A hole has been lenghtened here, tightened there to impose more demands on modern golf professionals whose equipment far outstrips the gutty balls and hickory shafts of the Havers-Hagen era.

Troon contains the shortest and longest holes in Open Championship golf in Britain. The tiny eighth is known as the Postage Stamp, as much for its diminutive proportions as for the perforated edging effect created by five deep bunkers. From the tee, the hole appears to offer no great problems, but a crowned green quickly guides anything less than a near-perfect shot into one of the five bunkers. In the 1950 Open an amateur from Germany hit into the sand off the tee shot and then leapfrogged from one deep pit to the next before finally completing the hole in 15 shots.

The eighth, measuring 126 yards, provided a nostalgic note of drama in the 1973 Open. Gene Sarazen, who was 21 when he had his first traumatic exposure to Troon, came back for what he announced would be his final competitive appearance. The attrition of age had shortened his swing a bit, but it was still stylish and classic, and the Scots thundered after the dapper 71-year-old man as he teed off on the opening round. At the eighth, which played directly into a strong wind, Sarazen punched a 5-iron shot that rolled into the cup for a hole-in-one. It was one of the great moments in the long history of the course. "When I made that double eagle at Augusta (in the 1935 Masters) it was seen by only a few people," Sarazen said. "This shot was seen by the whole world." The stroke had been recorded by the BBC cameras and relayed across the water via satellite. On the next day, as if to smile at history, Sarazen hit his tee shot into a bunker and then holed out for a deuce. In two rounds, he was three strokes under par on the Postage Stamp Hole.

In strict contrast is the 577-yard sixth hole, the longest of any British Open. Yet, in fast-running summer conditions, it seldom plays to its full length. When Arnold Palmer won the 1962 Open at Troon he reached the green in the final round with a drive and 3-wood. He set the Open record of 276 that year, and when the tournament returned to Troon in 1973. Tom Weiskopf matched that record score. It was the first major championship for Weiskopf, who learned quickly how to cope with Troon's tight driving areas and its treacherous bunkers.

Troon is in southwest Scotland, a bewildering density of golf courses — 140 in all — varying from true seaside links to parkland layouts. Troon hugs the beach and from the 10th hole you can see Prestwick, where the Open was first played in 1860. Troon is only overshadowed by its illustrious neighbor Prestwick in one respect, its relative lack of historical associations. The sea is in full view most of the way around and the first six holes run along the shore in a southeasterly direction toward Prestwick. Except for a few difficult holes, Troon is also a wonderful experience for the golfer on holiday.

—Keith Mackie

TROON SCORECARD*

Hole	Par	Yards	Hole	Par	Yards
1	4	362	10	4	437
2	4	391	11	5	481
3	4	381	12	4	432
4	5	556	13	4	468
5	3	210	14	3	180
6	5	577	15	4	457
7	4	389	16	5	542
8	3	126	17	3	223
9	4	427	18	4	425
	36	3,419		36	3,645

Totals: Par 72, Yards 7,064

*In Medal, or non-championship play, the 11th hole is played as a par-4, lowering total par to 71, with comparably lower total yardage.

BRITISH OPEN WINNERS

Year	Winner	Score
1923	Arthur Havers	295
1950	Bobby Locke	279
1962	Arnold Palmer	276
1973	Tom Weiskopf	276

Deep pot bunkers are scattered like moon craters over the Troon Golf Club course in western Scotland. This is a view of the seventh and eighth holes at this classic links.

193

At first glance, the Royal Liverpool Golf Club at Hoylake appears to be a rather meek site for the British Open. The course is extremely flat, there are no trees, and the superb greens promise to hold something less than the best-struck approach.

This appearance, however, is deceiving and holds true only on calm, sunny days which, to be truthful, are not exactly commonplace on the northwestern coast of England. When the wind comes howling in off the Irish Sea, Hoylake — few call the course by its correct title — turns into a monster, a brutal test of every ounce of a golfer's skill and courage. At almost any hole the slightest mistake can result in disaster. The fairways are narrow and bordered by vast areas of untended grass and rough, indigenous foliage. The greens are tantalizingly small. Artificial banks, or "cops," laterally define many holes.

At one time almost all of these banks represented out-of-bounds and it was possible to take a stroke-and-distance penalty 13 times in a round without repeating the mistake on any one hole or leaving the area of the course. Recent reflection by the Royal and Ancient Golf Club, which runs the British Open, has softened this threat, and now the chief problem for the off-line player is simply to find the ball! Two of the "cops" are still out-of-bounds, those lining the long, dogleg first and 16th holes. Few contenders, even in an Open Championship, are able to escape an encounter with their unique brand of perdition.

Hoylake's 6,940 yards are located a few miles south of Liverpool. Hefty, blood-colored villas almost surround the area, giving the course a definite suburban look. The houses have come to Hoylake, though, and not the other way around, for when the course was established at its present location in 1895, it was out in the country. Royal Liverpool itself was actually founded in 1869, making it a club of only middling vintage on this golf oriented island. The course was laid out by Robert Chambers Jr. and George Morris, a brother of Old Tom. The talented, energetic Harry Colt remodeled it in 1920.

The British Open was first played there in 1897. In almost all of the 10 Opens at Hoylake, the championship has been won or lost on the last four holes. For a player to have a chance for a good score, he must shoot well on the outward nine. The top players aim at 34. Then the going gets progressively more difficult.

The real crunch starts at 15, a 466-yarder which usually plays directly into the wind. Sixteen, a 513-yard dogleg with an out-of-bounds "cop" all the way on the right, tightens the player's skills. Approach shots on the 423-yard 18th seem a kind of horrible relief.

Since Walter Hagen won the second of his four British Opens at Hoylake in 1924 and Bobby Jones made a quarter of his Grand Slam there in 1930, Americans have not fared too well on this bleak stretch of one-time scrubland. The best showing was in 1947 when Frank Stranahan almost holed his second shot on the last hole, just missing a tie.

Peter Thomson, the Australian, won his third successive Open at Hoylake in 1956 with a score of 286. In 1967 the Open winner was Roberto deVicenzo, the Argentinian, with his score of 278. DeVicenzo was one of the most popular foreigners ever to compete in Britain. He was regarded with as much affection, in fact, as a native. Roberto had challenged for the Open Championship many times, and had found some way to lose it on each occasion, until he broke through at Hoylake.

There might be a few old-timers around who would compare the current stars to two of Hoylake's own champions, amateurs Harold Hilton and John Ball. Between them they won 15 British Open and Amateur championships between 1888 and 1915. There are those who say their ghosts still roam the wild Hoylake links as the western sun dips over the nearby estuary of the River Dee — sniggering, no doubt, at those golfers who find themselves entwined in the treacherous rough.

—Ken Bowden

BRITISH OPEN WINNERS			HOYLAKE (ROYAL LIVERPOOL) SCORECARD					
Year	Winner	Score	Hole	Par	Yards	Hole	Par	Yards
1897	Harold Hilton	314	1	4	421	10	4	404
1902	Alex Herd	307	2	4	426	11	3	201
1907	Arnaud Massy	312	3	5	491	12	4	460
1913	J. H. Taylor	304	4	3	196	13	3	158
1924	Walter Hagen	301	5	4	450	14	5	515
1930	Bobby Jones	291	6	4	389	15	4	459
1936	Alfred Padgham	287	7	3	193	16	5	529
1947	Fred Daly	293	8	5	492	17	4	418
1956	Peter Thomson	286	9	4	393	18	4	400
1967	Roberto de Vicenzo	278		36	3,451		36	3,544

Totals: Par 72, Yards 6,995

The Royal Liverpool Golf Club at Hoylake has never been known for its scenic virtues, but its grim architecture has an almost elemental appeal. Grass-covered dunes open to form a path for golfers playing one of the oldest courses in the world. Hoylake was founded in 1869.

muirfield

Muirfield has lasting qualities that have brought 11 British Open championships, seven British Amateurs and six Scottish Amateurs plus the Walker and Curtis Cup matches to its soil. Many of the most stirring chapters in modern golf have been written here since the club moved its headquarters down the coastline of the Firth of Forth from Musselburgh in 1891 — appropriately, too, since so much of the recorded history of the game in its beginnings is in the possession of the Honourable Company of Edinburgh Golfers.

The course evolved from a sand-strewn wilderness located amid three walls and a woods of buckthorn. Part of these remain, but the links, which have to bear less traffic than most, are now among the best maintained in the land and constitute a severe but honest test of golf. The present course was constructed in 1891, designed by Old Tom Morris. While it borders the sea, Muirfield has definite inland characteristics. The design is imaginative and convenient. Holes run in two circles of nine, the first clockwise and the second counter-clockwise inside. The first and 10th tees and the ninth and 18th greens are within a pitch shot of the clubhouse and no part of the course is more than a few minutes walk from this point.

For the watcher, there is a feeling of great space, yet for the player there is never more than a few yards between one green and the next tee.

Problems faced by golfers at Muirfield are almost always thoroughly exposed. The only blind shot is the drive at the 11th. Fairways are narrow, demanding precise tee shots to avoid the tough, rippling rough and the prolific bunkers. There are 164 bunkers although several in fairways fall into the category of "member bunkers" and seldom bother a pro. The greens are tightly guarded, though, and in winning his 1959 Open, Gary Player failed only once in the 12 times he was trapped to get down in two. He said bunker play was his key to victory.

Any obsession with length has been resisted. From the championship tees the course measures only 6,892 yards with a par of 71. One of the most famous and daunting holes in the world is the 495-yard ninth, which has so often swayed the tide of a British Open. If the wind is blowing

against the player, it becomes alarmingly evident that a wall runs the length of the hole down the left side. Drives must also avoid a large fairway bunker. Diagonal bunkers guard the green, including one that is camouflaged. Severe rough on both sides makes a player even more cautious.

The final sting in Muirfield's tail has proved many times to be painfully sharp. It was particularly so for Tony Jacklin in the 1972 Open. The target from the 18th tee is small, between three bunkers on the left and a deep one on the right. The shot to the flag is over two bunkers. There is another long one to the green's left and one on the right which is deeper and has an awkward island of grass. Jacklin needed a birdie three on this 429-yard hole for a playoff chance with Lee Trevino in the last round of the 1972 Open. He had held a one-stroke lead at the 71st tee, only to bogie weakly after Trevino shocked the world by chipping a 9-iron down a bank and into the hole at 17. At the 72nd, Jacklin fired his second shot at the pin, but the ball ran away, as it is prone to do, into the right-hand bunker. Only a counter-miracle could win the hole, and there was no such shot in his bag.

It was in that same 1972 event that Jack Nicklaus lost his dramatic bid for the modern grand slam, having won the Masters and the U.S. Open championships. Despite a courageous bid with a final round of 66, Muirfield stopped him. It is said that he played the course too carefully, that he attacked too late.

To visiting golfers who have endeavored to play at Muirfield it is often remembered as the most difficult course in Britain on which to gain admission. Unless you are accompanied by a member, your letter of introduction may well be lost or your entreaties fall on deaf ears. The Honorable Company of Edinburgh Golfers never has joined a golfing organization or union. It observes no formal handicapping system, and does not recognize handicaps acquired over other courses. When a club tournament is to be played at handicap, committee members sit over a drink and discuss the current form of the contestants.

"Well, dash it," one might say, "he played jolly well in his last two club matches. Let's give him an eight instead of a 10." His handicap has become eight—no argument allowed.

—Keith Mackie

196

BRITISH OPEN WINNERS				MUIRFIELD SCORECARD					
Year	Winner	Score	Hole	Par	Yards	Hole	Par	Yards
1892	Harold Hilton	305	1	4	453	10	4	475
1896	Harry Vardon	316	2	4	363	11	4	363
1901	James Braid	309	3	4	385	12	4	385
1906	James Braid	300	4	3	187	13	3	154
1912	Ted Ray	295	5	5	516	14	4	462
1929	Walter Hagen	292	6	4	473	15	4	407
1935	Alfred Perry	283	7	3	187	16	3	198
1948	Henry Cotton	284	8	4	451	17	5	528
1959	Gary Player	284	9	5	495	18	4	429
1966	Jack Nicklaus	282		—	—		—	—
1972	Lee Trevino	278		36	3,510		35	3,401

Totals: Par 71, Yards 6,892

Except for tournaments, play at the Muirfield course in Scotland is limited to members of the Honorable Company of Edinburgh Golfers and their guests. The venerable clubhouse looms behind the 447-yard 18th, one of the world's most vicious finishing holes due to prevailing crosswinds.

Among the hidden perils of Muirfield are bunkers like this one at
the 154-yard 13th, whose inside
edges are contoured with furrowed
ridges, an insidious presence that
poses a test of nerve for any golfer.

OTHER GREAT ENGLISH AND SCOTTISH COURSES

Ask six British golfers to name their country's two best courses, excluding British Open sites, and you will more than likely come up with a dozen different answers. England and Scotland have 1,200 courses in an area one third the size of Texas, and among them are scores of outstanding tests of golf.

All around the coasts are the links courses where the game of golf was born centuries ago, but there are also challenging inland tests—the British call them parkland courses—decorated by enchanting forests and great wind-swept heaths of gorse and heather. Golf in Britain is virtually a year-round game, very few days being lost because of snow.

In Scotland, where the game first took an identifiable shape 400 years ago, golf is the heritage of every man, woman and child in the land, and everyone can afford to play for an outlay of a few dollars a year. The cost of golf in England has not matched the rise in the cost of living, and the broadening distribution of wealth since World War II has brought golf within the financial scope of more people. Membership in a golf club, like that of the American country club, is a status symbol, although initiation fees are seldom more than $100 and annual dues, called "subscriptions," are usually under $150.

There are still clubs in Scotland where Spartan traditions survive. At the Royal and Ancient (St. Andrews), Troon and Prestwick, women are not normally allowed in the clubhouses. This is partly custom and partly due to lack of space. Scottish clubhouses usually are small and purely functional.

The turf on British courses may surprise the visitor. Fairway grass is finer, closer cut and not so lush in growth as in the U.S. where the smaller English ball would be impractical. In Britain both the big and small balls can be played with equal pleasure, save in a high wind, when the smaller ball is preferred. No British club waters all of its fairways. This would be a needless expense in a country of such temperate climate and consistent rainfall. However, increased watering and artificial treatment have altered the turf character of many great seaside courses over the year and as a consequence the ball will not roll or bounce as freely as before. When Bobby Jones came to St. Andrews in 1958, he remarked with surprise, and possible disappointment, how the Old Course's turf had toughened up since his visit there in 1927. However, the ball generally still runs farther on British courses than on those in America.

Many outstanding Scottish and English courses are clustered within a few miles of one another to form constellations of golf, often with one of the famous courses shining brightly among them. One of the exceptions is Gleneagles whose beautiful courses are miles apart from any others in the lowlands of Scotland. A look at this bright attraction in the firmament and some of the great courses in Scotland and England follows.

SCOTLAND

All the golfing world knows of Scotland's beautiful courses, more than 300 of them. Two of the best, Gleneagles and Turnberry, are owned by British Rail, the nationalized transport company. This helps account for two things. First, both complexes are known as hotel golf courses and, second, both offer the highest standards of service of any golfing resorts in Europe, one in the heart of the Highlands, the other on the west coast.

Gleneagles has two breathtaking courses nestled among the Perthshire mountain moorlands, the King's at 6,644 yards and the Queen's at 6,055, both laid out by James Braid just before World War I. The Gleneagles Hotel, a true gourmet's delight, opened its doors in 1924. So popular has it become that more than 60,000 rounds of golf are played on the two courses every year. A third course is being added.

Professional Ian Marchbank reckons that "Braid's Brawest" — the 13th on the King's Course—is the most difficult hole and, indeed, many regard it as the best and most testing inland hole in Britain. At this 465-yard hole, your drive must carry a ridge into which two large bunkers are set.

The name Turnberry is synonymous with golfing quality. The superb hotel overlooks the sea and both courses, which were completely rebuilt by MacKenzie Ross following World War II. The Ailsa course is the better known, playing 7,060 yards and having been host to many great golfing occasions, including the Walker Cup. It is mostly memorable for two reasons. First, it is a driver's course where the green is visible for every second shot. Second, the scenery, especially on the first nine, is spectacular. The ninth is the most famous. It was called the "greatest par-4 in golf" by Gene Sarazen, a man who won all of pro golf's Big Four. It has a tee high amongst the rocks from which you look down at breaking waves. Turnberry has now been awarded the supreme accolade, joining the British Open Championship rota in 1977.

If you do not feel up to the challenge of the Ailsa Course—especially off the back tees—the Arran Course, which is 6,350 yards long, is almost as tough and certainly as well kept as its championship sister.

To the north of Turnberry, nearer Glasgow, is old Prestwick, considered by some to be rather old-fashioned but by others a supreme test of golf. It possesses some outstanding holes, in-

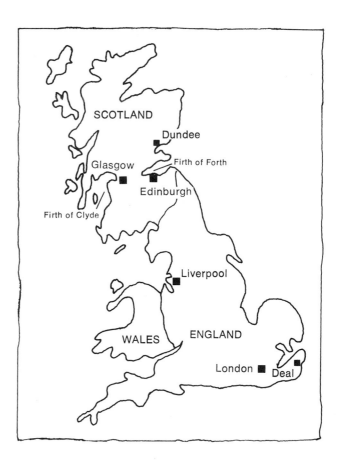

cluding the third, with a famous bunker called the Cardinal in which James Braid took eight strokes and still won the Open in 1908. Prestwick was the original British Open venue in 1860; it hosted the first 12 Opens, and 24 in all.

Perhaps the most varied concentration of Scottish courses can be found within range of Dundee on the east coast, not far from either Carnoustie or St. Andrews and within a short drive of tree-lined Rosemount, at Blairgowrie, which many regard as Scotland's most precious inland course. Royal Dornoch, near the sea and close to the Highlands, is the most northerly of the famous Scottish resort courses, with perhaps the most panoramic of views. It was laid out by Old Tom Morris with later modifications by J. H. Taylor.

ENGLAND

Within 25 miles to the southwest of central London, in Surrey, there is a strip of sandy, fir-clad land that contains some of the most imitated golf courses in the world. Among them are Wentworth, Sunningdale and Berkshire. Each has two courses.

Wentworth combines tradition and atmosphere with a modern outlook which makes it the nearest British equivalent to the American country club.

Here is the real attraction of true Scottish golf: a rugged beach bordering the Ailsa course at Turnberry. Located on Scotland's west coast off the Firth of Clyde, the Ailsa is not only long and tight, but contains thick growths of gorse just off its fairways. The ninth tee stands on high ground near the lighthouse at the upper left.

England's finest inland courses were built in the sandy woodlands of Surrey, southwest of London, and several have served to inspire some of America's best golf architecture. At Berkshire, above right, golfers stroll through typical unkept areas off the tee to the landing areas of their drives. At bottom right, the beautiful English course of Sunningdale with the first tee (left) and the 18th green merging near the clubhouse. In the photo at left is the elevated fourth green of the King's course at Gleneagles, an inland Scottish layout which resembles an American course. Note the umbrellas, a must for anyone undertaking a round of golf in Scotland.

Part of the tradition are the rhododendron bushes and silver birches which cover the courses. It also has what many consider the most beautiful clubhouse in England. Previously the home of Countess Morella of Spain, it stands in regal surroundings. Behind the outward scene lies a hive of country club industry with a swimming pool, tennis courts and a ballroom. There is hardly a course in the world which is regarded with such affection that even the pros call it by a nickname. But this is the case at Wentworth, with the West Course dubbed the "Burma Road" because of its length and toughness. It is 6,997 yards and even the strongest pros find it a tussle. The shorter East Course, (both were designed by H. S. Colt) is as exacting but a little more relenting. Wentworth has been the venue for both Ryder Cup and World Cup matches on the West Course and regularly hosts the Picadilly World Match Play Championships. The first Curtis Cup match took place on the East Course.

All you have to do is step inside Sunningdale's clubhouse and the atmosphere of traditional British golf envelops you. It is the epitome of the true English golf club, where it's the golf which counts, where the men-only bar beside the locker room is full of deep leather arm chairs, where pints of beer are served in traditional tankards.

The Old Course was originally designed by Willie Park in 1900. However, it was later fleshed out and put in its present state by H. S. Colt, who also designed the New Course in 1922. The Old Course is a marvelous inland layout over the dunes, from which elements appear at Pine Valley, N.J. The New Course is more open and considered slightly tougher than the Old and utilizes higher ground by offering commanding vistas. Across the road from the clubhouse is the Ladies Course, 18 holes of the highest quality but run as an independent entity. All in all, Sunningdale is a golfer's paradise and well deserves the reputation it has built up through the years. Those who can say they have played Sunningdale should know what English golf is all about.

The Berkshire course, situated in the same pine and heather country as Sunningdale and Wentworth, gives off the same sort of atmosphere as the other two, but in a less sumptuous way. The Red Course is the higher and hillier but, although more than 100 yards the longer, not necessarily the more difficult of the two. The composition of the holes on the Red is uncommon in that there are six par-3 holes. It is difficult to imagine there being a better sextet of short holes on a golf course than the second, fifth, seventh, 10th, 16th and 18th.

Almost back-to-back and stretched along the Kent coastline in Southeast England are three courses steeped in history, always a treat to play and true tests of skill. Royal St. George's at Sandwich, established in 1887, has been the scene of countless golfing incidents. Before the 1950s, the course was on the roster for British Opens. One of Britain's best known professionals, Henry Cotton, recorded his first big-time victory in the 1934 Open with a 283 there and had a round of 65, one of the lowest scores ever in a British Open. So highly was it regarded at that time that a manufacturer named a golf ball after it. It is known as the Dunlop 65.

Although taken off the Open roster of courses, Royal St. George's continues to play host to some of the biggest events on the British pro circuit including the British Masters. Hero in the 1967 Masters was young Tony Jacklin who broke the course record with 64 on his way to the title.

In a golfing sense, when looking at Royal Cinque Ports at Deal you either love it or hate it. Defended from the encroaching sea by a shingle bank, it is one of England's toughest tests of golf. The most difficult part about it is that the fairways are made of endless bumps and hallows.

At least when you near the greens on this 6,384-yard course you will find them fairly large, generally flat and in superb condition. A surprising fact about the history of this old course, designed in 1892 and given the Royal Seal of Approval 16 years later, is that the record is held by an amateur. Nobody has been able to tame it better than five-time British Amateur winner Michael Bonallack who went a round in 65 strokes in 1964. Prior to 1920, Deal also hosted two British Open championships.

Prince's, which shares the same stretch of linksland as Royal St. George's, was founded in 1905, but the bomb work of German planes during World War II almost obliterated it. However, the original architects would have been pleased with the amazing reconstruction job done by designers Sir Guy Campbell and John Morrison who turned the club into 27 holes of testing and enjoyable golf.

The Deal area is just one of the many great coastal constellations in England, rivalled in many ways by the areas surrounding Royal Birkdale and Royal Lytham in the west. Other British courses are listed in the Places to Play section of this book.
—*Keith Mackie*

IRELAND

The Emerald Isle might have been created just for golf. Some 200 courses scattered over Ireland's green, lush terrain take particular advantage of a topography and climate that lend themselves beautifully to the game. Notable influences are the winds blowing in off the Atlantic or the Irish Sea and wild rough nurtured by the island's moist climate. While Irish weather may not be ideal for all pastimes, it is usually warm enough for a sweatered round of golf and in the pleasantly dry months of September and October, golfing is nearly perfect. Irish golf clubs generally welcome visitors and local professionals are always happy to help you get up a game. Low greens fees and caddie fees are an added plus.

Portmarnock, which some consider the best course in the British Isles, is laid out on a narrow peninsula jutting out into Dublin Bay, just north of the city. Founded in 1894, Portmarnock, at almost 7,000 yards, is one of the longest courses in the Isles. When the wind blows in from the bay, as it does with alarming frequency, even the best golfers find their scores soaring. Henry Cotton, who once scored a seven on Portmarnock's dogleg 14th while losing the Irish Open, called the hole the greatest in the world. The beauty of Portmarnock is that it's not a tricky course, but rather a great natural test. Not only the wind, but the course's design—with a subtle change of direction on every hole—makes every club you select and every shot you play a critical strategic decision. The greens are soft, holding and true, and the fairway turf fine. In all, a perfect test of golf.

Within the boundaries of the city of Dublin is Ireland's oldest club, the Royal Dublin Golf Club, founded in 1885 and in its present site since 1889. The course is located on a small island, joined to the mainland by a causeway, and subject to the same winds that bedevil Portmarnock. A hilly course, with plenty of bunkers, it too requires careful shotmaking and imposes heavy penalties for bad judgment. On the western coast of Ireland, in County Clare, is another of the world's great links, Lahinch Golf Club. Well run and maintained, the course has undergone substantial alterations since Old Tom Morris laid it out, but its character—with rough hills, sandhills and sand pits and some of Ireland's loveliest and most rugged scenery—remains unchanged.

If ever there were an Irish sounding name it is Ballybunion; and if ever there were a true Irish seaside links, it is assuredly Ballybunion. On the southwest coast of the Shannon estuary facing

The rowdy spirit and brooding adventure of the Irish are symbolized in the glorious Ballybunion course whose 17th hole, pictured overleaf, runs between the Irish Sea and heather coated dunes, all resplendently and definitively Irish.

One of the newest Irish courses is Waterville Lake, designed by Eddie Hackett to be as rugged as the surrounding countryside. A modern resort hotel adjoins.

the blustery Atlantic, far from Ireland's metropolitan centers, Ballybunion is an absolutely beautiful adventure to play. Sited on choppy terrain atop high bluffs that tower over the ocean, the course offers no letup. Heather covered sandhills march away from the shoreline and many of the holes wend their way between the forbidding escarpments. The view from most tees gives the golfer a deceptive sense of security, for it would seem that an off-line drive would bounce down into the fairway. Not true. A hook or slice may well result in a ball lost in the vegetation. Although not a long course at only 6,500 yards, Ballybunion is a world class test that quickly separates the men from the boys.

Royal Portrush, in the very north of Northern Ireland, was the first Irish course to host the British Open in 1951. The club has three courses, the Dunluce at 6,809 yards, the championship links. The narrow curving fairways and multi-leveled sandhills make this a fearsome test, especially the fourth, Calamity Corner, an incredibly tough par-5. Portrush's smooth greens can be deceptive, as they are steeply sloped and all but the most precise putts slide off line.

One of the most scenic sections of Ireland is Killarney, an area of almost breathtaking beauty in the southwestern part of the country. Its famous lakes dot the green landscape, scattered among the rolling hills and forests and old mist-covered Irish castles. Killarney Golf Club, provides magnificent vistas of lake and mountains and while the scenery is hard to ignore, the course is a beauty in its own right, undulating around a lake. More a holiday course than the tough layouts at Portmarnock, Portrush, Ballybunion or Lahinch, it is usually played from the 6,000-yard front tees. While some of the holes are tricky—the eighth green, for instance, has a concealed stream in the foreground—it is a splendid golfing treat.

Virtually all of Ireland's courses have very modest clubhouses, no showers or locker rooms of the sort with which Americans are familiar. An exception is the new (1973) Waterville Lake Hotel and Golf Course on Ireland's famed Ring of Kerry on the southwest coast. With probably the finest new course in all of Europe and possibly the longest (7,116 yards, par-73 from the back), with an elegantly luxurious hotel situated between the Atlantic coastline and a lake that's a trout fishing paradise, and with other resort facilities that include boating, horses and swimming, Waterville Lake becomes a destination itself in the tradition of world class resorts.

—Howard R. Gill

4. THE WORLD OF GOLF

australia

Golf was played in Australia in 1848 by a small group of enthusiasts presided over by Lt. Col. J. H. Ross. They practiced their skills on a plot of ground that was later to become part of the inner city of Melbourne. That was 40 years before the father of American golf, John Reid, made the first joyous swipes at Yonkers, N.Y., establishing the game in the United States.

By 1855 golf had also been established in Sydney, but it was not until 1882 that the first official golf club was formed there. This was the Australian Golf Club, now at Kensington near Sydney's International Airport. It is a course that today remains one of this nation's great tests. The Australian Golf Union which administers the nation's golf activities was instituted in 1898.

An estimated 750,00 Australian golfers enjoy the game on some 1,300 courses. Australians are noted for their love of sports, and the number who play golf reflects this general interest. Almost one out of every 10 Australians play the game. In the United States the ratio is about one to 20. Australian clubs stage competitions every weekend, and the courses are usually crowded from dawn to dusk.

An island continent dwarfed by the Pacific and Indian oceans, Australia encompasses three million square miles, almost the area of the continental United States. And although much of the land is uninhabited, the more populated areas boast a wide variety of golf courses, many of them of high caliber.

Australian golfers are enthusiastic and do not require sleek, manicured courses on which to play. They'll play anywhere. For instance, at the Bourke Golf Club, 500 miles northwest of Sydney in New South Wales, the tees are concrete blocks covered with corded rubber, the fairways are grassless baked ground and the greens are

The elegance of Royal Sydney, one of Australia's oldest clubs, is captured in morning sunlight in this view of the clubhouse from the first green. Narrow fairways and perilous rough add bite to this popular tournament course.

treated sand. The members, zealous golfers, enjoy a local rule which reads, "If any foliage other than a tree interferes with the stance or swing it may be removed without penalty."

Since Joe Kirkwood won the 1920 Australian Open and left for the United States to become golf's first well-known trick shot stylist, Australia has produced a series of world class golfers. The acerbic Peter Thomson has been the most successful. Twice the Australian Open winner, Thomson has won five British Opens. Only the legendary Harry Vardon has won more—six. Norman Von Nida, a three-time Australian Open winner, is one of the golf world's most sought-after teachers. Kel Nagle and Jim Ferrier achieved great success in the United States and throughout the world. Today Aussies Bruce Dev-

lin, Bruce Crampton and David Graham are often found among the U.S. Professional tour leaders. Both Devlin and Thomson have expanded their interests to golf course architecture.

The Australian summer is from November through April. Prominent American and world golfers are frequent competitors in the Australia Open, Dunlop International, Chrysler Classic and the Wills Masters, held late in the year, making for outstanding fields in these tournaments. South Africa's Gary Player and the United States' Jack Nicklaus and Arnold Palmer are examples of past Australian Open champions.

The process of selecting the 10 most challenging and interesting tests in Australia is strongly influenced by two factors. One is that Dr. Alister Mackenzie, the famed Scot golf course architect,

was consulted on many of the best Australian courses. His genius is reflected in five of the selections that follow. The other factor is the 25-square mile area south of Melbourne known as the Sand Belt which is a mother lode of excellent courses. This undulating golf countryside, covered with fine English grasses and native ti-tree pines and gums, contains 16 championship courses. One could be excused if all 10 of Australia's best were selected from this area. However, the other states boast their great courses and these should not be ignored.

1. ROYAL MELBOURNE GOLF CLUB

The most celebrated club in this illustrious group is Royal Melbourne Golf Club in Black Rock, Victoria, which has two courses. Dr. Mac-

Australian courses have a special charm, and here are two of the more elite clubs in the Melbourne area. At left, the seventh of the West Course at Royal Melbourne, located in the Sand Belt area. Above, typically treacherous but beautifully bunkered is the ninth at Commonwealth, another Sand Belt course. Despite the dry soil, the turf is lush and verdant and the foliage plentiful.

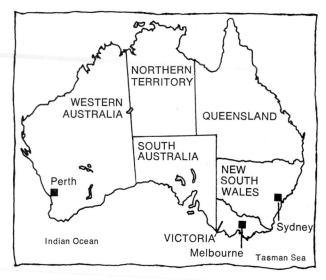

kenzie designed the West Course in 1929 with the able cooperation of Alex Russell who laid out the East Course in 1931. The two are similar and bear a striking resemblance in bunkering and greens contour to Augusta National. The tee-shot areas are tight and the large, sloping greens extremely fast. A composite of these two courses was used for the 1959 and 1972 Canada Cup (now World Cup) matches, and the 1968 World Amateur Team championship for the Eisenhower Trophy.

2. METROPOLITAN GOLF CLUB

The Metropolitan Golf Club, in South Oakleigh, Victoria, another in the Sand Belt area, exhibits a decided American architectural influence. The original part of the course features small, savagely trapped greens with fierce rough choked with ti-trees. In the 1960s the loss of part of the course necessitated alterations and Dick Wilson, the well-known American architect, was asked to undertake the task.

Wilson introduced the modern concept of strategic fairway bunkering and large, undulating greens. The blend of old and new holes has produced a finely balanced test that can be played at 7,000 yards with a par of 72. It was here in 1951 that Peter Thomson gave promise of his future greatness by winning the Australian Open.

3. KINGSTON HEATH GOLF CLUB

Aptly named, the 6,900-yard, par-72 Kingston Heath course in Cheltenham, Victoria, abounds in native heath and bush which tender stern hazards. The former Australian Open champion, Des Souter, built the original course and Alister Mackenzie laid his imprimatur on the fairways,

bunkering and greens. Also in the Sand Belt area, Kingston Heath has been a frequent Australian Open venue since its first in 1948. That Open marked the return to Australia of Jim Ferrier fresh from his 1947 PGA victory. Winning scores so often around the 280s attest to the course's demanding challenge.

4. COMMONWEALTH GOLF CLUB

In East Oakleigh, Victoria, Commonwealth is another of the famous Melbourne Sand Belt courses. A committee of four of its members, after traveling to many courses to inspect their designs and challenges, planned and built this fine test. Although only moderately long at 6,713 yards, Commonwealth's par-72 course has held even the best players at bay. The fairways are narrow and no less than six holes have the added danger of out-of-bounds. A lake that cuts across the northern section of the course makes the final holes difficult to negotiate. Sharp-faced bunkers guard the small, irregularly shaped and rolling greens which are glassy fast.

5. ROYAL SYDNEY GOLF CLUB

Situated on Sydney Harbor at Rose Bay, 15 minutes from downtown Sydney, the Royal Sydney Golf Club has been at its present location since 1894. There are 27 holes spread over 350 lush acres of elegant parkland, laid out by one of its original members, S. R. Dobbie. Through 1974 the Australian Open had been played here eight times, and the Australian Amateur 11 times. Clearly a favorite, the 6,688-yard, par-72 course used for tournament play is not long by modern standards, and despite its proximity to the harbor has no water hazards. Narrow fairways and tigerish rough, however, punish the loose shot and the small, fast greens require great attention. Gary Player scored 288 to win the last Australian Open there in 1969.

6. AUSTRALIAN GOLF CLUB

In Kensington, New South Wales, the Australian Club is the oldest and longest of Australia's top courses. It was formed in 1882 and its present course was originally designed by Dr. Alister Mackenzie in 1926. In 1967 the course was renovated under the direction of Sloan Marpeth, a fine amateur golfer, when a new freeway forced redirection and alterations. The course now measures 7,148 yards from the back tees, playing to a par of 72. Numerous water hazards and a number of raised greens, much like those at

A view from behind the green on the third hole at the Royal Adelaide in Australia. The hole measures only 301 yards, a short par-4 by any standards, but Norman Von Nida once took an 11 here.

215

The first tee at Lake Karrinyup which snakes its way though rugged, desert scrub near Perth in Western Australia, features surprisingly dense foliage and, in season, a gorgeous panorama of wild flowers. Jack Nicklaus won the Australian Open here in 1968.

Winged Foot, make it one of the toughest tests in the country. The Australian was the site of the first Aussie Open in 1904, won by Michael Scott, an imposing figure in early Australian professional golf. He returned home to Britain to become the oldest player to win the British Amateur Championship in 1933.

7. NEW SOUTH WALES GOLF CLUB

New South Wales Golf Club is another of Alister Mackenzie's architectural creations, a Scottish-type links on a headland in Matraville, overlooking Botany Bay near Sydney. A classic seaside links, it snakes through rolling sandhills which are covered with Australian scrub and "pigface" (called ice plant in America). An errant shot into this wild country is irretrievably lost, but it is the ever-present wind which finally is the most demanding hazard the golfer faces. It's so windy that it's been remarked that even the birds walk out there. The course has a permanent link with Australian history for in 1770 Captain Cook landed in Botany Bay laying claim to the land for the British Crown. He found water below what is now the 17th tee. The course's tournament yardage is 6,687 yards, with a par-72.

8. ROYAL ADELAIDE GOLF CLUB

Another Mackenzie course, Royal Adelaide in Seaton, South Australia, was opened for play in 1892 as the Adelaide Club. It is a searching test combining the best of classic architecture with modern demands for length and accuracy from the tees. The critical run home from the 220-yard, 12th hole, a par-3, is through typically narrow, sandy terrain bordered by pines and rough which resemble unkempt bunkers. The last Australian Open played there in 1962 was a triumph for tenacious Gary Player, whose 281 gave him the edge over Kel Nagle.

9. KOOYONGA GOLF CLUB

In 1923 a member of Adelaide Club, H. L. Rymill, formed a new club called Kooyonga in Lockleys, South Australia. Rymill was the club's architect and its first president and the course is acknowledged as probably the finest conditioned in Australia. Gary Player remarked after winning the 1965 Australian Open that the greens were the finest on which he had ever putted. That year he scored two incredible rounds of 62 in a 72-hole winning score of 264. This extraordinary total does not indicate the strength of the course which has hosted many other championships.

10. LAKE KARRINYUP GOLF CLUB

Encompassing a large lake that lends both beauty and hazardous conditions to the course, Lake Karrinyup in Perth was constructed by course architect Fred Summerhayes in 1926 on towering sand dunes covered with native trees and scrub. The Indian Ocean is not far away and wind is often a factor on this par-72 course where Jack Nicklaus won the 1968 Australian Open with a 270. Lake Karrinyup was also the site of the 1952 Australian Open, won by Norman Von Nida, and the 1960 Open, won by then-amateur Bruce Devlin.

OTHER OUTSTANDING AUSTRALIAN COURSES

Royal Queensland Golf Club. Renovated under the supervision of Alister Mackenzie in 1926-7, this 6,825-yard, par-72 course situated in Hamilton, Queensland, winds alongside the Brisbane River.

Victoria Golf Club. One of Melbourne's fine Sand Belt courses in Cheltenham, Victoria plays to 6,850 yards and par-72. Peter Thomson was influential in altering the original course. The club has a unique record: in 1954 both the British Open and the British Amateur were won by club members Peter Thomson and Douglas Bachli, respectively.

Huntingdale Golf Club. At over 7,000 yards, this par-73 course in South Oakleigh, Victoria, features large, rolling and lightning fast greens. It was designed with the assistance of Mr. Berriman who also helped in the construction of the Commonwealth course. —*Thomas L. Crow*

new zealand

Although boasting no courses of world championship stature, New Zealand is a pressureless paradise for a majority of golfers. There are almost 400 courses in a nation of less than 3,000,000 inhabitants. Greens fees average $1.50. "Ours is also a nation without pollution, unemployment or poverty," says New Zealander Bob Charles, a former British Open champion and the greatest left-handed golfer ever. "Our two islands have as much land area as England and only as many people as Philadelphia."

Most courses are relatively short with small greens. They would offer little challenge to a Jack Nicklaus, a Lee Trevino or even a Bob Charles. But the scenery is spectacular, the price is right and there is plenty of trouble for the amateur golfer.

Paraparaumu Beach Golf Club near Wellington is perhaps the finest golfing test in New Zealand. It is a seaside links, very British in layout and measures 6,500 yards from the longest tees. "The fifth hole, a 160-yard par-3, is equal to any short hole I've played in the world," says Charles. "The superb bunkering and terrain make it impossible to get close to the hole if you don't reach the green with your tee shot." Paraparaumu, playing to par 71, has been a popular site for the New Zealand Open in recent years.

Wairakei International Golf Course is a newer, more Americanized course although designed by British architect Frank Harris. It is a fine test of golf and, by New Zealand standards, extremely long at 6,903 yards. The par-71 layout sits at the foot of a mountain range and near Lake Taupo, one of the finest fishing spots in the south Pacific.

Rotorua's Arikikapakapa course offers some unusual challenges even though its length is only 6,000 yards at par-70. There are geysers spitting spirits from below at several points on the course and it can be an intriguing shot if you slash your ball into a hazard that is actually a boiling mudpool. "There's only one way to play those hazards," says Charles. "You mark another stroke on your card and drop a new ball." What this ancient course lacks in length is made up for by the magnificent scenery.

Although courses on the North Island dominate the offerings of New Zealand, there is class on the South Island with the Christchurch and Otago golf clubs.

Christchurch Golf Club is the longest course in the country at a maximum of 7,000 yards. It is a links course mixed with parkland and has also been the scene of several New Zealand Opens.

Otago in Dunedin is extremely hilly and features one of the most challenging holes anywhere. The 350-yard 11th, a par-4, has a steep grade on the right side plus out-of-bounds and a creek to the left. "Although it has been the downfall of many fine players, Arnold Palmer and I played an exhibition here once," recalls Charles, "and Arnold drove the green on the hole."

If you plan to golf in New Zealand, you had best get your legs into condition. There are no power cars and no caddies. You either carry your bag or pull a cart on the predominantly rolling courses. "The worst feature of golf in the United States," Charles says, "are the golf cars that allow you to play 18 holes without spending any energy. In New Zealand, golf is good exercise. You don't see many overweight golfers."

—Hubert Mizell

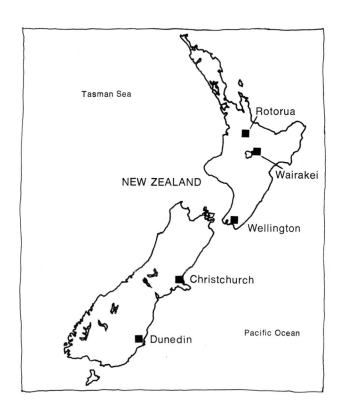

This is New Zealand golfing scenery at its best. Above is the 14th hole at Wairakei International, a public course near the resorts of Lake Taupo. Below, golfers head for home and the clubhouse at the Paraparaumu course.

japan

Imagine a golf resort charging greens fees of $23 on weekdays, $40 on weekends and requiring reservations for starting times as much as six months in advance.

So it is at Karuizawa 72, a complex of four 18-hole courses, as its name implies, located 125 miles north of Tokyo. It was developed by the same visionary Japanese businessman who created the first three-tiered driving range in Tokyo 15 years ago. Karuizawa 72 is an attractively modern development, with 36 holes designed by Robert Trent Jones and the other 36 by his son, Bob Jr. The extravagance and popularity of its facilities somewhat characterize modern golf in Japan. Demand for golf so outstrips supply that remarkable things have resulted.

"Gorufu," which is the colloquial Japanese name for golf, was first played nearly 75 years ago in Japan. However, "gorufu fever" did not begin rising until the 1950s, as it did in America about the time Arnold Palmer began captivating audiences. In 1957 the World Cup matches (then known as the Canada Cup) came to Kasumigaseki Golf Club. Japan won the event, a complete surprise to everyone, and a year later sent a team to the World Amateur playoffs at St. Andrews, Scotland. By then, millions of Japanese had begun to patronize the two- and three-tiered driving ranges that sprang up in metropolitan areas. "Gorufu fever" had reached epidemic proportions.

It is not known how many Japanese golfers never get closer to playing the game than hitting balls at a practice range; those who promote the game estimate as many as 10,000,000 "golfers." The Japan Golf Ass'n reports that there are 1,100,000 established Japanese players. It is a known fact that there are under 800 golf courses to play on. By comparison, this means that Japan has as many as seven times the number of golfers per course as the United States, with its 12,000 courses for 13,000,000 golfers.

A cherry tree, symbol of the scenic elegance found on so many golf courses in Japan, drapes gently over a fairway at the Abiko Golf Club near Tokyo, one of the most prestigious courses in Japan.

Only the well-to-do can afford to play. Club memberships average between $2,500 and $25,000, and there are very few public courses. Weekday greens fees are seldom less than $17, and a weekend tee-off time costs at least $25—if you can get one. One of the few inexpensive aspects of golf in Japan is caddies, who are predominantly women averaging $3 a bag, plus a dollar if it rains. To accommodate the heavy play, most of the courses feature double greens, one of korai grass, similar to bermuda, for summer, and another of bentgrass for winter.

Probably the most prestigious of clubs in Japan is the Koganei Country Club, located 10 miles from Tokyo, the closest course to the center of the city. It was completed in 1937 and based on a design rendered by American golfing great Walter Hagen. From the Japanese-style clubhouse, you look out onto fairways curtained on both sides with forest called "musashino." The 6,755-yard layout looks deceptively easy, but golfers find it difficult to shoot good scores. Membership to the Koganei Country Club, limited to important individuals, now costs about $115,000, the most expensive in Japan.

The Tokyo area probably contains the top five clubs in Japan, if not in championship quality, certainly in prestige. In addition to Koganei, they include Kasumigaseki, designed by amateur golfer and businessman Kinya Fujita in the late 1920s. Its superb East Course at just under 7,000 yards is the nation's most famous championship site and the West Course is shorter but more interesting. Others include the old line Tokyo Country Club started in 1913; the Sagami Country Club, whose membership includes leading bankers, actors and actresses; and the Abiko Golf Club, a masterful design of 1930 vintage by R. Akaboshi, who honed his techniques in the United States, ranging from 6,175 to 6,700 yards in length.

The consensus is that the best test of golf in the nation is Hirono, near Kobe in western Japan. The course was designed by the English architect C. H. Allison. Unimpeded by the sloping land, he patterned each of the holes after another of international repute. A believer in penal architecture, he created some treacherous bunkers and utilized deep, wild rough to punish errant tee shots. Most Japanese golfers dream of a chance to tackle this 6,950-yard test at least once.

All sides of Mt. Fuji, 75-100 miles south of Tokyo, abound in golf courses. The most famous are the two at the Kawana Golf Club, a resort overlooking the Pacific Ocean.

In the last 15 years, golf courses have been going in around the base of Mt. Fuji at the rate of one a year, most of them expensive membership clubs. This proliferation of golf course developments has created a backlash by local governments — prefectures — designed to protect agricultural land and potential housing sites from "gorufu kogai" — golf pollution. Together with the scarcity of available property, it has driven the Japanese to invest heavily in golf course resorts and properties abroad — particularly in Hawaii and California. For example, the conglomerate which sponsors the $300,000 Japanese Masters, held annually at its own course, the Sohbu Club, in Tokyo, now owns the Peacock Gap Golf Club, in Marin County, north of San Francisco, and plans three more courses in the bay area.

Such forays into foreign countries are simply an extension of the Japanese addiction to the game. Golf course development within Japan continues unabated into mountainous areas once regarded as too remote to attract anyone. For example, some 2½ hours from Tokyo in the Tochigi prefecture, both Arnold Palmer and Jack Nicklaus have been engaged by different promoters to design and put in golf courses. One of those courses assigned to the Jack Nicklaus organization in conjunction with golf architect Desmond Muirhead is the new St. Andrews, a modified replica of the Old Course in Scotland. The large double greens, nothing new to the Japanese, will be used on the same 14 holes where they became famous, but the fairways will slope and the flowers and trees which line them will be meticulously maintained.

After all, what would a Japanese golf course be like without horticultural beauty?

—*William H. Davis*

The Fuji course at the 36-hole Kawana resort under the shadow of the famous volcano is one of the most majestic and difficult in Japan. Nearly every hole features rolling terrain, easily discernible here. On the next page, the top photo shows the Kasumigaseki Country Club with one of its many water hazards. The bottom photo is an aerial view of the four 18-hole courses of the "Karuizawa 72" golf complex in northern Japan.

south africa

There's more to South African golf than Gary Player.

"As much as I enjoy the great courses of America, Great Britain, Japan, Australia and the rest of the golfing world," says Player, "I'm always proud to show what we have back home. There is great challenge, balance, beauty and design at most of our courses. Most of the courses are extremely long, but that isn't important since the altitude causes shots to carry so far. It is not uncommon to drive a ball 350 yards and hit a 9-iron 175."

Player, along with most South African golf experts, rates the Durban Country Club as the showplace of that country's golf world. "There are bush roughs and small greens to make it interesting," he says. "Durban is our seacoast resort and compares to Florida in terrain. Durban Country Club is a gorgeous, tropical layout that even has monkeys running wild on the course. It is not uncommon to hit your drive and then find a monkey has grabbed your golf ball and wants to play games." Another feature of the Durban club is some of the finest food south of Paris.

Johannesburg, Player's hometown, has over 80 golf courses within a 60-mile area. Royal Johannesburg Golf Club is one of the finest, but unlike most South African courses it is private and not as available for play by visitors. Most courses welcome tourists. Royal Jo-Burg, as the natives call it, has two outstanding courses including a 7,283-yard test that may be the toughest in the country. Although Royal Jo-burg has hosted the South African Open, it generally prefers not to associate with professional events.

Houghton Golf Club, also in Johannesburg, is filled with stately trees and measures a healthy 7,115 yards. "That's about like 6,500 yards in the States," says Player. "The distances are very misleading. You can ask Jack Nicklaus, who could hardly find a club to hit from 100 yards. Everything he took out of the bag hit the ball too far. Maybe he should putt from that distance in South Africa."

Perhaps the most unusual course design is at Royal Durban. This relatively short 6,538-yard course is located in the infield of a race track. Since trees and other large hazards might either ruin the looks of the Turf Club or block the view of races, the rough is almost nonexistent. But, it is still a sufficient golfing challenge and par is 74.

East London Golf Club is located in another coastal resort area some 400 miles around the bend from Durban. The Indian Ocean is visible, but doesn't come into play. Nine holes are links style and the other side is flatter with troublesome sandhills and willow scrub.

There are more than 300 courses in South Africa. They are especially plentiful along the coast. Almost every hotel has a course of some kind. There are no powered golf cars, however, so the exercise value is high. Caddies are numerous and among the most helpful you will find in the world, especially when figuring distance on the long courses.

South Africa is moving to the metric system and scorecards at some clubs carry hole distances in both yards and meters. However, if a Westerner plays at one that is meters-only, a caddie will be a must for figuring club selection.
—*Hubert Mizell*

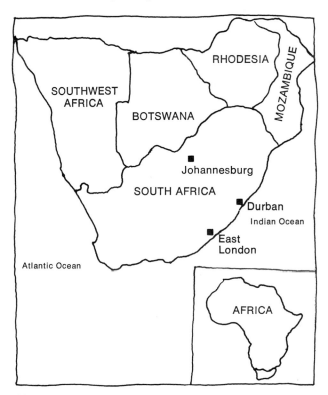

Against the background of luxury resorts lining the beach of the Indian Ocean, a foursome plays out the 13th hole at East London Golf Club in South Africa, which offers scenic views of the coast on several holes.

europe

Golf on the continent of Europe is in many ways quite different from the game in the rest of the western world. Except in the resort areas, it is still largely a game for the very wealthy, the very social, or the very adventuresome. Until the late 1960s, little emphasis was placed upon building golf courses of what would be regarded as championship caliber by international standards.

Unlike the large golfing nations (United States, Great Britain, Australia and South Africa), the countries of Europe boast relatively little golf near their great capital cities. The area around Paris is the exception with 20 courses, yet Hamburg has only six, Madrid five, Brussels three and Rome two. Rather, the courses and clubs are widely spread across each nation. In most of Europe, golf is a game of narrow fairways and troublesome rough and woods. It is a game of accuracy, not power. Many of the better-known European courses are situated in or near the ski towns of Austria's Tyrol and the Swiss and French Alps; in towns like Kitzbuehl, Badgastein and Innsbruck in Austria; Crans, Davos and St. Moritz in Switzerland; and Megève in France.

With the growth of international competition and travel, some very high caliber courses are being built. An important stimulus to golf on the Continent has been the growth of the European golf tour, an adjunct to the British PGA schedule of events. In 1974, nine tournaments with a total purse of over $250,000 were scheduled.

The greatest growth in European golf facilities is taking place in the resort areas, particularly along the Mediterranean. Virtually all of these new facilities are being built by professional architects such as Robert Trent Jones whose organization has a full-time office in Marbella, Spain. Robert Dean Putnam, George Fazio, Desmond Muirhead and Ron Kirby, an American for-

It's easy to see why the Crans Golf Club, Crans-sur-Sierre in the Swiss Alps, has played host to so many major European golf events. Not only is it a beautiful course, but it is also a measure of skillful shot-making.

EUROPE'S TOP 40 COURSES

COURSE	LOCATION*	PAR/YARDAGE
AUSTRIA		
Golf Club Seefeld-Wildmoos	Innsbruck	72/6,965
BELGIUM		
Royal Antwerp G.C.	Antwerp	73/6,660
Royal Golf Club de Belgique	Brussels	73/6,700
Royal Waterloo G.C.	Brussels	74/6,789
Royal Zoute G.C.	Knokke-Le Zoute	72/6,681
DENMARK		
Rungsted Golf Klub	Rungsted Coast	72/6,425
Silkeborg Bryghus Golf Klub	Silkeborg (Jutland)	74/7,025
FRANCE		
Golf Club du Touquet (New)	Le Touquet (Dieppe)	74/6,500
Golf de Chantilly	Chantilly (Paris)	71/6,750
Golf de Saint-Cloud	Saint-Cloud (Paris)	72/6,592
Golf de Saint-Nom-la Bretèche (Red)	Versailles	72/6,713
GERMANY		
Club zur Vahr	Bremen	74/6,980
Frankfurther G.C.	Frankfurt-am-Main	72/6,400
Refrath	Cologne	72/6,650
GREECE		
Glyfada G.C.	Athens	72/6,715
ITALY		
Circolo Golf Olgiata	Rome	72/6,879
Golf Club Biella	Magnano (Torino)	72/6,804
Golf Club Milano	Milan	72/6,900
Golf Club Torino	Torino	72/6,804
Pevero G.C.	Costa Smeralda (Sardinia)	72/6,643

COURSE	LOCATION*	PAR/YARDAGE
NETHERLANDS		
Eindhovensche G.C.	Valkenswaard	70/6,322
Haagsche Golf en C.C.	Wassenaar (Hague)	72/6,077
Hilversumsche G.C.	Amsterdam	73/6,805
NORWAY		
Oslo G.C.	Oslo	71/6,580
PORTUGAL		
Club de Golf Vale do Lobo	Albufeira (Algarve)	73/6,910
Club de Golf Vilamoura	Almansil (Algarve)	72/7,030
Penina G.C.	Portimao (Algarve)	73/7,480
SPAIN		
Club de Golf Sotogrande (Old)	Cadiz	72/6,887
La Manga Campo de Golf (South)	Murcia	72/6,855
Nueva Andalucia G.C. (Old)	Marbella	72/6,736
Real Automovil Club de España	Madrid	72/6,550
Real Club de Campo	Madrid	72/7,150
Real Club de Golf El Prat	Barcelona	72/6,517
Real Club Puerto de Hierro	Madrid	72/6,860
SWEDEN		
Falsterbo Golfklubb	Falsterbo (Malmo)	71/6,627
Halmstad Golfklubb	Tylosand	73/6,600
SWITZERLAND		
Crans G.C.	Crans-sur-Sierre	74/6,932
Golf Club de Genève	Geneva	72/6,875
Golf Club Lausanne	Lausanne	72/6,760
Golf & C.C. Hittnau-Zurich	Zurich	72/6,518

* To help locate courses, nearest large city or region is indicated in parentheses.

merly with Trent Jones who is in partnership with Gary Player, are among the other American architects who are undertaking courses on the continent, formerly the bastion of such British designers as Commander John Harris and former British Open champion Henry Cotton. The quality of their efforts is often in direct proportion to the funds they are given to work with. One of the finest new courses in the works may turn out to be the Pebble Beach of the Continent if Trent Jones has his way. It is the Troia Golf Club at Setubal, near Lisbon, Portugal, and it is situated on the ocean where wild brush, sandy loam and rocky precipices form a magnificent golfing landscape.

Europe has many absolutely beautiful looking golf courses that do not measure up as great tournament courses under strong competition. Typical would be Biella in northern Italy, not far from Lake Como. Golf at Biella is a marvelous adventure in maneuvering a golf ball through beautiful, winding terrain. Its 7,100 yards were well thought out some 17 years ago by British golf architect John Morrison. This superb parkland course offers many doglegs and the four par-5s are as good as you will find anywhere.

With so many charming courses, yet so few which severely challenge the abilities of today's top players, selecting the great European tests for this volume became a particularly difficult task. We originally set out to establish the 25 "best" with the help of colleagues abroad in the golfing profession and the well-traveled editors of the golfing publications of Europe. Unfortunately, it was impossible to find 25 courses that met American and British standards as great tests of golf; and by easing the criteria it was impossible to confine the selection to 25. The list we ended up with consists of the 40 courses nominated by more than one of the following European golf magazine editors as "the top in Europe."

Horst T. Ostermann, *Golf*, Germany
Gaetan Mourgue d'Algue, *Golf Européen*, France
Piero Mancinelli, *Golf Selezione*, Italy
Anders P. Janson, *Svensk Golf*, Sweden
—*William H. Davis*

A links-type course on the North Sea, the Royal Zoute Golf Club (above) at Knokke-Le Zoute in Belgium offers 6,700 yards of trouble. Located in a resort area just an hour from Brussels, the Royal Zoute once served as the site of a tournament held exclusively for owners of Mercedes cars. At left, the Glyfada Golf Club near Athens, on the magnificent Aegean Sea coastline.

Evergreen trees frame the green on this par-3 hole at the Frankfurter Golf Club at Frankfurt-am-Main in Germany. At right, a panoramic scene of the Pevero Golf Club on the island of Sardinia. Pevero, blessed by natural hazards such as ravines and streams, was designed by Robert Trent Jones.

mediterranean gateway

The fastest growing area in the game of golf outside the United States is along the coasts of Portugal, Spain and Morocco. You never know quite what you'll uncover when you hit a golf shot fat along the southern coast of Europe. Just off the course at Vilamoura on the Algarve in Portugal, the ruins of a Roman fishing village recently were discovered only divot-deep. They date back to the time of Christ, when the Romans ruled much of the western world.

Golf in any foreign land has special romantic qualities for most Americans. Playing for the first time at St. Andrews, Scotland, is a baptismal experience—something you have heard about since you first took up the game—but you know what to expect, and the whole scene seems as natural as southern accents in Georgia. By contrast, golf along the Mediterranean Gateway is a fascinating incongruity. Here you are swinging away at a golf ball in a setting where the vestiges of one civilization defending itself against another are still widely visible. A thousand years ago, the lands along the Mediterranean and Atlantic coast east and west to Gibraltar as far as soldiers could march were occupied by the Moors. Ruined watchtowers and stone embattlements still jut from the horizon.

Although Spain and Portugal are today proudly distinctive nations and Morocco is as different from either as Christianity is from Islam, all three show interesting similarities from a golfing viewpoint. The most compelling of these is the marvelous climate along the coastal areas near Gibraltar . . . not too hot in the summer nor too cold in the winter. It is weather for olives and almonds, and symmetrical rows of olive trees sometimes stitch the landscape as far as you can see. The almond trees in bloom provide an accent on beauty and color similar to the dogwood of America, but they are more widely grown. And then there are the mountains which sweep down to the sea, spectacularly along most of the southern coast of Spain, gently at the Algarve in Portugal, abruptly in parts of Morocco.

Golfing tourists are certain to find another amusing, if somewhat frustrating, similarity—the caddies. They cost from a norm of $2.00 to no higher than $3.50 a round. You get what you pay for. There are no Scottish Tip Andersons among them. They are uniformly inept, mainly because they have picked up all the wrong information on the game very quickly. "Aqui, aqui (here, here)!" they will yell excitedly in Spain as they point out your line of putt, illegally tamping the green with a club. And you're apt to get a 7-iron with which to hit a 4-iron shot.

From a practical point of view, many American tourists who travel to that area visit both Spain and Portugal. With increasing frequency, they are taking side trips to Morocco. The coastlines to the east and west of Gibraltar abound with unusual holiday golf at remarkably low prices, particularly if you know when and how to travel. In addition to Malaga, there are major airports at Alicante and Murcia on the Costa Blanca of Spain and at Faro on the Algarve of Portugal. Whatever you do, rent a car. It is inexpensive and gives you freedom to explore. From Malaga, you can drive to most of the courses on the Costa del Sol in less than an hour; to Lagos, the farthest golfing point on the southern coast of Portugal, in six hours. (See map, p. 262).

A hydrofoil boat from the Costa del Sol to Tangier in Morocco takes an hour and a half, a ferryboat ride that accommodates your car takes only a couple of hours and costs under $5.

SPAIN

The golf explosion along the Costa del Sol truly began after 1965 when Joseph McMicking, a Philippine-born World War II U.S. Air Corps officer, opened Sotogrande, a magnificent development in the shadow of Gibraltar. The success of Sotogrande, which recently added its second Robert Trent Jones course, has helped to inspire a half dozen outstanding new golf resorts and real estate developments along the Mediterranean coast of Spain between Gibraltar and Malaga 90 miles to the east. American enterprise and tourism have contributed greatly to the boom.

Most of the major golf resorts and developments are in the area of Marbella, the attractive

Long carries over water to large, rolling greens are common at the tough Nueva Andalucìa Golf Club at Marbella on Spain's Costa del Sol. The Sierra Blanca mountains backdrop this view of the green at the 385-yard eighth.

and swinging social center of the Costa del Sol. Each of the courses has been built by a different architect and possesses a unique personality. The oldest, Guadalmina (1959), winds like a snake over miles of gentle land near the sea, but most of the newer courses have been built over rugged terrain. The Rio Real course in Marbella, laid out in an old river gulch, reportedly cost over $4 million to build in 1965. The two courses at Nueva Andalucia, designed by Robert Trent Jones, also traverse rugged land along the foothills of the mountains. The first of them, a modern monster with vast sloping greens and sinister water hazards, was the site of the 1973 World Cup matches.

An interesting new development is La Manga Campo de Golf, about 200 miles east of Malaga on that part of the Spanish coastline called the Costa Blanca. This 1,100-acre property, owned by an enterprising American named Greg Peters, opened in October, 1972, and gained the distinction of being the first golf club in Europe to start play with 36 holes. The North Course was the site of the 1973 Spanish Open and is considered by many a peer of the best courses on the continent. It was designed by Californian Robert Dean Putnam.

PORTUGAL

If Robert Trent Jones has left his mark on the Costa del Sol, the Algarve of Portugal is the land of "Cotton." Until 10 years ago, the Algarve which stretches for 100 miles along the Atlantic coastline, belonged strictly to history, fishermen and farmers. Then Sir Thomas Cootain, a wealthy British builder, virtually discovered it, purchasing several thousand acres near Faro. He subsequently hired his favorite golf professional, Henry Cotton, to design a golf course. It is called Vale do Lobo, one of the truly spectacular courses of the world. The front nine of Vale do Lobo traverses undulating wooded land down to the cliffs of the sea. Here Cotton created one of the most photographed holes in the world, the 180-yard, par-3 seventh, on which the tee shot must fly over two yawning chasms and a cliff.

However, it is the original 18-hole course at nearby Penina which Henry Cotton considers his finest accomplishment. When he was hired he phoned his wife and said, "I have been contacted to build a golf course on water." Over what was low swampland, inland a few miles from the sea, Cotton plowed and filled furrows, planted 365,000 trees over 340 acres and built a golf course which stretches for 7,480 yards. It is the scene of many major European championships. An additional 18 holes was completed in 1974 at the Penina.

Portuguese enterpreneurs soon decided to get into the act and created Vilamoura, a beautiful 4,000-acre resort between Vale do Lobo and Penina. And recently a group launched Palmares, designed by Frank Pennink, just east of Penina along the ocean near Lagos.

MOROCCO

While American military personnel stimulated the growth of golf in Morocco after World War II, the game took a big leap forward when King Hassan II ascended to the throne in 1961. He plays nearly every day on one or another of four courses within palace walls at Rabat, Skhirat, Fez and Meknes. In recent years he has fathered and financed the development of some first class golf facilities for tourists.

One is the seaside links course of the Royal Mohammedia Golf Club on the Atlantic, the scene of one of the matches in Shell's old television series, "Wonderful World of Golf." Another is just outside the colorful city of Marrakech, 1,300 feet high, where the snow-capped Atlas Mountains overlook the city. But the most spectacular of all is the King's new golf course in Rabat, called the Royal Golf Rabat, Dar-Es-Salam.

The annual Morocco International Grand Prix Tournament, begun in 1971 and held at Rabat, invites professionals from all over the world. The best four-round score posted over the 7,500-yard layout was by Billy Casper in 1973 with 71-70-71-76—288. You can guess who designed it—Robert Trent Jones, whose reputation for building tough golf courses is now rooted on both sides of the remarkable gateway to the Mediterranean.

—*William H. Davis*

The Penina Golf Club (above) at Algarve, Portugal, is long and flat, but adventure is built into the course with clever use of water hazards and dog-legged fairways. The straight-away 18th hole which heads toward the hotel on the left is a classic at 482 yards. Also on the Algarve is the Vale do Lobo Golf Club whose 200-yard seventh hole (left) is among the most spectacular in the world, requiring a shot over a crevasse along the Atlantic Ocean. Former British Open champion Henry Cotton designed both courses.

237

great golf is everywhere

The urge to play anywhere and everywhere is often as inexplicable as it is irresistable, exemplified by this intrepid pair, goggled and dwarfed by the mountainous dunes somewhere in the Namib Desert of South Africa.

238

There once were those who believed that only mad dogs and Englishmen would go out in the noontime heat of the tropics or the midnight cold of the Arctic to beat away at a golf ball. This belief was inspired largely by British colonists who would play golf wherever they could dig a hole in the ground.

Henry Longhurst, the British golf writer and commentator, writes with nostalgia about man's primitive fascination with golf, which he describes as "the pleasure to be derived from starting at A and holing out at B, overcoming as best you can the hazards encountered on the way." It was with this simple objective in mind that most of the early courses of the Mid-East and Africa were built, often with asphalt "greens" covered with sand or sand greens covered with oil. It was often said in Persia (now Iran) that men who went into the wilderness in search of oil, many of them Scots, would build themselves a hut, erect their drilling gear and lay out nine holes, in that order.

Longhurst tells of a course at El Fasher, capital of the Province of Darfur, in the heart of darkest Africa, "An unlikely spot, perhaps, in which to play golf but those who did were all the keener for that. They had nine flattened-out patches of sand for greens, but no clubhouse and no tees. Like the earliest golfers, when you finished one hole you simply teed up nearby and started the next. They had one red flag which was brought out by a small boy when anyone wanted to play. It was no good having regular flagsticks since, if they were made of wood, the ants would eat them and, if of metal, the locals would instantly melt them down for spears. The boy would hold the flag in the first hole till one was near enough for an enormous, very black Sudanese caddie to angle his feet behind the hole, at which point the boy would rush off with the flag and hold it on the second green."

India claims the oldest golf course in the world outside the United Kingdom, the Royal Calcutta Golf Club, built in 1829 by Scottish troops. Nearly 150 years later, the 1974 Indian Open, a stop on the Asian professional tour, was held there, following the lengthening of the course to 7,053 yards. The winning score of 287 attests to the current difficulty of Royal Calcutta.

While golf courses have existed in many parts

The Andes provide a rugged mountain background for the Country Club of Bogota in Colombia, above. The course, flanked by rugged cliffs, is built on a flat shelf of land 8,500 feet above sea level. Below, the 12th green at Los Leones in Chile, fronted by a lovely little canal.

Flanked by a double hazard, the unusual Royal Bangkok Sports Club's golf course nestles inside a race track and a canal. The par-66 course also runs alongside cricket and hockey fields.

The Delhi Golf Club of India (above)
claims to be the oldest course in the
world outside Scotland. It was built
by Scottish troops garrisoned at Calcutta in the 1830s. Below, a scenic
view of the Valley Golf Club in the
Philippines, built in 1964. Special
grass from Champions Club in Houston was imported for the greens.

of the world for 50 to 75 years, after World War II international golf competition between nations on both amateur and professional levels has significantly widened and intensified interest in the game. The 92-part television series, "Wonderful World of Golf," sponsored by the Shell Oil Company from 1962 to 1970, drew wide attention to the beauty of golf courses in 46 different countries.

The World Team Amateur matches, in which four-man teams compete against one another, were inaugurated in 1958, under the guidance of Joe Dey, former executive secretary of the United States Golf Ass'n. Twenty-nine teams played the first year in Scotland. The most recent matches in 1972 drew representation from 32 nations.

The World Cup competition (formerly called the Canada Cup) of the International Golf Ass'n, originated in 1953 by Canadian industrialist John Jay Hopkins, is contested annually by two-man teams of professionals from different countries. The number of nations competing has grown from eight the first year to 47 in 1973, and the list now includes a team from the "iron-curtain" country of Rumania. While the victory by the Japanese team playing in its own country in 1957 triggered an unprecedented golf boom in Japan, the 1972 victory by a team from Taiwan competing in Melbourne strongly reminded the world that golf in Asia had come of age.

Today, the game of golf throughout the Orient has become a strong symbol of sophistication if not a cult among Oriental royalty, politicians and ranking businessmen. As a result, in the last 20 years many new courses of excellent caliber by international standards have been built.

Perhaps the most interesting courses in Asia are in Singapore, Thailand and the Philippines. Singapore is an island where modern office buildings merge with ageless sampans in the crowded harbor, and the smells of Madras curries and frangipani blossoms fill the air. The Singapore Golf Club came into existence in 1891, when Scottish jute traders were spreading their national game and their trade throughout the Far East. In 1924, it was moved from its original site to a new location it now occupies, seven miles from the center of Singapore. The "new" course was laid out by James Braid through nearly 300 acres of almost impenetrable jungle. Another 18 holes were added six years later. The Old Course now offers visitors a taste of typically British golf in the midst of Asian jungle, for when Braid had the land cleared he imported a wide variety of trees from Britain to give the course a truly English flavor.

Singapore Island Club is a tough par-72 layout of 6,470 yards with rolling terrain and sloping fairways lined with trees. When the wind comes whipping in off the South China Sea, the back nine is as tough as any in the Far East.

Bangkok, capital of the Kingdom of Thailand, is like Venice, intertwined with drainage ditches. On its lowlands are two of the most unusual golf courses anywhere. The most famous is the Royal Bangkok Sports Club, whose golf course is alongside a racetrack, which it occasionally crosses. The newest, called Navatanee, is a country club community developed by Sukum Navapan, president of the Thai Military Bank, and named jointly after his wife Tanee and himself. It was designed by Robert Trent Jones Jr. on land, all 6,500 yards of it, below water level. Both the clubhouse area and the home of Navapan look like modern castles virtually surrounded by moats. Navatanee is an engineering miracle in converting mush to lush.

The Wack-Wack Golf Club in the Philippines, frequently the site of international matches, is a fine golf course, beautifully landscaped and maintained, but not so exciting as Luisita in the high country or the Valley Club, a rolling, modern course designed by Japanese Seichi Inoye, about an hour drive from Manila.

The British also brought the game to much of South America, where today you can find some of the world's most beautiful courses. Among them are Los Leones in the Chilean Andes, where 6,700 yards of fairway snake through a forest of trees so thick that the only light seems to come from overhead, and Gavea, outside Rio de Janeiro, Brazil, where the mountain foothills meet the Atlantic Ocean and wild orchids grow in the rough. The 6,914-yard Country Club of Bogota in Colombia, and the two 18-hole courses at the Jockey Club in Buenos Aires, Argentina, are among the best tests of golf on that continent. The Red Course at the Jockey Club was designed by the gifted and peripatetic Alister Mackenzie.

Today, mad dogs and Englishmen are not alone in chasing after golf balls in far away places. They are in the company of millions of golfing enthusiasts from nearly every foreign country in the world, all sharing a common insanity.
—*William H. Davis*

5.
COURSE
DIRECTORY
AND
CHARTS

a directory of over 900 courses you can play

This directory of more than 900 places you can play around the world is based on an annual feature that appears in *Golf Digest* magazine. These listings are designed to assist the traveling golfer with valuable introductory information about enjoyable places to play and stay. The courses included in this list usually offer accessible accommodations nearby and are for the most part open to the visiting golfer, as qualified in the comments and legend symbols. The information can be subject to change. Locator maps have been provided with flag numbers corresponding to the numbers in front of each course listed to help you locate each course geographically.

LEGEND: Each course in this directory is described by one of the following symbols: R—resort course; SP—semi-private; MU—municipal; PU—public; Mil—Military; PR—private (most of the private courses listed extend playing privileges to guests of hotels or motels or to potential buyers of adjacent properties).

COURSE LOCATION, TYPE	HOLES/PAR LENGTH

Hawaii

Oahu

1 Makaha Inn — West: 18/72 / 6,427
Makaha—R
Older of 2 Bill Bell courses. Fine greens. Bent. Really tough at 7,252 from back.
East: 18/71 / 6,092
Tight hillside course on lower slopes of Waianae mountains. Bermuda greens.

1 Pearl C.C. of Hawaii — 18/72 / 6,481
Aiea—SP
Hilly course with spectacular views. Formerly called the Francis H. I. Brown course.

2 Ted Makalena G.C. — 18/71 / 6,296
Waipahu—MU
Flat but tricky Bob Baldock course. 7 water holes; 9 O.B.

3 Mililani G.C. — 18/72 / 6,369
Waipio—PR
Bob Baldock course 19 miles from Waikiki in residential community. Open to the public.

3 Hawaii Country Club — 18/71 / 6,000
Kunia—SP
Sporty with rolling terrain, trees. Special golf packages.

4 Barber's Point G.C. — 18/71 / 6,455
Barber's Point—Mil
Developing course recently expanded to 18. Good greens, few traps.

5 Oahu C.C. — 18/71 / 5,955
Honolulu—PR
Lush, exquisitely manicured private course on slopes of valley.

5 Ala Wai G.C. — 18/71 / 6,392
Waikiki—MU
Flat, poorly conditioned course with heaviest play in the islands.

5 Waialae C.C. — 18/72 / 6,608
East of Diamond Head—PR
Flat oceanside course apt to be windy with dry fairways in summer.

6 Hawaii-Kai G.C. — 18/72 / 6,562
Kalama Valley—PU
Meanders across gently sloping terrain and offers mountain and ocean views.

6 Olomana Golf Links — 18/71 / 6,321
North of Waimanalo—SP
Scenic Bob Baldock course 18 miles from Diamond Head.

7 Mid-Pacific C.C. — 18/72 / 6,576
Lanikai—PR
Course in top condition. Trees, water hazards, rolling terrain. Limited visitor privileges on Mon., Tues. & Fri.

8 Pali Golf Course — 18/72 / 6,493
At foot of Pali Cliffs—MU
Best of Oahu's municipal courses. 20 minutes from Waikiki. Lush, but weedy fairways.

9 Kuilima G.C. — 18/72 / 6,420
Kahuku—R
George Fazio course in new Del Webb resort complex.

Kauai

1 Kauai Surf G. &.C.C. — 18/72 / 6,900
Near Nawiliwili Harbor—R
Pleasant resort course with rolling terrain, water.

2 Wailua G.C. — 18/72 / 6,631
4 miles south of Lihue—MU
Sporty oceanside course, tight greens, trees. Near hotels.

3 Princeville G.C. — 27/72-36 / 6,530-3,260
Hanalei—SP
Challenging Robert Trent Jones, Jr., layout on beautiful site overlooking ocean.

Hawaii

1 Mauna Kea Beach Hotel & G.C. — 18/72 / 6,488
Near Kamuela—R
One of world's toughest oceanside courses, built by Robert Trent Jones on rugged lava flow. Lush fairways, greens, and fabulous views.

2 Waikoloa Village G.C. — 18/72 / 6,715
Kamuela—SP
R.T. Jones course in big Boise Cascade planned resort community.

3 Keauhou Kona G.C. — 18/72 / 6,329
Keauhou Bay near Kailua-Kona—R
Black lava rough makes it tough. Rolling and scenic. 6,814 from back.

4 Volcano G.C. — 18/72 / 6,119
29 miles south of Hilo—SP
On slopes of Mauna Loa Mt. Beautiful scenery, lush fairways.

5 Hilo Municipal G.C. — 18/72 / 6,427
Hilo—MU
Large greens, flat, wide fairways, no bunkers.

6 Seamountain Ninole G.C. — 18/72 / 6,492
Pahala—R
J. Snyder course, ocean view, monkey pod trees. Open '74. New resort development.

Maui

1 Royal Kaanapali G.C. — 18/72 / 6,336
Kaanapali Beach—R
Championship tees of this Robert Trent Jones course play to 7,179 yards. It has all the elements for great golf: water, trees, terrain, wind and scenery. Also 18-hole, 4,300-yard course.

2 Waiehu G.C. — 18/72 / 6,565
Waiehu—MU
9 on ocean and 9 in hills. Sporty and fun.

3 Wailea G.C. — 18/72 / 6,700
Kihei—R
Little wind on this resort community test. Beautiful setting.

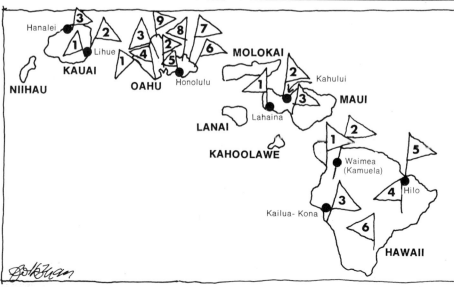

244

Washington

1 Alderbrook Inn & G.C. — 18/73
Union—R — 6,376
Wooded course with view of Olympic Mts. All fairways separate.

2 Tumwater Valley — 18/72
Olympia—PU — 6,441
Two extra par-3s in new recreation complex.

2 Capitol City G.C. — 18/71
Olympia—PU — 6,438
Monthly rates available.

3 Meadow Park G.C. — 27/72-31
Tacoma—MU — 6,158-1,775
Tree-lined, narrow. Extra nine is short, sporty.

3 Brookdale G.C. — 18/71
Tacoma—PU — 6,035
Well equipped public course.

4 Sahalee C.C. — 18/72
Redmond—PR — 6,555
Cut from forest overlooking lake. Year-round recreation complex.

4 Jefferson Park G.C. — 27/70-28
Seattle—MU — 6,315-1,450
Tree-lined, hilly. Short and tight. Built in 1915.

4 Foster G.C. — 18/68
Seattle—PU — 5,800
Short course outside city. Green River comes into play on 10 holes.

4 Earlington G.C. — 18/69
Renton—PU — 5,200
Easy walking course near Seattle. Open since 1894. Play year-round.

4 West Seattle G.C. — 18/72
Seattle—MU — 6,400
Public course with practice facilities.

4 Port Ludlow G.C. — 18/72
Seattle—SP — 6,800
Robert Muir Graves course overlooks harbor, Hood Canal. Wooded, rugged terrain.

5 Ocean Shores G.C. — 18/72
Ocean Shores—R — 6,130
Year-round coastal course with accommodations.

6 Cedarcrest G.C. — 18/69
Marysville—SP — 5,165
Rolling hills with bent greens and tees. Very sporty. Motels nearby.

7 Indian Canyon G.C. — 18/71
Spokane—MU — 6,380
One of three city-owned layouts. Fairways pitch uphill, downhill, sidehill. Very picturesque.

7 Downriver G.C. — 18/71
Spokane—PU — 6,150
Spokane's oldes "muni." Tight course, easy to walk.

7 Esmeralda G.C. — 18/70
Spokane—PU — 6,300
Rolling pastureland, wide fairways, big greens. Open all year.

7 Wandermere G.C. — 18/70
Spokane—PU — 6,200
Public course with practice area north of city limits. Spring-fed swimming lake and trout stream.

7 Sun Dance G.C. — 18/70
Spokane—PU — 6,200
Charming course built by non-golfer Dale Knott.

7 Hangman Valley G.C. — 18/71
Spokane—PU — 6,500
Course winds along gentle slopes on Hangman Creek. Pastoral setting.

7 Liberty Lake G.C. — 18/70
Spokane—PU — 6,050
County-owned course. Flat and short with small greens.

8 Veterans Memorial G.C. — 18/72
Walla Walla—PU — 6,400
Year-round course on edge of town. Rolling contour, variety of shots. Renowned for conditioning.

Oregon

1 Gearhart G.C. — 18/72
Gearhart—R — 6,125
Seaside links built in 1890s, flat, windy. Hotel adjoins; beaches near.

2 Pleasant Valley G.C. — 18/72
Clackamas—PR — 6,500
View of Mt. Hood from all holes. Condominiums and par-3 planned.

2 Broadmoor G.C. — 18/72
Portland—PU — 6,155
Lush, sporty course in beautiful natural setting. Four water hazards. All year play.

2 Colwood G.C. — 18/72
Portland—PU — 6,432
Water and trees add interest.

2 Rose City G.C. — 18/72
Portland—PU — 6,376
Centrally located course with many trees. Long par-4s. Very picturesque. Year-round play.

2 Glendoveer National G.C. — 36/74-72
Portland—MU — 6,368-6,066
Outstanding scenic views. Towering fir trees make it extra tough.

2 Eastmoreland G.C. — 18/72
Portland—PU — 6,142
Fairly exacting public course; front nine flat, tree-lined. Back known as "Ball-Hawk Monster"—water hazards on 6 holes.

2 Rock Creek C.C. — 18/72
Somerset West—SP — 7,128
Pleasant country club atmosphere. Near Portland.

2 Progress Downs G.C. — 18/72
Progress—MU — 6,480
Fairly open course near Portland. Rolling hills, tree-lined, 2 lakes. Lighted driving range.

2 West Delta Park G.C. — 18/72
Portland—MU — 6,400
R. T. Jones, Jr., course designed for international competition. Water hazards threaten half of course.

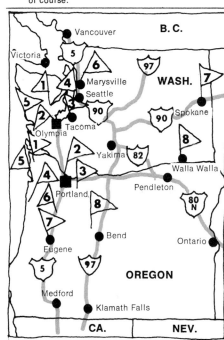

2 Oregon City C.C. — 18/70
Oregon City—PU — 5,871
Sporty course south of Portland. Rolling with many doglegs and trees.

2 Top O' Scott G.C. — 18/70
Portland—PU — 5,544
Tree-lined fairways. Good for average golfer. Open all year.

3 Bowman's Mt. Hood G.C. — 18/70
Wemme—R — 6,428
Beautiful hilly year-round golf and ski resort at foot of Mt. Hood.

4 Salishan Golf Links — 18/72
Gleneden Beach—R — 6,437
Narrow, well-landscaped. Course overlooks Pacific Ocean. Hotel.

5 Alderbrook G.C. — 18/71
Tillamook—PU — 5,810
Course set in natural surroundings. Lots of trees; ocean breeze.

5 Forest Hills G.C. — 18/72
Cornelius—SP — 6,244
One of most beautiful in Northwest. Somewhat hilly. Many traps and trees.

6 Salem G.C. — 18/70
Salem—PU — 6,205
Outstanding course with share of interesting holes.

6 McNary G.C. — 18/72
Salem—SP — 6,850
Huge, smooth greens. Luxurious facilities.

6 Battle Creek G.C. — 18/71
Salem—SP — 6,020
Course five miles south of Salem. Fairly flat with 2 creeks and 2 lakes.

6 Santiam G.C. — 18/71
Stayton—PU — 6,245
Public course with lake and two creeks.

7 Oakway G.C. — 18/72
Eugene—PU — 6,500
Well-maintained course near city.

8 Sunriver G.C. — 18/72
Sunriver—SP — 6,660
Large resort complex. Lodge. Private paved lighted airstrip. Near Bend.

8 Black Butte Ranch G.C. — 18/72
Black Butte—SP — 6,880
Near town of Sisters amid stands of Ponderosa Pine. Part flat, part wooded hills. By Robert Muir Graves.

Nevada

1 Black Mountain C.C. — 18/72
Henderson—SP — 6,397
First 9 short, easy; back side long and tough.

1 Las Vegas C.C. — 18/71
Las Vegas—PR — 6,665
Fine desert course. Can putt on tees. 1969 U.S. Sr. Open site.

1 Craig Ranch G.C. — 18/70
Las Vegas—R — 5,703
Short and simple. No traps. Caters to women and novices.

1 Desert Inn C.C. — 18/72
Las Vegas—R — 6,778
Tournament course. Flat. More trees than usual desert layout. Big tees. LPGA tour stop.

1 Dunes Hotel & C.C. — 18/72
Las Vegas—R — 6,564
Long (7,240 yards) from back tees. Long par-5s and par-3s. Many traps.

1 Las Vegas G.C. — 18/72
Las Vegas—MU — 6,457
Good test on back side. Small greens. Co-site of Sahara Pro-Am.

1 Paradise Valley C.C. — 18/72
Las Vegas—SP — 6,568
Good tournament course with country club feel. Site of '73 U.S. Nt'l Sr. Open.

1 Sahara-Nevada Hotel & C.C. — 18/71
Las Vegas—R — 6,800
Tough driving course with some water. Recently remodelled.

1 Tropicana Hotel & C.C. — 18/70
Las Vegas—R — 6,427
More character than usual desert course. Tough on hookers.

1 Winterwood G.C. — 18/71
Las Vegas—MU — 6,427
Good bent grass greens. Wide open. County course.

1 Fairway-To-The-Stars — 18/70
Las Vegas—SP — 6,300
Novel resort course designed by bandleader Louis Prima.

2 Lake Ridge G.C. — 18/72
Reno—SP — 6,378
Water and sand on rolling Trent Jones layout.

2 Brookside G.C. — 18/70
Reno—SP — 6,500
Flat with large greens. Some water.

2 Washoe County G.C. — 18/72
Reno—MU — 6,550
Easy to walk. Tree-lined. 3 lakes. 1 mile west of Reno airport.

2 Washoe County Stead G.C. — 18/72
Reno—PU — 6,219
Good greens, some water, north of Reno.

3 Incline Village G.C. — 18/72
Incline Village—SP — 6,723
Magnificent setting on shores of Lake Tahoe. Trent Jones layout in resort development.

4 Edgewood-Tahoe G.C. — 18/70
Stateline—R — 6,734
Stiff challenge designed by George Fazio on south shore of Lake Tahoe.

5 Spring Creek C.C. — 18/71
Elko—R — 6,540
Many natural hazards, doglegs. A McCulloch Properties development.

California

1 Lake Shastina G.C.   18/72
Mt. Shasta—PU   6,620
    Partly open, partly wooded. Robert Trent Jones course opened in 1972.

2 Peacock Gap C.C.   18/71
San Rafael—SP   6,503
    Not too tough, but interesting. All facilities.

3 Silverado C.C.   36/72-72
Napa—PR   6,849-6,602
    Tough championship courses. Open to guests staying on premises. Site of Kaiser Open.

3 Chimney Rock G.C.   18/72
Napa—SP   6,537
    Course overlooks vineyards and orchard. Two lakes, many trees.

3 Napa Municipal G.C.   18/72
Napa—MU   6,498
    Designed by J. Fleming. Fifteen water holes.

3 Sonoma National G.C.   18/72
Sonoma—PU   6,408
    Rolling terrain, woods, water. Some elevated greens. Interesting challenge built in 1928 by Sam Whiting.

4 Blue Rock Springs G.C.   18/72
Vallejo—MU   6,352
    J. Fleming course five miles outside of Vallejo.

4 Walnut Creek G.C.   18/72
Walnut Creek—PU   7,020
    Long course has driving range with night lighting.

4 Franklin Canyon G.C.   18/72
Rodeo—MU   6,354
    Four water holes, five par-3s and five par-5s.

5 Lew F. Galbraith G.C.   18/72
Oakland—MU   6,750
    Well laid out course on rolling tree-lined fairways.

5 Alameda G.C.   36/71-72
Alameda—MU   6,417-6,615
    Completely renovated North Course; 5 artificial lake hazards.

5 Lake Chabot Municipal G.C.   18/72
Oakland—MU   6,180
    Hilly municipal layout. Also has par-3 course.

5 Tilden Park G.C.   18/70
Berkeley—MU   5,813
    Scenic course in park; rolling hills, tree-lined fairways.

5 Skywest Public G.C.   18/72
Hayward—PU   6,636
    Adjacent to Hayward Municipal Airport.

5 Hayward G.C.   18/72
Hayward—PU   6,230
    Relatively flat, tree-lined course. Several water hazards.

6 San Mateo Municipal G.C.   18/70
San Mateo—MU   5,779
    Short, flat course. Many accommodations nearby.

6 Silver Pines G. & C.C.   18/72
Newark—PU   6,585
    Course has all facilities and swimming.

6 Palo Alto Municipal G.C.   18/72
Palo Alto—MU   6,418
    Municipal course has driving range with night lighting.

7 Harding Park G.C.   27/72-32
San Francisco—MU   6,700-2,500
    Outstanding municipal course. Narrow, tree-lined.

7 Lincoln Park Municipal G.C.   18/69
San Francisco—MU   5,277
    Short municipal course near coast.

8 Sharp Park Public G.C.   18/71
Pacifica—PU   6,240
    Seaside links course south of San Francisco.

8 Half Moon Bay Lodge G.C.   18/72
Half Moon Bay—R   7,105
    New Palmer-Duane course. Very scenic. Contoured greens; stiff off-shore breezes.

8 Crystal Springs G.C.   18/72
Burlingame—SP   6,654
    Semi-private course with many facilities.

9 Sunnyvale Municipal G.C.   18/70
Sunnyvale—MU   6,406
    Municipal course west of San Jose.

9 Fairway Glen G.C.   18/70
Santa Clara—PU   6,120
    Public course with driving range.

10 Las Positas G.C.   18/72
Livermore—MU   6,790
    Good test; fairly long front 9; rolling back 9. Water hazards.

10 Rancho Murietta G.C.   18/72
Sacramento—PU   6,997
    Bert Stamps course in foothills 25 miles southeast of town. Lakes, traps, fine test.

10 Sunol Valley G.C.   36/72-72
Sunol—SP   6,671-6,341
    One 18 completely surrounds the other.

11 Oak Ridge G.C.   18/72
San Jose—PU   6,585
    Rolling fairways. Driving range.

11 Cambrian G.C.   18/70
San Jose—PU   5,647
    Short course with driving range.

11 Pleasant Hills G.C.   18/72
San Jose—SP   6,888
    Relatively flat, but difficult and well-maintained course.

11 San Jose Municipal G.C.   18/72
San Jose—MU   6,450
    Well equipped municipal course.

11 Santa Teresa G.C.   18/72
San Jose—PU   6,800
    Front side flat but long; back nine hilly and more tricky.

11 Thunderbird G. & C.C.   18/65
San Jose—PU   4,802
    Also has driving range with night lighting.

12 Pasatiempo G.C.   18/71
Santa Cruz—SP   6,274
    Fine, old Alister MacKenzie layout overlooking Monterey Bay.

13 Laguna Seca G.C.   18/71
Monterey—R   6,500
    Trent Jones course with many bunkers. 2 lakes.

13 Pebble Beach G.C.   18/72
Pebble Beach—R   6,747
    Borders ocean, one of world's best. Del Monte Lodge guests only. Site of 1972 U.S. Open.

13 Del Monte G.C.   18/71
Monterey—SP   6,173
    Near Del Monte Hyatt House. Oldest of the Peninsula seacoast courses.

13 Spyglass Hill G.C.   18/72
Pebble Beach—SP   6,810
    Very tough Robert Trent Jones course. Site of Bing Crosby Pro-Am.

13 Pacific Grove Municipal G.C.   18/70
Pacific Grove—MU   5,493
    Jack Neville course along sand-duned shore of Monterey Bay. Front nine true links; back nine inland.

14 Carmel Valley G. & C.C. — 18/72
Carmel—PR — 6,756
Flat, beautifully maintained Robert Muir Graves course. Pastoral environment with 100-room lodge. Available to guests of Quail Lodge.

15 Corral de Tierra C.C. — 18/72
Salinas—PR — 6,284
Bob Baldock course near Monterey Peninsula. Members of out-of-town clubs may play.

15 Ridgemark — 18/72
Hollister—SP — 6,900
R Bigler course on 500-acre resort development on old turkey farm. Rolling hills, large greens.

15 Salinas Fairways G.C. — 18/72
Salinas—PU — 6,555
Located adjacent to Salinas Municipal Airport. Fairly flat. One of best public courses in Cal.

16 Rancho Canada G.C. — 36/72-71
Carmel Valley—PU — 6,613-6,400
East course nation's 10,000th. Gently rolling terrain on Carmel River. Pebble beach sand. Lakes.

17 San Luis Bay Inn & G.C. — 18/71
Avila Beach—R — 6,341
New resort. Olin Dutra, pro. Tennis, fishing, swimming, sailing. Open all year.

18 Alisal G.C. — 18/72
Solvang—R — 6,400
Tree-lined, 9 fairways cross river. Combined ranch-hotel facility.

18 Sandpiper G.C. — 18/72
Goleta—PU — 6,977
Bill Bell seaside course with sweeping fairways. and spacious greens reminiscent of Scotland. Lodging nearby.

19 Ojai Valley C.C. — 18/71
Ojai—R — 6,351
Surrounded by mountains, course circles Ojai Inn. Picturesque and tough. Complete resort facilities.

19 Valencia G.C. — 18/72
Valencia—SP — 6,700
Rugged Trent Jones layout with 12 doglegs. Motel adjoins.

20 Los Robles Greens G.C. — 18/71
Thousand Oaks—SP — 6,529
Oak studded course. 7 holes play around thoroughbred ranch. Large tees. Driving range.

21 Brookside G.C. — 36/72-70
Pasadena—MU — 6,600-6,100
Testing muny course. New clubhouse. North of Rose Bowl.

21 Azusa Greens Public G.C. — 18/70
Azusa—PU — 6,068
Flat, but very tight B. Baldock course. Good view of mountains.

21 De Bell G.C. — 18/71
Burbank—PU — 5,432
Also has 9-hole par-3 course; driving range.

22 Rancho Park G.C. — 18/71
Los Angeles—MU — 6,600
Busy, beautiful tournament course in heart of L.A.

22 Harding Municipal G.C. — 18/71
Los Angeles—MU — 6,610
In Griffith Park.

22 Wilson Municipal G.C. — 18/72
Los Angeles—MU — 6,954
In Griffith Park.

22 Western Avenue G.C. — 18/70
Los Angeles—PU — 6,084
Course has driving range with night lighting.

22 Alondra Park C.C. — 18/72
Lawndale—PU — 6,309
Course by C. B. Hollingsworth near Los Angeles. Also has 18-hole par-3 course.

23 Recreation Park G.C. — 18/72
Long Beach—PU — 6,157
Also has 9-hole course and driving range.

23 Skylinks G.C. — 18/72
Long Beach—PU — 6,201
Course by Bill Bell with number of lakes. Accommodations nearby.

23 El Dorado Park G.C. — 18/72
Long Beach—PU — 6,704
Has driving range.

24 Anaheim Hills Municipal G.C. — 18/72
Anaheim—PU — 6,257
Richard Bigler course near Disneyland. Hilly, very challenging.

24 Corona National G.C. — 18/72
Corona—PU — 6,661
Course offers driving range; swimming.

24 Green River G.C. — 36/71-71
Corona—PU — 6,200-6,200
River runs through picturesque course set among mountains. Easy to walk.

24 Anaheim Municipal G.C. — 18/70
Anaheim—MU — 6,017
Dick Miller course in Disneyland area.

25 Costa Mesa G. & C.C. — 36/71-70
Costa Mesa—MU — 6,400-5,005
Lush club and facilities. Huge practice area.

25 Huntington Beach C.C. — 18/71
Huntington Beach—PU — 5,879
Short public course.

25 Huntington Seacliff C.C. — 18/72
Huntington Beach—PU — 6,481
Course also has driving range.

25 Rancho San Joaquin G.C. — 18/72
Newport Beach—SP — 6,402
Slightly rolling. Three holes play over water.

26 Apple Valley Inn — 18/71
Apple Valley—R — 6,765
Sprawling resort course, open year around.

26 Hesperia G. & C.C. — 18/72
Hesperia—SP — 6,708
Course lies between two mesas. Country club open all year.

27 Spring Valley Lake G.C. — 18/72
San Bernardino—SP — 6,200
Short course on lake. Wide fairways.

27 San Bernardino Public G.C. — 18/71
San Bernardino—PU — 6,100
Relatively short, but interesting course. Well groomed. Near new Hilton Inn.

28 Seven Hills G.C. — 18/72
Hemet—PU — 6,310
Short but sporty well-trapped course. Trees, lakes and undulating greens.

28 Massacre Canyon Inn — 27/72-23
Gilman Hot Springs—R — 6,978-2,960
Flat and long, 2 lakes, many trees. At foothills of mountain range.

28 Murietta Hot Springs C.C. — 18/72
Murietta—SP — 7,160
R. T. Jones course built around six lakes and resort development.

28 Soboba Springs C.C. — 18/72
San Jacinto—SP — 6,726
Muirhead creation is flat but challenging, with huge rolling greens and 6 water holes.

29 Pala Mesa Inn & G.C. — 18/72
Fallbrook—R — 6,400
Championship course; distinctly separate 9s; one hilly, the other woodsy.

29 Rancho California G.C. — 18/72
Temecula—R — 6,800
New course in 9,500-acre Kaiser Aetna resort development. Lodge.

29 Fallbrook G. & C.C. — 18/72
Fallbrook—SP — 6,169
Well trapped. Flat. Lake on front side, trees on back nine.

30 Whispering Palms G. & C.C. — 18/71
Rancho Sante Fe—SP — 6,319
Excellent greens. Level lies.

30 La Costa C.C. — 18/72
Rancho La Costa—R — 6,642
Top Dick Wilson course. Fine resort hotel and spa. Site of Tournament of Champions.

30 Rancho Bernardo Inn & C.C. — 36/72-72
Escondido—R — 6,735-6,400
Two courses in long, winding valley. 150-room resort inn.

30 San Vincente C.C. — 18/72
Ramona—SP — 6,630
New resort-home community with Ted Robinson course in rolling meadowland. Al Geiberger is golf director.

30 Lake San Marcos C.C. — 18/72
Lake San Marcos—R — 6,400
Flat, open course north of San Diego adjoining Quails Inn Motel.

30 Rancho Sante Fe G.C. — 18/72
Rancho Sante Fe—R — 6,610
Affiliated with Rancho Sante Fe Inn. Fine, interesting course.

30 Circle R Golf Resort — 18/71
Escondido—R — 6,401
Well-manicured, fairly flat. Lake and trees. Lodge adjoins.

31 Torrey Pines Inn & G.C. — 36/72-72
La Jolla—R — 6,363-6,727
Choice of two challenging Billy Bell courses. PGA tour stop.

32 Balboa Park Municipal G.C. — 27/72-32
San Diego—MU — 5,995-2,197
Short and tight municipal course. Slightly hilly. Near zoo and city center.

32 Coronado Municipal G.C. — 18/72
Coronado—MU — 6,378
Undulating fairways, elevated greens. Trees.

32 Ohula Vista Municipal G.C. — 18/73
Bonita—MU — 6,646
Beautiful greens. Well-trapped.

32 Rancho de los Penasquitos C.C. — 18/70
San Diego—SP — 5,877
Rolling greens. Pine trees come into play.

32 Stardust C.C. — 18/72
San Diego—PR — 6,633
Flat and well bunkered. Four teaching professionals. On Hotel Circle.

33 Carlton Oaks C.C. and Lodge — 18/72
Santee—R — 6,960
Twelve holes affected by water. Greens more undulating than most in area.

33 Cottonwood C.C. — 36/73-72
El Cajon—SP — 7,112-6,116
Large acreage with 4,000 trees, three lakes.

33 Singing Hills C.C. — 54/73-72-61
El Cajon—SP — 6,800-6,500-4,200
Resort courses for guests of Singing Hills Lodge.

34 Warner's Golf Resort — 18/72
Warner Springs—R — 6,550
Spacious fairways. Flat. Trees.

34 De Anza Desert C.C. — 18/72
Borrego Springs—PR — 6,518
Nicely manicured oasis. Flat. Guests of member hotels may play.

35 Whitewater C.C. — 18/71
Palm Springs—PR — 6,164
Recently improved. Open to members of out-of-town clubs.

35 Riviera Hotel & C.C. — 9/30
Palm Springs—R — 1,490
Short course on grounds of hotel. Open to public.

35 Biltmore Hotel G.C. — 9/30
Palm Springs—R — 1,235
Finely conditioned little course. On hotel grounds. Open to public.

35 Canyon C.C. (North) — 18/72
Palm Springs—PR — 6,763
One of best in area. Open to out-of-town club members.

35 Canyon C.C. (South) — 18/71
Palm Springs—PR — 6,700
Open to public during slow seasons. Challenging layout.

35 Palm Springs G.C. — 18/72
Palm Springs—MU — 6,500
Outstanding city course. Good test. Open to public.

36 Mission Hills G. & C.C. — 18/72
Cathedral City—PR — 6,454
Lush Desmond Muirhead course. Visitors need approval. Much water.

36 Desert Island C.C. — 18/70
Cathedral City—PR — 5,656
Rolling Desmond Muirhead course. Open to out-of-town club members.

37 Desert Air C.C. — 18/71
Rancho Mirage—SP — 6,835
Well-conditioned. Plays long. Rolling. Open to public on approval. Landing strip.

37 Shadow Mountain G.C. — 18/69
Palm Desert—PR — 5,339
Open to members and guests of some hotels.

37 Del Safari C.C. — 18/72
Palm Desert—PR — 6,760
Course open to out-of-town club members on limited basis. Beautiful clubhouse. Lakes.

37 Palm Desert C.C. — 18/70
Palm Desert—SP — 6,396
Several lagoons. Excellent greens. In housing project. No clubhouse.

37 Indian Wells C.C. — 27/72-36
Indian Wells—PR — 6,732-3,540
Fine course; co-site of Hope Classic. Open to out-of-town club members.

37 Bermuda Dunes C.C. — 27/72-36
Bermuda Dunes—PR — 6,375-6,765
Constructed on rolling sand dunes. Open to visiting club members.

38 La Quinta C.C. — 18/72
La Quinta—PR — 6,900
Excellent test. For guests of La Quinta Hotel.

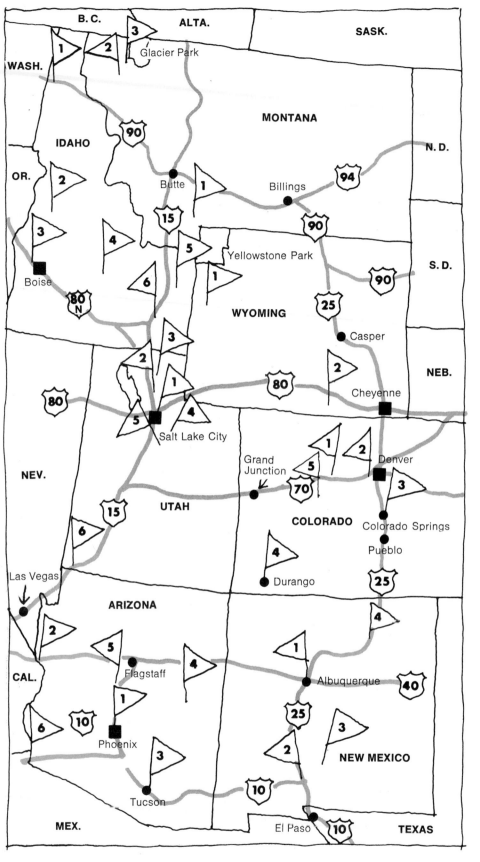

| 1 | Golden Hills C.C. & Resort | 18/71 |
| | Mesa—R | 6,560 |

Accommodations on course; rates include golf; extra large greens.

| 1 | Apache Wells C.C. | 18/70 |
| | Mesa—SP | 5,745 |

Well-groomed desert course amid housing development.

| 1 | Thunderbird C.C. | 18/71 |
| | Phoenix—SP | 6,375 |

Rolling desert course built in foothills of South Mountain.

| 1 | Arizona Biltmore C.C. | 18/72 |
| | Phoenix—R | 6,440 |

Mountain and desert setting for fine course.

| 1 | Mountain Shadows C.C. | 18/56 |
| | Scottsdale—R | 2,635 |

Executive course run by Mountain Shadows Resort.

| 1 | Scottsdale Inn & C.C. | 18/70 |
| | Scottsdale—R | 6,015 |

Course not difficult but tricky; 4 water holes.

| 1 | Pima Inn & Golf Resort | 18/71 |
| | Scottsdale—SP | 6,491 |

Good test on Indian reservation. Desert-mountain vistas. Formerly called Roadrunner.

| 1 | McCormick Ranch G.C. | 27/72-36 |
| | Scottsdale—R | 6,350-3,200 |

In resort-residential community. 17th and 18th finish over 40-acre lake.

| 1 | Sun City G.C. | 90 |
| | Sun City—SP | holes |

4 full-length courses and one executive-length par-60 layout in retirement community.

| 1 | San Marcos Hotel G.C. | 18/72 |
| | Chandler—R | 6,500 |

Plush resort course, bordered by tall tamarack trees.

| 1 | Goodyear G. & C.C. | Gold: 18/72 7,105 |
| | Litchfield Park—R | Blue: 18/70 6,107 |

Gold course designed by Robert Trent Jones extremely difficult. Blue course short and simple. For club members and Wigwam guests.

| 1 | Desert Forest G.C. | 18/72 |
| | Carefree—PR | 6,831 |

Tough desert course puts emphasis on strategy. Carefree Inn nearby.

| 1 | Maryvale G.C. | 18/72 |
| | Phoenix—MU | 6,223 |

Popular city course. Front nine includes many water hazards.

| 1 | Estrella Mountain G.C. | 18/70 |
| | Goodyear—MU | 6,600 |

Good city course with practice area and eating facilities.

| 1 | Moon Valley C.C. | 18/72 |
| | Phoenix—PR | 6,600 |

Limited guest privileges. Contact club in advance.

| 1 | Encanto Muni. G.C. | 18/70 |
| | Phoenix—MU | 6,245 |

Good test. Near downtown area. Also includes a 1,730-yard 30-par layout.

| 1 | Century C.C. | 18/72 |
| | Scottsdale—SP | 6,783 |

Excellent course. Very challenging.

| 1 | Camelback Inn C.C. | 18/72 |
| | Scottsdale—R | 6,687 |

Fine new course for Camelback Inn guests. Elevated greens. Lush.

| 1 | Valley C.C. | 18/72 |
| | Scottsdale—SP | 6,150 |

Scenic course. Guests of several inns have preferred starting times.

| 1 | Papago Park G.C. | 18/72 |
| | Phoenix—MU | 6,690 |

Wide fairways. Large greens. Site of 1971 U.S. Publinx event.

| 1 | Mesa C.C. | 18/72 |
| | Mesa—PR | 6,750 |

Scenic course with limited guest privileges.

| 2 | Lake Havasu G. & C.C. | 18/72 |
| | Lake Havasu—MU | 6,382 |

Every hole a dogleg except par-3s. Part of resort community. London Bridge is here. Another 18 going in.

| 3 | The Forty-Niners G.C. | 18/72 |
| | Tucson—SP | 6,228 |

Rolling terrain, trees, 4 water holes. Complete resort, dude ranch.

| 3 | Skyline C.C. | 18/70 |
| | Tucson—R | 6,344 |

Cottage colony in Catalina Mts. with real estate development.

| 38 | Westward Ho G.C. | 18/72 |
| | Indio—SP | 6,640 |

Public welcome at this established desert course. Little waiting.

| 39 | Horse Thief G. & C.C. | 18/72 |
| | Tahachapi—SP | 6,710 |

Hilly course, no fairway bunkers. Many trees. Part of Stallion Springs community.

Arizona

| 1 | Fountain Hills G.C. | 18/71 |
| | Fountain Hills—R | 6,331 |

Laid out along bottom of series of ravines and gullies.

3 El Rio G.C. 18/70 6,418
Randolph South G.C. 18/70 6,400
Randolph North G.C. 18/72 6,973
Tucson—MU
    Three public courses available to visitors.

3 Kino Springs 18/72
Nogales—R 6,520
    Front nine in rolling meadowland, back nine rough and hilly in 6,000-acre home development. Hotel and spa.

4 Pinetop C.C. 18/71
Pinetop—PR 6,690
    Challenging second home development course in White Mountains near Show Low.

5 Antelope Hills G.C. 18/72
Prescott—PU 6,900
    L. Hughes course at 5,000 feet. Fairly flat. Lodging nearby.

6 Desert Hills Municipal G.C. 18/72
Yuma—PU 6,815
    Gently rolling course open 1973. Very pretty. Lodging nearby.

Utah

1 Bonneville G.C. 18/72
Salt Lake City—PU 6,522
    Closed December-February.

1 Glendale Park Municipal G.C. 18/72
Salt Lake City—MU 6,432
    Billy Bell course. Flat with great views of Salt Lake City and mountains.

1 Meadow Brook G.C. 18/72
Salt Lake City—MU 6,900
    Flat, lush course. Wide fairways. Motels nearby.

1 Mountain Dell G.C. 18/71
Salt Lake City—PU 6,100
    In mountain setting east of city.

1 Rose Park G.C. 18/72
Salt Lake City—PU 6,436
    City course closed during winter.

1 Stansbury G.C. 18/72
Stansbury Park—PU 6,400
    New course west of Salt Lake City near Great Salt Lake.

2 Patio Springs C.C. 18/72
Ogden—PR 6,600
    Lush mountain course. Good test. Large greens, lakes, streams.

2 White Barn G.C. 18/71
Ogden—PU 6,300
    Flat course with private club on premises.

2 Ben Lomond G.C. 18/72
Ogden—PU 6,166
    Public course with practice facilities.

2 Davis County G.C. 18/72
Kaysville—PU 6,600
    Good test. Heavily played. Between Ogden and Salt Lake City.

3 Logan G. & C.C. 18/71
Logan—SP 5,796
    Short but interesting course. Beautiful scenery.

4 Park City Resort G.C. 18/72
Park City—R 6,400
    Course recently remodeled at base of mountain ski area. Condos and homes.

4 Wasatch Mountain State Park G.C. 27/72-36
Wasatch Mountain State Park 6,765-3,525
    Seven lakes, two streams on three W. Neff 9's set between two mountains. Lodging on site and nearby.

5 Tri-City G.C. 18/72
American Fork—PU 6,752
    Joe Williams course, wooded and hilly with 5 lakes.

5 Timpanogos G.C. 18/72
Provo—PU 6,600
    Public course closed in winter.

Colorado

1 Vail G.C. 18/71
Vail—PU 6,156
    Set at foot of mountains. River crosses course twice.

2 Hiwan G.C. 18/70
Evergreen—SP 6,673
    Long, narrow, rolling course in foothills of Rockies.

2 Inverness C.C. 18/70
Denver—SP 7,000
    Resort development on 600 acres southeast of Denver. J. P. Maxwell course open late '74.

2 Heather Ridge C.C. 27/70-32
Denver—SP 5,896-2,230
    Tight course, eight lakes. Many sand traps. Also 9-hole executive course.

3 Broadmoor G.C. 36/72-72
Colorado Springs—R 6,531-6,542
    Both 18s at Broadmoor Hotel resort are fine tests.

4 Pagosa Pines G.C. 9/36
Pagosa Springs—R 3,694
    J. Bulla course in 29,000-acre resort development. Tight with narrow approaches. Second 9 planned.

4 Tamarron 18/72
Durango—R 6,800
    Arthur Hills course 7,000 feet above sea level. Condominium resort by same group that built Innisbrook. Lodge.

5 Snowmass G.C. 18/71
Aspen—SP 6,354
    Course 8,000 feet above sea level. Rolling hills and fast greens. Many lakes.

Wyoming

1 Jackson Hole G. & Tennis C. 18/72
Jackson—R 6,600
    Course rebuilt by Robert Trent Jones backed by majestic Grand Teton range. 2 lodges.

2 Old Baldy Club 18/72
Saratoga—PR 6,600
    Lush, rolling course in exclusive resort. Mountain backdrop.

New Mexico

1 Paradise Hills G. & C.C. 18/72
Albuquerque—PR 7,060
    Level resort development course on 16,000 acres by Red Lawrence. Lake and 80 traps.

1 U. of New Mexico G.C. 18/72
Albuquerque—SP 6,698
    Rugged test in desert terrain; driving range. Open to public. Stretches to 7,258 yards.

1 Panorama G. & C.C. 18/72
Albuquerque—SP 6,600
    Desmond Muirhead course loops across sandy hillside. Panorama Inn.

2 New Mexico State U. G.C. 18/72
Las Cruces—MU 6,672
    All 18 holes can be seen from clubhouse. Site of 1968 NCAA.

3 Cloudcroft Lodge G.C. 18/68
Cloudcroft—R 4,693
    Highest course in America at 9,200 feet. Hilly.

4 baca grande-angel fire g.c. 9/36
Eagles Nest—R 3,239
    Seventy-two room condo-hotel. Luxury facilities.

Montana

1 Big Sky 18/72
Big Sky—PU 6,725
    Frank Duane course in mountain meadow. Open mid-1974. Black Otter Lodge.

2 Whitefish Lake G.C. 18/72
Whitefish—PU 6,277
    Picturesque course in tourist area. Lodging nearby.

3 West Glacier G.C. 18/68
West Glacier—PU 4,941
    "Players may move ball without penalty to avoid elk tracks. Do not throw clubs or ball at tame deer."

Idaho

1 Coeur d'Alene Municipal G.C. 18/72
Coeur d'Alene—MU 6,248
    Course winds through pines beside beautiful lake. Practice facilities available.

1 Avon Dale on Hayden Lake G.C. 18/72
Coeur d'Alene—PU 6,500
    Good course on lovely lake. Picturesque.

1 Stoneridge G.C. 18/72
Blanchard—PU 6,407
    Course partly in forest, mostly in lush meadowland along Blanchard Creek. Good test from the back.

2 McCall Municipal G.C. 18/70
McCall—MU 6,010
    Located one mile from town.

3 Plantation G.C. 18/72
Boise—SP 6,500
    Near town; public can play.

3 Purple Sage G.C. 18/71
Caldwell—SP 6,425
    Course has large greens, wide fairways.

3 Warm Springs Municipal G.C. 18
Boise—MU holes
    New municipal course on east side of city.

4 Sun Valley G.C. 18/71
Sun Valley—R 6,499
    Ski mecca has 18-hole course for May to October season. Well maintained and fun. Another 18, called Elkhorn, open 1974.

5 Pinecrest Municipal G.C. 18/70
Idaho Falls—MU 6,600
    Municipal course has trees, medium size greens.

6 Highlands G.C. 18/73
Pocatello—PU 6,720
    Long course with practice area.

Texas

1 Sherrill Park G. Cse. 18/72
Richardson—PU 6,400
    Gently rolling terrain with 9 water hazards. Fourteen holes completely tree-lined.

1 Tenison Park Mem. G.C. 18/70
Dallas—MU 6,578
    Difficult muny course. Site of 1968 Publinx.

2 Lakeway Inn & G.C. 18/72
Austin—SP 6,395
    Water, woods overlooking beautiful lake. All resort facilities.

3 Pecan Valley C.C. 18/71
San Antonio—PR 6,750
    Always open. Challenging wooded layout. Site of '68 PGA tourney.

4 Kerrville Hills C.C. 18/72
Kerrville—SP 6,400
    New residential resort in Texas hill country. Inn and private airport.

5 Hilltop Lakes G.C. 18/72
Hilltop Lakes—R 6,316
    Old West flavor at this new resort located between Houston and Dallas.

6 Bear Creek G.C. 36/70-72
Houston—PU 6,473-7,100
    Two J. Riviere courses give good variety. 20 miles from downtown Houston.

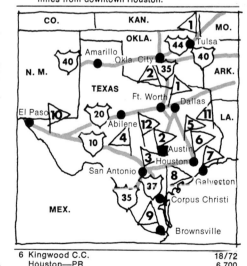

6 Kingwood C.C. 18/72
Houston—PR 6,700
    Joe Finger course part of 54-hole development on 14,000 acres. Reciprocal club privileges.

6 Memorial Park G.C. 18/72
Houston—MU 6,500
    Wooded course, 5 water hazards.

6 Columbia Lakes 18/72
West Columbia—R 7,198
    Residential-recreational development includes stylish clubhouse.

7 Clear Lake C.C. 18/72
Galveston—PR 6,821
    J. Riviere course in residential development near Johnson Space Center. Reciprocal club privileges.

7 Sun Meadow G.C. 18/72
Friendship—R 6,500
    Front 9 open, back 9 hilly. Open to guests of Hotel Galvez.

7 Galveston C.C.   18/72
   Galveston—R   6,291
    Straight fairways. Palms and oleanders. Open to guests of Hotel Galvez.

7 Galveston Municipal G.C.   18/70
   Galveston—MU   6,700
    Seaside course played along sea wall fronting Gulf of Mexico. Hotels, motels nearby.

8 Padre Island C.C.   18/71
   Corpus Christi—R   6,990
    Links in natural dunes setting. Inn nearby.

9 Valley International C.C.   18/70
   Brownsville—R   6,857
    Interesting and tight, with water on 12 holes. Also 9-hole par-3 course. Fairway cottages and inn. Southernmost course in continental U.S.

9 Rancho Viejo C.C.   18/72
   Brownsville—R   6,807
    Testing Dennis Arp course cut out of Rio Grande Valley citrus grove. Inn and fairway cottages.

10 Sierra Blanca C.C.   18/72
   Sierra Blanca—R   7,000
    Bill Cantrell course open 1973.

10 Mile High C.C.   2 courses
   Mile High—R   planned
    On I-10, 95 miles east of El Paso. Big Diamondhead Corp. development. Open 1974.

11 Woodland Hills G. C.   18/72
   Nacogdoches—PU   6,566
    Don January, Bill Martindale course carved out of the pine hills of east Texas. Natural hazards, tree-lined fairways. Accommodations nearby.

11 Fairway Farms G.C.   18/71
   San Augustine—PR   6,572
    Visiting club members may play. A brutal 7,352 yards from back. Lodge facilities.

12 Horseshoe Bay G.C.   18/72
   Lago Vista—R   6,839
    R. T. Jones test with 7 lakes; in hill country of central Texas on Lake LBJ. Condos, tennis and pool.

12 Lago Vista C.C.   18/72
   Lake Travis—R   6,632
    Hilly course. Condos, pool and tennis. New 18 under construction.

Oklahoma

1 Shangrila G. & C.C.   18/72
   Afton—R   6,435
    Tree-lined, hilly course adjoining lake in picturesque resort.

2 Falconhead   18/72
   Burneyville—R   6,468
    Flat front nine, rolling tree-lined back side. Clever bunkering and water provide a few flights. Resort hotel.

Arkansas

1 Dawn Hill C.C.   18/72
   Siloam Springs—R   6,390
    Enjoyable, fairly flat; runs through valley in Ozarks; creek, many trees.

1 Paradise Valley G.C.   18/71
   Fayetteville—MU   6,005
    Wooded, rolling course with eleven water holes. Several motels nearby.

2 Cherokee Village G.C.   18/72
   Cherokee Village, Hardy—R   6,252
    Interesting course flanked by river in Ozark retirement village.

3 Rebsamen Park G.C.   18/71
   Little Rock—MU   6,207
    Flat, wooded course on Arkansas River.

4 Belvedere C.C.   18/72
   Hot Springs—SP   6,750
    Rolling, interesting course, recently renovated.

4 Hot Springs G. & C.C.   45
   Hot Springs—R   holes
    Famous health spa has wide choice in courses. Arlington Hotel adjoins.

4 Hot Springs Village C.C.   18/72
   Hot Springs—R   6,770
    New Edmund Ault course. Six water holes framed by pines, white sand bunkers.

5 Eden Isle G.C.   9/36
   Heber Springs—R   3,376
    Rolling, forested course in mountains. Cliffs and water.

Missouri

1 Lake Valley G. & C.C.   18/70
   Camdenton—PU   6,041
    Near Lake of the Ozarks.

1 Dogwood Hills G.C.   18/71
   Osage Beach—SP   6,090
    Near Tan-Tar-A resort in Ozarks.

1 Lodge of the Four Seasons G.C.   18/71
   Lake Ozark—R   6,700
    R. T. Jones 18 open spring 1974. Variety of holes; valley, ridges, lake come into play. Also have extra nine. Complete resort facilities.

2 Chapel Woods G.C.   18/72
   Lee's Summit—SP   6,306
    Outside of Kansas City. One nine each side of road which bisects course. One nine rolling, other hilly. Water holes.

2 Shamrock Hills G.C.   18/71
   Lee's Summit—PU   6,100
    Open course with excellent greens. Fun to play. Lodging facilities nearby.

Iowa

1 Okoboji Vu G.C.   18/71
   Spirit Lake—R   6,215
    Has par-3 19th hole for playoffs.

2 Pheasant Ridge G.C.   18/72
   Cedar Falls—PU   6,550
    Near Waterloo. Undulating greens, rough and trees make the course.

Illinois

1 Macktown G.C.   18/72
   Rockton—R   5,935
    Wagon Wheel Lodge adjoins. Excellent food, rustic atmosphere.

2 Cog Hill G. & C.C.   72
   Lemont—SP   holes
    All four courses wooded. Tough No. 4 has 101 bunkers. Watered fairways.

2 Chicago
    The Chicago-Cook County area contains more semi-private courses available to golfers on a greens-fee basis than any major city in the U.S.

3 Pheasant Run Lodge   18/73
   St. Charles—R   6,043
    Lodge is convention center. Has own shops, entertainment.

Indiana

1 French Lick-Sheraton Hotel   36
   French Lick—R   holes
    Hill course tougher; easier valley course free to hotel guests. 485 rooms.

2 Christmas Lake G. & C.C.   18/72
   Santa Claus—MU   6,500
    Testing Edmund Ault layout on Christmas Lake. Watered fairways. Play year-round.

Minnesota

1 Bemidji C.C.   18/72
   Bemidji—SP   6,309
    Hilly, wooded. All out-of-town guests may play.

2 Enger Park G.C.   18/72
   Duluth—MU   6,105
    Pine-surrounded hilly course. Many accommodations nearby.

3 Madden G.C.   18/72
   Brainerd—R   6,400
    Gentle hills, plenty of trees. Also 2 9-hole par-3s.

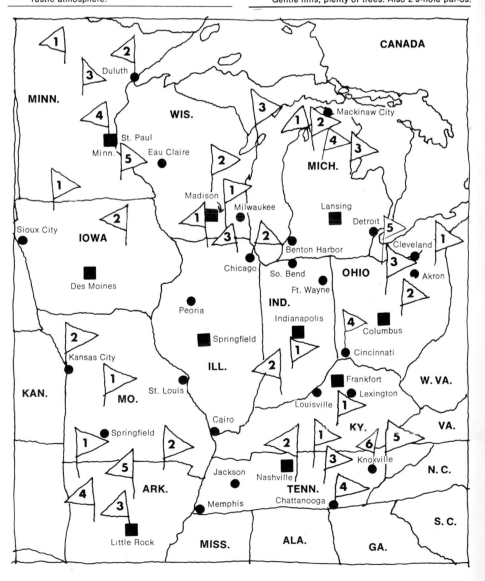

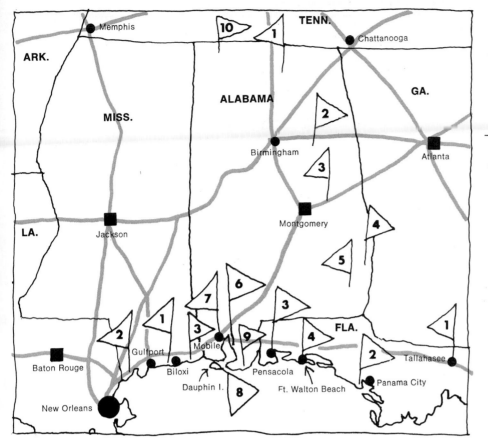

TENN.
Memphis
ARK.
Chattanooga
ALABAMA
GA.
MISS.
Birmingham
Atlanta
LA.
Jackson
Montgomery
Baton Rouge
Gulfport
Mobile
FLA.
Biloxi
Pensacola
Tallahasee
Dauphin I.
Ft. Walton Beach
Panama City
New Orleans

3 Madden Pine Beach G.C.   36/72-63
Brainerd—SP   6,100-3,541
Rolling terrain; short 18 adjoins. Pine Beach Inn on Gull Lake offers various facilities.

4 Sundance G. & C.C.   18/72
Osseo—PU   6,489
Gently rolling course with 12 lakes and ponds.

4 Coon Rapids G.C.   18/72
Coon Rapids—MU   6,610
Three lagoons affect 7 holes. Tree-lined fairways, rolling terrain, elevated greens. Driving range, practice greens.

4 Francis Gross G.C.   18/70
Minneapolis—MU   6,361
Tree-lined. National Publinx Championship once held here.

4 Keller G.C.   18/72
St. Paul—MU   6,557
Twice site of PGA Championship. Well-trapped, long par-4 holes.

4 Meadowbrook G.C.   18/72
Hopkins—MU   6,474
Rolling, well-trapped course with many dogleg holes. Creek runs through course.

4 Eden Prairie G.   27/72-32
Hopkins—MU   6,374-2,012
Level, fairly easy layout.

5 Maple Valley G. & C.C.   18/72
Rochester—SP   6,975
Scenic, challenging course in Root River Valley. Hotel and motel facilities nearby.

Wisconsin

1 Scotsland G.C.   18/72
Oconomowoc—R   6,700
Course features par-6, 666-yard hole. Lakes; stream in play on 7 holes. Complete facilities include hotel, theater, health spa.

1 Lake Lawn G.C.   18/71
Delavan—R   6,100
Rolling course, good greens. Many nearby accommodations.

1 Playboy Club—Hotel G.C.   36/71-72
Lake Geneva—R   6,700-6,800
Robert Bruce Harris and Pete Dye courses surround Bunny Hutches.

1 Abbey Springs C.C.   18/72
Fontana-On-Lake Geneva—PR   6,335
Course has undulating fairways in secluded setting. Resort-condo community.

2 Lawsonia Links   18/72
Green Lake—SP   6,620
Fine test in resort run by Baptist Assembly. Lodge and cabins. Public welcome.

3 Alpine Lodge and Cottages   18/71
Egg Harbor—R   6,200
Well-maintained course with many trees. Elevated greens. Lodge and cottages.

3 Bay Ridge G.C.   9/35
Sister Bay—PU   2,840
Gently rolling open fairways. Small greens.

3 Maxwelton Braes C.C.   9/35
Bailey's Harbor—R   6,045
Well-manicured course, open fairways, 68 bunkers. Resort accommodations.

3 Peninsula State Park G.C.   18/71
Ephraim—MU   6,450
Scenic, hilly course. Many trees, huge bunkers.

Michigan

1 Boyne Highlands G.C.   36/72-72
Harbor Springs—R   6,400-6,550
R. T. Jones did first course, W. Newcombe, second. Heavily wooded, rolling, water.

2 Boyne Mt. Alpine G.C.   18/72
Boyne Falls—R   6,627
Wooded course plays from mountain to lakefront. Also 9-hole executive-length course.

3 Bay Valley G.C.   18/72
Bay City—R   6,809
Desmond Muirhead course. Sculptured terrain, long curved tees, much water.

4 White Deer C.C.   18/74
Prudenville—R   6,300
Winds along Houghton Lake. Very large greens.

Ohio

1 Avalon Lakes G.C.   36/71-72
Warren—R   6,102-6,468
Tree-lined courses. Well-trapped, 8 water hazards. Avalon Inn adjoins.

2 Granville Inn G.C.   18/71
Granville—SP   6,417
Fine, rolling course with Granville Inn.

3 Whetstone River G.C.   18/72
Caledonia—SP   6,256
Lodging facilities and camping close by this course.

4 Golden Bear Golf Center   18/72
Kings Island-Cincinnati—R   6,410
Nicklaus course, part of Kings Island theme park. Also, 3,736-yard illuminated short course.

5 Sawmill Creek G.C.   18/70
Huron—SP   6,351
On Lake Erie. Well-trapped with water and marsh areas. 212 rooms on site.

Kentucky

1 General Burnside State Park   18/70
Burnside—R   5,869
Island resort course. Gently rolling with small greens.

Tennessee

1 Ironwood G.C.   18/72
Cookeville—PU   6,105
Wesley Flatt, Bobby Nichols course. Lodging facilities nearby.

2 Henry Horton State Park   18/72
Chapel Hill—MU   6,570
Huge greens and bunkers. Wide fairways. Elevated tees.

3 Fall Creek Falls State Park G.C.   18/72
Pikeville—PU
Scenic Joe Lee course cut in virgin forest atop Cumberland Mountains.

4 Brainerd G.C.   18/72
Chattanooga—MU   6,800
Many tees on long, rolling terrain. Tough par-4s.

5 Cobbly Nob   18/72
Gatlinburg—R   6,456
Davis-Kirby-Player course in resort area. Creek and lakes add to challenge.

5 Gatlinburg G.C.   18/72
Gatlinburg—MU   6,000
At foot of Great Smoky Mountains. Hilly terrain with big greens.

6 Dead Horse Lake G.C.   18/71
Knoxville—PU   6,225
Wooded course built around Dead Horse Lake. Accommodations nearby.

Alabama

1 Point Mallard G.C.   18/72
Decatur—PU   6,820
Carved from woodland in family recreation complex. 10 water holes.

1 Jetport G.C.   18/72
Huntsville—MU   6,470
Adjoins Skycenter Hotel at Air Terminal. Practice range, pool.

2 Alabama International C.C.   36/71-71
Talladega—R   6,646-6,682
Two tree-lined Robert Trent Jones courses opened in '72. Hotel planned.

2 Pine Harbor Champions C.C.   18/71
Pell City—PR   6,720
Adjoins Pine Harbor Motel. Open to members and guests of the motel.

3 Still Waters G.C.   18/72
Dadeville—PR   6,918
A mountain course by George Cobb with tight fairways in a 3,000-acre home community.

4 Lakepoint Resort G.C.   18/72
Eufaula—PU   7,026
Tom Nieol course in resort development. Water hazards.

5 Olympia Spa & C.C.   18/72
Dothan—R   6,600
Rolling fairways, several water holes on this resort course. Motel.

6 Lakewood G.C.   27/70-36
Point Clear—R   6,429-3,177
Excellent tree-lined courses with 12 doglegs. Grand Hotel owns course. Superb resort.

6 Lake Forest   18/72
Daphne—R   6,700
Hilly test.

7 Langan Park G.C.   18/72
Mobile—MU   6,383
Fine municipal course. Opening nine hilly, second fairly level. No water.

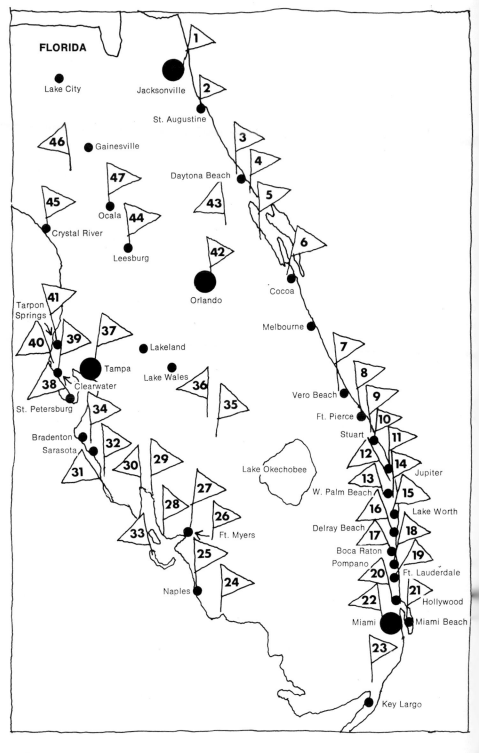

FLORIDA

```
8 Isle Dauphine C.C.                    18/72
  Dauphin Island—PR                     6,596
     Devilishly tough course overlooks Gulf of Mex-
     ico; sand dunes, water.
9 Gulf State Park G.C.                  18/72
  Gulf Shores—PU                        6,730
     Earl Stone course. Wide fairways, three lakes
     make six water holes. Greens well-trapped.
10 MacFarland Park G.C.                 18/72
  Florence—PU                           6,660
     Tree-lined fairways, 8 lakes, designed by Earl
     Stone. Camp grounds on site.
```

Mississippi

```
1 Gulf Hills Dude Ranch C.C.           18/72
  Ocean Springs—R                       6,294
     Beautiful woodland setting. Gently rolling fair-
     ways.
1 Edgewater Gulf C.C.                   18/72
  Biloxi—R                              6,314
     Edgewater Hotel gone but Buena Vista guests
     have privileges here and elsewhere.
1 Broadwater Beach G.C.              36/71-72
  Biloxi—R                         6,100-6,530
     Sea course flat, open, cute. No water. Sun
     course a tough test. Also 18-hole lighted par-3.
1 Sunkist C.C.                          18/72
  N. Biloxi—SP                          6,121
     Delightful, rolling test with level fairways and
     smallish greens.
1 St. Andrews on Gulf                   18/72
  Ocean Springs—R                       6,700
     New course, part of residential development.
     Second 18 planned.
2 Pass Christian C.C.                   18/72
  Pass Christian—PR                     6,400
     Private course. Guests of members only.
2 Banyan View C.C.                      18/71
  Gulfport—MU                           6,622
     Young course. Three water holes. Driving range.
2 Diamondhead G.C.                      18/72
  Bay St. Louis—R                       6,547
     Part of large recreational home development.
     Long tees, roller-coaster greens. Second 18
     planned.
3 Hickory Hill C.C.                     18/72
  Pascagoula—SP                         6,632
     Water, including two large lakes, dominates
     seven holes on this rolling Earl Stone course.
```

Florida panhandle

```
1 Killearn G. & C.C.                    18/72
  Tallahassee—PR                        6,316
     Guest play by invitation. Hotel, good food.
     Site of Tallahassee Open.
1 Winewood G.C.                         18/72
  Tallahassee—SP                        6,215
     L. Packard course runs through live oak and
     pine. Resort development, lodging nearby.
2 Bay Point Yacht & C.C.               18/72
  Panama City Beach—PR                  6,398
     Willard Byrd design. Tight course, heavily water-
     ed. Residential resort. Second 18 under con-
     struction.
2 Colony Club Gulf & Bay               18/72
  Panama City Beach—SP                  6,800
     Condominium development with beach and ma-
     rina. Hubert Green, touring pro.
3 Perdido Bay Inn C.C.                  18/72
  Pensacola—R                           6,411
     Overlooks gulf in resort community with inn,
     homes and homesites.
4 Sandestin                             18/72
  Ft. Walton Beach                      6,800
     Tom Jackson resort community course. Opened
     spring 1974.
```

Florida

```
1 Amelia Island Plantation           27/72-36
  Amelia Island—R                 6,900/3,400
     Pete Dye course opened fall 1973. Beach and all
     resort facilities plus homesites, condominiums.
1 Baymeadows G.C.                       18/72
  Jacksonville—SP                       6,800
     Residential-resort complex. Motel and con-
     vention center adjoins.
1 Ponte Vedra Club                      18/72
  Ponte Vedra Beach—PR                  6,485
     Lush oceanside course laced with lagoons.
     Ponte Vedra Inn guests only.
```

```
1 Jacksonville Beach G.C.               18/72
  Jacksonville Beach—PU                 6,350
     Good public course in beach town.
2 Ponce de Leon C.C.                    18/71
  St. Augustine—PR                      6,485
     Tight greens, well-trapped links. Hotel with
     convention facilities adjoins. Guests may play.
3 Fly-In Spruce Creek                   18/72
  Daytona Beach—SP                      6,800
     Fly-in golf resort at Spruce Creek Airport. Open
     Fall '74. Front 9 has water, back 9 wooded.
3 Daytona Beach G.C.                       36
  Daytona Beach—SP                       holes
     Four par-36 nines, interesting and tricky. Mo-
     tels nearby.
3 Ormond Beach                          18/71
  Ormond Beach—SP                       6,133
     Rolling terrain. Pro shop, swimming pool, rid-
     ing and tennis.
```

```
4 Sugar Mill C.C. & Estates             18/72
  New Smyrna Beach—SP                   6,550
     Joe Lee course in sand-pine country with tree-
     lined fairways and good elevations.
5 Royal Oak C.C. & Lodge                18/71
  Titusville—R                          6,615
     Challenging vacation course near Cape Ken-
     nedy. Deluxe lodge, condominiums adjoin.
6 Cocoa Beach G.C.                      18/72
  Cocoa Beach—MU                        6,768
     Minutes from beaches. Surrounded by Banana
     River.
7 John's Island Club                 36/72-71
  Vero Beach—PR                    6,582-6,400
     Two Pete Dye courses are tough, beautiful. Con-
     dominiums, homesites.
7 Riomar C.C.                           18/72
  Vero Beach—SP                         5,535
     Non-residents who are members of USGA-
     member clubs may play.
```

8 Indian Hills G. & C.C. — 18/72
Ft. Pierce—SP — 6,240
Rolling course among the sand dunes.

9 St. Lucie Hilton Inn & C.C. — 36/72-72
Port St. Lucie—R — 6,429-6,717
Saints and Sinners courses, both good. Water, tree-lined fairways. Also 18-hole par-3 course.

10 Martin County G. & C.C. — 18/71
Stuart—SP — 6,441
Well-established course with trees, greens slightly elevated.

11 Turtle Creek C. — 18/72
Tequesta—PR — 6,550
Residential community. Fine course designed by Joe Lee. Top condition.

12 Lost Tree Club — 18/72
Lost Tree Village—PR — 6,849
Beautiful course, 9 holes on ocean. Open to accredited club members.

12 JDM C.C. (formerly PGA National) — 54 holes
Palm Beach Gardens—PR
Three fine courses at site of 1971 PGA Championship. East course is toughest.

12 North Palm Beach C.C. — 18/71
North Palm Beach—SP — 6,575
Rolling terrain. Recently improved. Olympic-size swimming pool.

13 The President C.C. — 36/72-72
West Palm Beach—SP — 6,600-6,150
Two Bill Mitchell courses, including senior layout.

13 Palm Beach Lakes G.C. — 18/68
West Palm Beach—SP — 5,505
Tight course designed around two lakes, adjacent to Ramada Inn.

13 Breakers West G.C. — 18/71
West Palm Beach—SP — 6,388
First of two Willard Byrd courses for Breakers Hotel.

13 West Palm Beach G. & C.C. — 18/72
West Palm Beach—MU — 6,745
Excellent public course, steep bunkers, fast greens, disturbing rough.

14 Breakers Ocean G.C. — 18/70
Palm Beach—R — 6,008
Short but tough older course for guests at Breakers Hotel only.

14 Royal Palm Beach G. & C.C. — 18/72
Royal Palm Beach Village—PU — 6,452
Large greens, well trapped, fairway bunkers. Second 18 for this carefully planned community open in 1974. Inn adjoins.

15 Lake Worth G.C. — 18/70
Lake Worth—SP — 5,654
Pleasant, demanding short course with five holes along lake.

15 Palm Beach Nat'l G. & C.C. — 18/72
Lake Worth—SP — 6,575
Homesites surround course. Lots of water.

15 The Fountains of Palm Beach — 27/71-36
Lake Worth—PR — 7,042-3,575
Von Hagge-Devlin course in resort community. Water on 14 holes, 122 traps. Members, guests, prospective buyers.

16 Atlantis C.C. — 27/72-36
Lantana—R — 6,625-3,325
Scenic tree-lined course with accommodations at Atlantis Inn.

16 Cypress Creek C.C. — 18/72
Boynton Beach—SP — 6,808
Interesting layout. Condominium villas. Homes.

16 Delray Dunes G. & C.C. — 18/71
Boynton Beach—PR — 6,500
Clustered condominum villas and homesites. Pool, tennis.

16 Delray Beach C.C. — 27/72-36
Delray Beach—SP — 6,987-3,270
Courses suit both long and short hitters.

16 Quail Ridge — 18/71
Delray Beach—PR — 6,450
Designed by Joe Lee. Water, fairway bunkers, elevated greens.

16 The Hamlet — 18/72
Delray Beach—SP — 6,840
New course by Joe Lee has pines, palms and cypress trees, puts emphasis on playing strategy.

17 Deer Creek G. & C.C. — 18/72
Deerfield Beach—SP — 6,439
Unusually wooded and hilly for southern Florida.

17 Kimberly of Boca Raton — 18/72
Boca Raton—MU — 6,840
Open 1974 with 16 holes flanked by water. Tom Bolt, golf director.

---

17 Sandalfoot Cove G. & C.C. — 18/72
Boca Raton—SP — 6,874
Woods, water and sand. Homes and homesites.

17 University Park C.C. — 18/72
Boca Raton—SP — 6,589
Canals and lakes add to sporty character.

17 Southern Manor C.C. — 18/71
Boca Raton—SP — 6,836
Well-groomed course with fine elevated greens, water on 16 holes.

17 Boca Teeca G. & C.C. — 27/72-36
Boca Raton—R — 6,165-6,400
Fourth nine to be completed soon. 3rd course planned.

17 Boca Raton Hotel & C. — 27/71-29
Boca Raton —R — 6,500-2,000
Well-trapped throughout, three water holes. Condominium apartments.

17 Boca Raton West — 36/72-72
Boca Raton—R — 6,165-6,400
Desmond Muirhead courses in large resort community affiliated with Boca Raton Hotel.

18 Colony West C.C. — 18/72
Pompano Beach—SP — 6,686
Well wooded with water on 6 holes. Good challenge, designed by Von Hagge-Devlin.

18 Oriole Golf & Tennis C. — 18/72
Margate—SP — 6,400
Golf cars only, but have another 9 at 1,700 yards, par-30 for walking.

18 Broken Woods — 18/69
Coral Springs—PR — 5,238
West of Pompano. Narrow fairways, water hazards. Emphasis on accuracy, not length. Need introduction from member.

18 Pompano Beach G.C. — 36/72-72
Pompano Beach—SP — 6,753-6,275
Longer Pines course, narrow, water. Palms course more open.

18 World of Palm Aire — 72 holes
Pompano Beach—R
Huge resort development on 2,500-acre site. All activities, including health spa. 5th course planned.

18 The Woodlands C.C. — 36/72-72
Pompano Beach—SP — 6,955-6,750
Pleasant, well conditioned Robert Von Hagge layouts in resort complex.

18 Crystal Lago C.C. — 36/72-72
Pompano Beach—R — 6,884-6,780
Lodge adjoins. Four housing developments surround both layouts.

19 Jacaranda C.C. — 18/72
Plantation—SP — 6,900
First of 2 Mark Mahannah courses in real estate development.

19 Inverrary C.C. — 36/72-71
Lauderhill—SP — 6,444-6,715
Trent Jones courses in posh new development. Also 18-hole executive-length course.

19 Plantation G.C. — 18/72
Ft. Lauderdale—SP — 6,925
Winding streams come into play on most holes.

19 Lago Mar C.C. — 18/72
Ft. Lauderdale—PR — 6,750
Private course for members and guests of Lago Mar Hotel.

19 Bonaventure C.C. — 18/72
Ft. Lauderdale—SP — 6,515
Seigneurie course features par-3 over waterfall. Villas, townhouses, homesites.

19 Arrowhead C.C. — 18/71
Ft. Lauderdale—PR — 6,388
Condominium apartments flank fairways. Par-5s and par-3s are testing.

19 Sunrise C.C. — 18/72
Ft. Lauderdale—SP — 6,900
Water, rough and fairways skillfully blended. Bill Watts, architect.

19 Oak Ridge C.C. — 18/72
Ft. Lauderdale—SP — 6,517
Pleasant golf. Modern hotels nearby.

19 Rolling Hills Lodge & C.C. — 18/72
Ft. Lauderdale—R — 6,500
Lush, landscaped facility also has swimming, riding. 70-unit lodge.

20 Foxcroft G. & Tennis — 18/72
Hollywood—SP — 6,417
Excellent drainage. Playable after hardest rain.

20 Hollywood Lakes C.C. — 36/72-72
Hollywood—SP — 6,238-6,660
14 lakes, wooded rough. Fine condition. Holiday Inn adjoins.

---

20 Diplomat Resort & C.C. — 36/72-72
Hollywood—R — 6,552-6,702
Two championship courses. Presidential and Diplomat. Also par-3.

20 Hollywood Beach C.C. — 36/70-72
Hollywood—R — 6,479-6,350
On ocean. Newer 18 has island green.

20 Hillcrest East G. & C.C. — 27/72-33
Hollywood—PR — 6,725-2,300
High-rise apartments in park-like environment. Also executive nine by Mark Mahannah.

20 Orange Brook G.C. — 36/72-71
Hollywood—MU — 6,307-6,109
Many waterways; tropical foliage is plentiful.

20 Emerald Hills C.C. — 18/72
Hollywood—PR — 6,850
Lovely homesites surround testing Von Hagge layout.

20 Aventura G.C. — 18/72
Biscayne Village—SP — 6,377
New Trent Jones course, core of high-rise development. Julius Boros, host pro.

21 Normandy Shores G.C. — 18/71
Miami Beach—SP — 6,055
On Isle of Normandy in Biscayne Bay. Water everywhere.

21 Bay Shore Municipal — 18/72
Miami Beach—MU — 6,893
Von Hagge layout with rolling fairways, mounds and lakes.

22 Costa Del Sol G. & Racquet — 18/72
Miami—SP — 6,500
Challenging but not frustrating. 5,000 fruit trees.

22 Kendale Lakes G. & C.C. — 27/72-36
Miami—SP — 6,805-3,580
Sporty test—canals and lakes. 1974 LPGA Burdine's Invitational site and school.

22 Key Biscayne G.C. — 18/72
Key Biscayne—MU — 6,579
Unique Robert Von Hagge course laid out amid mangrove flats. Beautiful, eerie and tough test.

22 Le Jeune G.C. — 18/72
Miami—MU — 6,400
Gently rolling terrain. Near Miami Airport.

22 Miami Shores C.C. — 18/71
Miami Shores—PR — 6,473
Members and their guests only.

22 Miami Springs G. & C.C. — 18/71
Miami Springs—SP — 6,730
Former site of Miami Open.

22 North Dade G. & C.C. — 18/72
Miami—SP — 6,300
Layout richly landscaped with tropical palms.

22 C.C. of Miami — 63 holes
Miami—SP
Fine resort course and clubhouse. Newest 18 by Bill Dietsch. Homes, townhouses, homesites.

22 Miami Lakes Inn & C.C. — 36/72-54
Miami—SP — 6,700-2,185
Challenging courses with elevated tees and greens, wandering streams and lakes.

22 Doral Hotel & C.C. — 81 holes
Miami—R
Outstanding resort. Great golf. Gold Course is for men only. Blue course a great one.

22 King's Bay Yacht & C.C. — 18/72
Miami—PR — 6,834
Challenging scenic course open to members and hotel guests.

22 Palmetto G.C. — 18/71
South Miami—MU — 6,669
Canal runs through course which has wide fairways, 13 water holes.

22 Fontainebleau C.C. — 18/72
Miami—R — 6,800
Mark Mahannah course with seven lakes, rolling fairways.

22 Biltmore G.C. — 18/71
Coral Gables—MU — 6,563
Picturesque course in lush surroundings; some tricky water holes.

23 Redlands G. & C.C. — 18/72
Homestead—SP — 6,700
Well-maintained, contoured greens; well-conditioned.

23 Ocean Reef C. — 27/71-36
North Key Largo—PR — 6,324-3,313
Newly redesigned by Robert Von Hagge and Bruce Devlin.

24 Marco Island G.C. — 18/72
Marco Island—R — 6,650
Excellent resort course with complete facilities. Huge new hotel.

25 Palm River G. & C.C. 18/72
Naples—SP 6,575
Hard to handle what with well-conceived design, length.

25 Lely G. & C.C. 18/72
Naples—SP 6,201
Good enough test without being too tough on older legs.

25 Golden Gate C.C. 18/72
Naples—R 6,602
Has some contour, and good length. In development, with hotel.

25 Naples Golf & Beach C. 18/72
Naples—R 6,470
Doglegs, water, sand backbone layout. 18th is tough. Hotel adjoins.

26 Mirror Lakes C.C. 18/72
Lehigh Acres—R 6,722
Mark Mahannah course. Well-designed, rolling, demanding.

26 Lehigh Acres C.C. 18/72
Lehigh Acres—R 6,710
Scenic, wooded, sporty course amidst large development area.

27 Lochmoor C.C. 18/72
N. Fort Myers—SP 7,020
Bill Mitchell course opened late 1972. Pines, palms and lakes. Residential resort.

27 Cypress Lakes C.C. 18/72
Fort Myers—MU 6,430
Canal affects play on 16 holes of this scenic Dick Wilson course.

27 Fort Myers C.C. 18/71
Fort Myers—MU 6,105
Attractive Donald Ross course opened in 1918. Small greens, sporty.

27 Seven Lakes C.C. 18/60
Fort Myers—PR 4,115
Well-trapped course in condominium community. Open to residents and guests.

27 San Carlos Park G.C. 18/72
Fort Myers—SP 6,700
New course with 7 water holes, 7 miles south of Fort Myers.

28 Rotonda West G.C. 18/72
Rotonda West—R 6,622
First of seven courses in America's first city-in-the-round. Second course under construction.

28 Cape Coral C.C. 18/72
Cape Coral—R 6,827
107 bunkers, much water on good Dick Wilson course. Hotel adjoins.

29 Punta Gorda C.C. 18/72
Punta Gorda—PR 6,000
Tricky course with small greens in natural setting. Seasonal memberships available.

29 Punta Gorda Isles G.C. 18/71
Punta Gorda—PR 6,850
Cut through orange grove in development.

30 Port Charlotte C.C. 18/71
Port Charlotte—SP 6,643
Established course with tall trees everywhere. Doglegs rampant.

30 C.C. of No. Port Charlotte 18/72
No. Port Charlotte—SP 6,700
Contoured fairways. Lots of water. Affiliated with Ramada Inn in Port Charlotte.

31 Englewood C.C. 18/71
Englewood—SP 6,412
Several man-made lakes make this course interesting.

32 Mission Valley G. & C.C. 18/72
Venice—PR 6,438
Open course but has some contour, well-placed bunkers.

32 Lake Venice G.C. 18/72
Venice—MU 6,902
Long test with challenging 17th, 18th holes.

33 South Seas Plantation 9/36
Captiva Island—R 3,150
6 holes on Gulf, 3 on Island in Bay. 59 traps. Scenic.

34 El Conquistador G. & C.C. 18/72
Bradenton—R 6,771
Mark Mahannah course on Sarasota Bay opened fall 1973. Pines, water, apartments and condos.

34 Forest Lakes C.C. 18/71
Sarasota—PR 6,050
Full facility family country club. Guests of members are welcome.

34 Sarasota G.C. 18/72
Sarasota—SP 6,900
Long course but not too severely bunkered.

34 Palma Sola G.C. 18/71
Palma Sola—SP 6,352
North of Sarasota. Set amidst citrus groves, lakes and streams.

34 Longboat Key G.C. 18/72
Sarasota—R 6,890
Twisting fairways, numerous water hazards. Fabulous clubhouse. Lido Biltmore guests may play.

34 Bobby Jones G.C. 36/72-72
Sarasota—MU 6,388-6,080
Heavily played by 1,400 members and tourists. Steep bunkers. Trees.

34 Rolling Green G.C. 18/72
Sarasota—SP 6,500
Good length but flat, wide open. Comfortable course. Restaurant.

34 Palm Aire West C.C. 18/72
Sarasota—SP 6,927
Formerly DeSoto Lakes course, re-worked late '69.

34 Sun City G.C. 18/72
Sun City Center—SP 6,875
Mature trees line fairly wide fairways; 8 holes with water.

34 Sunrise National G.C. 18/72
Sarasota—SP 6,523
R. A. Anderson course carved from pine and palm jungle. 240-yard 6th a real beaut.

35 Placid Lakes G. & C.C. 18/71
Lake Placid—R 6,433
Boating, fishing, swimming pool, entertainment nightly. Hotel adjoins.

36 Harder Hall Hotel 18/72
Sebring—R 6,793
Dick Wilson course with 7 lakes, trees. Summer golf camp. Pool, tennis, entertainment.

36 Kenilworth Lodge & G.C. 18/72
Sebring—R 6,600
Fairly open course with large greens.

37 Rogers Park G.C. 18/71
Tampa—MU 6,677
Well-kept public course with good length.

37 U. of So. Fla. G.C. 18/72
Tampa—SP 6,962
Fine course, surrounded by swamp. Tight par-5 14th a "monster."

37 Pebble Creek G. & C.C. 18/72
Tampa—SP 6,147
Creek wanders through relatively flat course. Fair enough test.

37 Quail Hollow G.C. 18/72
Tampa—SP 6,739
18 natural lakes. Alligator "Olly" eats from your hand. Lounge, snack bar, practice range.

37 Rocky Point G.C. 27/72-36
Tampa—SP 6,122-2,456
Narrow fairways with out-of-bounds everywhere. Trees, water, some sand.

38 Bardmoor C.C. 27/72-36
St. Petersburg—SP 6,800-3,285
Real "19th hole" for special events. Homesites and condominiums.

38 Airco Flight 18 G.C. 18/72
St. Petersburg—SP 6,100
Flat course near airport. 3rd 9 in works.

38 Pasadena G.C. 18/71
St. Petersburg—SP 6,226
"Old-fashioned" open fairways, tiny greens. Walter Hagen was first pro.

38 Seminole C.C. 18/72
St. Petersburg—SP 6,500
Tight course with numerous out-of-bounds areas, water hazards.

38 Sunset G.C. 18/71
St. Petersburg—SP 6,288
Oldest city course in area. Minarets on interesting clubhouse. Open to guests of Vinoy Park Hotel.

38 Tides Inn & Country Club 18/72
St. Petersburg—R 6,400
Beautiful and challenging course. Four holes surrounded by water—trees and lagoons.

39 Tampa Airport Resort Golf & Racquet Club 18/72
Clearwater—PU 6,625
Flat course adjoining property of Tampa Airport. 11 water holes, many traps on open island.

39 Clearwater C.C. 18/72
Clearwater—SP 6,100
Well-bunkered. Creek runs through back nine.

39 Cove Cay G. & T.C. 18/70
Clearwater—SP 5,796
David Wallace course in recreation-condominium community.

39 Belleview-Biltmore Hotel & G.C. 54
Clearwater—R holes
Creek wanders through rolling East & West courses, set atop bluff. Top condition. Open Jan.-mid-April. West and Pelican courses open year-round. Grand resort hotel.

40 Dunedin C.C. 18/72
Dunedin—SP 6,600
Former PGA National course, interestingly designed. 4 water holes.

41 Innisbrook G. & C.C. Island: 18/72
Tarpon Springs—PR 6,745
Heavily wooded, hilly and a great test in private resort. Mike Souchak, pro.
Sandpiper: 18/71 5,900
Copperhead: 18/71 6,800
Sandpiper tough short course. Copperhead tough tournament course. Each has separate clubhouse.

42 Errol Estate Inn & C.C. 18/72
Apopka—R 6,800
Joe Lee course with big bunkers, oak, pine and wild plum trees on rolling terrain.

42 Poinciana Golf & Racquet C. 18/72
Kissimmee—SP 6,997
Devlin-Von Hagge course opened 1973. Built in and around a cypress hammock. Trees and water.

42 Sheoah G.C. 18/72
Winter Springs—PU 6,550
Testing and picturesque daily fee course surrounded by residential community. Some extremely tough holes.

42 Winter Springs G.C. 18/72
Winter Springs—PR 6,360
Superbly laid out by Joe Lee in rolling parkland on old estate.

42 Bay Hill Club 27/72-36
Dr. Phillips—R 6,347-3,500
Superb Dick Wilson course with lodge. Great golfing atmosphere. Arnold Palmer is owner.

42 Alhambra G. & C.C. 18/72
Orlando—MU 6,750
1,500 apartments. Driving range has closed-circuit TV to view swing.

42 Cypress Creek G.C. 18/72
Orlando—SP 6,465
Fairly wide open and flat, but water lurks off 16 holes. Fine clubhouse. Guests of affiliated hotels may play.

42 Walt Disney World G.C. 54
Lake Buena Vista—R holes
Two distinct styles designed by Joe Lee. Magnolia course is longer and more open. Palm course shorter, tighter. Buena Vista newest.

42 Deltona G. & C.C. 18/72
Deltona—SP 6,689
One of region's finest tests, this David Wallace design winds through hills and pines. Deltona Inn nearby.

42 Mission Inn & C.C. 18/70
Howey-in-the-Hills—R 6,122
Beautifully conditioned course winds among four lakes. Attractive Spanish-style inn, restaurant and convention center.

43 Mayfair C.C. 18/72
Sanford—SP 6,400
Good parkland layout formerly owned by N.Y. Giants. Holiday Inn nearby.

44 Silver Lake G. & C.C. 18/72
Leesburg—SP 6,403
Rolling, difficult course with especially testing par-3s.

44 Wildwood C.C. 18/72
Wildwood—R 6,274
New Ronald Garl layout with tree-lined fairways. Camping facilities.

45 Plantation Hotel C.C. 18/72
Crystal River—R 6,838
No parallel holes on Mark Mahannah course; long tees, water. Hotel.

46 Williston Highlands G.C. 18/72
Williston Highlands—SP 6,446
Wide fairways. Rolls through oaks and pines in housing development.

47 Silver Springs Shores C.C. 18/71
Ocala—SP 6,745
80 acres of lakes on this rolling Muirhead creation. Panorama Inn adjoins.

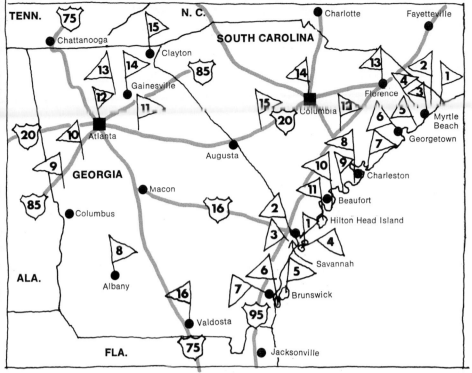

Georgia

1 Savannah Inn & C.C. — 18/72
Wilmington Island—R — 6,750
Well-designed, lush course, with lots of variety. Fair and testing.

2 Bacon Park G.C. — 18/71
Savannah—MU — 6,318
Well-trapped, with few hazards. Surrounded with woods. Flat.

2 Savannah G.C. — 18/70
Savannah—SP — 6,291
Large greens and narrow, tree-lined fairways. Six doglegs.

3 Henry Ford Plantation — 18/72
Richmond Hill—R — 6,500
Scheduled to be home of LPGA. Open fall '74.

4 The Landings — 18/72
Skidaway Island—R — 6,600
Palmer-Duane resort development course on wooded island.

4 Skidaway Island Plantation — 18/72
Skidaway Island—R — 7,000
Bill Byrd course to open mid '73. Dense oak and pine wooded.

5 St. Simons Island G.C. — 18/72
St. Simons Island—R — 6,800
Fine Joe Lee course. Open fall '74. On ocean, but well wooded.

5 Sea Palms G. & C.C. — 18/72
St. Simons Island—R — 6,765
Very scenic; water holes; beautiful oaks, tall pines, inn and villas. Condominiums.

5 Sea Island G.C. — 36
St. Simons Island—R — holes
Spectacular site on old plantation; accommodations at Cloister Hotel. Superb links at one of America's great resorts.

6 Jekyll Island G.C. — 45
Jekyll Island—R — holes
Fine courses, inexpensive. Daily fees or package at 5 motels. Formerly millionaires' hideaway.

7 Brunswick C.C. — 18/72
Brunswick—SP — 6,500
Flat, coastal course built around five small lakes.

8 Radium Springs C.C. — 18/72
Albany—R — 6,125
Some tricky left and right doglegs.

9 Callaway Gardens — 63
Pine Mountain—R — holes
Outstanding resort with complete facilities. Holiday Inn, cottages on premises.

10 Canongate G.C. — 18/72
Palmetto—SP — 6,365
Gently rolling course with wide fairways. Not too tough but nice test. Great practice range.

11 Hard Labor Creek G.C. — 18/72
Rutledge—R — 6,308
Well-equipped state park with cottages, mobile homes, camping. Enjoyable course with four water holes.

12 Stone Mountain Park G.C. — 18/70
Stone Mountain—MU — 6,831
Tough Trent Jones mountainside layout in 3,800-acre Confederate memorial park.

12 Adams Park G.C. — 18/72
Atlanta—MU — 6,600
Good layout, but sometimes crowded.

12 North Fulton G.C. — 18/71
Atlanta—MU — 6,600
Former site of Atlanta Open. Good layout in spotty condition.

12 Browns Mill G.C. — 18/72
Atlanta—MU — 6,535
Rolling George Cobb course surrounded by 5 lakes. Open year-round.

12 Snapfinger G.C. — 18/72
Snapfinger—SP — 6,400
Joe Lee layout opened in 1972 as part of huge new development.

12 East Lake C.C. — 18/72
Atlanta—PR — 6,515
Fine old Donald Ross course where Bobby Jones learned to play. Open to guests of certain hotels.

12 Bobby Jones G.C. — 18/71
Atlanta—MU — 6,300
Tough and hilly. Creek crosses course five times.

12 Mystery Valley G.C. — 18/72
Atlanta—MU — 6,628
Good Dick Wilson course in rolling terrain and thick pine forest.

12 Fairington G. & T.C. — 18/72
Atlanta—PR — 6,400
Rees Jones course surrounded by condominium apartments. Interesting test.

13 Canongate-on-Lanier G.C. — 18/72
Cumming—SP — 6,330
Rolling, wooded Joe Lee course with plenty of variety and challenge.

14 Chattahoochee G.C. — 18/72
Gainesville—MU — 6,535
Tree-lined fairways. In foothills of Blue Ridge Mountains.

15 Kingswood C.C. — 18/70
Clayton—PR — 5,785
Small resort with spectacular scenery in mountains. Guests of hotels may play.

16 Francis Lake C.C. — 18/72
Valdosta—R — 6,800
Willard Byrd course in 350-acre resort development. Lodging nearby.

South Carolina

1 Cypress Bay G.C. — 18/72
North Myrtle Beach—PU — 6,502
Russ Breeden course opened summer '72. Championship with many lakes and streams.

1 Eagle's Nest G.C. — 18/72
North Myrtle Beach—SP — 6,900
Open to guests of member motels. No. 16 doglegs across beautiful lake.

1 Bay Tree Golf Plantation — Gold: 18/72 6,527
Myrtle Beach—R — Green: 18/72 6,426
— Silver: 18/72 6,280
Three courses designed by George Fazio and Russell Breeden. Accommodates beginner to expert. Complete facilities.

2 Beachwood G.C. — 18/72
North Myrtle Beach—R — 6,730
High handicapper's delight. Not demanding, fun. Double-dogleg 14th unique.

2 Azalea Sands G.C. — 18/72
N. Myrtle Beach—PU — 6,165
Gene Hamm course on Highway #17 in city limits. Two blocks from ocean. Lodging facilities nearby.

2 Robber's Roost G.C. — 18/72
Ocean Drive Beach—R — 6,440
Challenging design. Water a constant threat. Lengthy par-5s make it tough.

2 Possum Trot G.C. — 18/72
Crescent Beach—R — 6,966
Not overly difficult, but enjoyable. Water guards four greens.

2 Surf G.C. — 18/72
Ocean Drive Beach—R — 6,740
Most greens permit run-up approaches. Interesting. Par-3 18th outstanding.

3 Arcadian Shores G. Club — 18/72
Arcadian Shores—PU — 7,080
Rees Jones course open summer 1974. Water courses and lakes. Many trees, seashore sandhills. Hilton Hotel complex.

3 Pine Lakes International C.C. — 18/72
Myrtle Beach—R — 6,680
Narrow pine-lined fairways, small greens. You must play carefully.

3 Myrtlewood G.C. — 18/72
Myrtle Beach—R — 6,510
Left-to-right doglegs abound. Trees special obstacles. Tennis. Building second 18.

3 Deer Track C.C. — 18/72
Myrtle Beach—PR — 6,650
J. P. Gibson course open summer '74. Guests of member motels may play.

3 Dunes G. & Beach C. — 18/72
Myrtle Beach—R — 6,450
One of nation's best. Many elevated greens. You'll love dogleg 13th.

4 Myrtle Beach National G. Club — 18/72
Myrtle Beach—PU — 6,950
Duane-Palmer course on sand pine ridge with lakes.

4 Quail Creek G.C. — 18/72
Myrtle Beach—SP — 6,238
Big flat greens invite good scores. Several water hazards.

5 Sea Gull G.C. — 18/72
Pawley's Island—R — 6,910
Good layout. Back nine rolls. 12th has two greens.

5 Litchfield C.C. — 18/72
Litchfield Beach—R — 6,751
Tight fairways, numerous water hazards. Most green entrances wide open.

6 Wedgefield C.C. — 18/72
Georgetown—R — 6,571
Tait-Toski-Gibson course on the Black River. Open spring '74.

7 Snee Farm — 18/72
Charleston—R — 6,800
George Cobb course. Homesites and villas. Par 3 11th a beaut. Seawater lagoon.

7 Charleston G.C. — 18/72
Charleston—MU — 6,350
Narrow fairways provide the challenge. Flat, few traps.

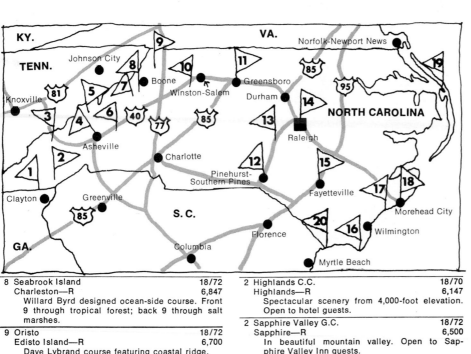

10 Tanglewood Park G.C.   36/72-72
Clemmons—SP   6,480-6,057
     Also has 18-hole par-3 lighted course. Lodge in park-like setting. Site of 1974 PGA.

10 Bermuda Run   18/72
Clemmons—PR   6,427
     Fine new Ellis Maples course in private resort-home complex, next-door to Tanglewood.

11 Green Valley G.C.   18/71
Greensboro—SP   6,200
     Lush course. Fine clubhouse with hotels, motels nearby.

11 Pine Tree G.C.   18/71
Kernersville—PU   6,589
     Well trapped and pretty. Lodging nearby. Gene Hamm course.

12 Seven Lakes G.C.   18/72
West End—SP   6,865
     Blend of traditional and modern design by Peter Tufts on rolling sand hills. Six miles west of Pinehurst in new resort community. Open Nov. 1974.

12 Pinehurst C.C.   90
Pinehurst—R   holes
     Outstanding golf complex. Open to guests of nearby inns. No. 2 course one of 10 best in U.S.

12 Mid Pines Club   18/72
Southern Pines—R   6,628
     Donald Ross-designed layout. New clubhouse.

12 Pine Needles Lodge & C.C.   18/72
Southern Pines—R   6,905
     Rolling, Donald Ross course at complete resort. Cozy accommodations.

12 Whispering Pines G.C.   36/72-71
Whispering Pines—SP   6,172-6,358
     On 3,000-acre community development.

12 Foxfire G. & C.C.   18/71
Pinehurst—SP   6,644
     Lush, rolling course adjoining Foxfire Inn. Private airport.

12 Southern Pines C.C.   18/71
Southern Pines—SP   6,425
     Relatively hilly, interesting doglegs, water on four holes.

12 Highland Hills   18/72
Southern Pines—R   6,425
     Tom Jackson course part of Whispering Pines Motor Lodge. 13 mile skyline view.

13 Carolina Trace C.C.   18/72
Sanford—SP   6,600
     Wooded layout by Trent Jones along 300-acre lake. Guests welcome.

14 Eagle Crest G.C.   18/71
Raleigh—MU   6,253
     Bent grass greens. Wide fairways, water hazards.

15 Cypress Lake G.C.   18/72
Fayetteville—MU   7,240
     Motels nearby. Green fees, electric golf cars.

16 Oak Island G.C.   18/72
Southport—R   6,608
     Lovely, seaside course. Open year-round. Lodging nearby.

17 Star Hill G. & C.C.   18/71
Cape Carteret—SP   6,837
     Part of new residential resort-community. Third nine planned.

18 Brandywine Bay C.C.   18/72
Moorehead City—R   6,900
     Open summer 1974, by Von Hagge-Devlin on beautiful bay.

19 Duck Woods G.C.   18/72
Kitty Hawk—SP   6,599
     Ellis Maples course on Outer Banks amid lagoons and lakes.

19 Sea Scape   18/71
Kitty Hawk—SP   6,122
     A true links built on dunes overlooking Atlantic Ocean, and a pure delight to play.

20 Carolina Shores G.C.   18/72
Calabash—SP   6,871
     T. Jackson course intertwines resort development. Open mid-1974.

Maryland

1 Ocean Pines G. & C.C.   18/72
Ocean City—R   6,625
     Trent Jones course for guests of Ocean City hotels. Billy Casper, touring pro.

2 Needwood G.C.   18/71
Rockville—MU   6,701
     Rolling, 2 lake holes, trees, big greens.

---

8 Seabrook Island   18/72
Charleston—R   6,847
     Willard Byrd designed ocean-side course. Front 9 through tropical forest; back 9 through salt marshes.

9 Oristo   18/72
Edisto Island—R   6,700
     Dave Lybrand course featuring coastal ridge.

10 Fripp Island G. & C.C.   18/72
Fripp Island—R   6,850
     Excellent seaside course by George Cobb; lagoons, many trees.

10 Royal Pines C.C.   36/72-72
Beaufort—PR   7,140-6,470
     Picturesque, well-treed, some water. In resort development. Some condominiums for rent.

11 Hilton Head Plantation   18/72
Hilton Head Island—R   6,600
     Designed by Ron Kirby and Gary Player. Open early '74.

11 Sea Pines Plantation G.C.   72
Hilton Head Island—R   holes
     Fine resort; Harbour Town Links site of Heritage Classic. Hilton Head Inn, fairway homes, condominiums adjoin.

11 Port Royal Plantation G.C.   27/72-36
Hilton Head Island—R   6,424-3,271
     Fourth 9 due '74 at this picturesque resort. Excellent facilities.

11 Palmetto Dunes   36
Hilton Head Island—R   holes
     Challenging Jones course. New Fazio course is tremendous. Bob Toski, golf director.

11 Hilton Head G.C.   18/72
Hilton Head Island—R   7,003
     This fine course available to guests of adjacent Adventure Inn. Full facility resort.

12 Santee-Cooper   18/72
Santee—R   6,800
     Overlooks huge Lake Marion. Also 18-hole executive length course.

13 C.C. of South Carolina   18/72
Florence—PR   6,611
     Varied course, many bunkers. Visitors may play.

14 Coldstream C.C.   18/71
Columbia—R   6,430
     Amid woodlands and tumbling streams. Truly beautiful.

15 Palmetto C.C.   18/72
Aiken—SP   6,365
     Handsome course. Quite hilly with many elevated tees and greens.

15 Midland Valley C.C.   18/72
Aiken—SP   6,823
     Rolling fairways, big trees and greens. Motels nearby.

North Carolina

1 Chatuge Shores   18/72
Hayesville—MU   6,792
     View of lake and mountains. Large greens. Motel planned.

2 High Hampton Inn & C.C.   18/71
Cashiers—R   5,904
     Gently rolling with beautiful mountain views. A pleasure to play.

---

2 Highlands C.C.   18/70
Highlands—R   6,147
     Spectacular scenery from 4,000-foot elevation. Open to hotel guests.

2 Sapphire Valley G.C.   18/72
Sapphire—R   6,500
     In beautiful mountain valley. Open to Sapphire Valley Inn guests.

3 Waynesville C.C. Inn   18/71
Waynesville—SP   6,015
     Hotel and dining room open. May-Oct. Few bunkers, 2 water holes.

3 Maggie Valley C.C.   18/71
Maggie Valley—SP   6,431
     A 52-unit motor lodge, offering year-round golf special, adjoins course. Villas available.

4 Beaver Lake G.C.   18/72
Asheville—R   6,556
     Bent greens. Has longest par-5 hole in country at 690 yards.

5 Wolf Laurel G.C.   18/72
Wolf Laurel—R   6,431
     Year round vacation retreat in laurel and rhododendron valley at 4,300 ft. Highest hole east of the Rockies.

6 Black Mountain G.C.   18/71
Black Mountain—R   6,837
     No. 17 hole is world's longest at 745 yards, par-6. Open year-round.

6 C.C. of the Mountains   18/72
Lake Lure—R   6,805
     Water and woods make this a challenging test. Not overly hilly. Excellent greens.

7 Beech Mountain G.C.   18/72
Banner Elk—R   6,474
     Highest course east of Rockies. Chalet rentals, 3 mountaintop inns.

7 Grandfather G. & C.C.   18/72
Linville—R   6,880
     At base of Grandfather Mtn. Long, tough and beautiful.

7 Linville G.C.   18/72
Linville—R   6,750
     Fine course high in mountains. Eseeola Lodge adjoins.

8 Seven Devils Resort   18/71
Boone—R   6,300
     Lodge, cottages planned. Surrounded by building sites.

8 Boone G.C.   18/71
Boone—PU   6,388
     Good standby resort course. Short, but challenging. Open Apr.-Nov.

8 Blowing Rock C.C.   18/70
Blowing Rock—R   6,100
     Tricky, windy mountain course with small greens, narrow fairways. Motels nearby.

8 Hound Ears Lodge C.C.   18/72
Blowing Rock—R   6,359
     Fine scenic resort course with streams, lakes and a few hills.

9 High Meadows G.C.   18/72
Roaring Gap—R   6,650
     Rolling terrain and lakes characterize this mountain layout.

9 Roaring Gap G. & C.C.   18/72
Roaring Gap—R   6,400
     Scenic mountain course open to guests of nearby Graystone Inn.

2 Northwest Park G.C. — 18/72
Wheaton—MU — 7,320
  Rolling, narrow, wooded course, 68 bunkers.

2 Washingtonian G.C. — 36/72-70
Gaithersburg—PR — 6,400-6,640
  Rolling, wooded, four large lakes. Motel has 100 rooms.

3 Hunt Valley Inn & G.C. — 18/72
Hunt Valley—SP — 6,588
  Open to Inn guests. Carol Mann assistant golf director.

3 Pine Ridge G.C. — 18/72
Lutherville—MU — 6,820
  Many doglegs, much water. One of the finest public courses anywhere.

4 Dwight D. Eisenhower G.C. — 18/71
Annapolis—SP — 6,900
  Many doglegs, much water.

5 Martingham G.C. — 18/71
St. Michaels—SP — 6,700
  Pete Dye's front 9 wide, links-type checkered with traps, back 9 through woods.

West Virginia

1 The Greenbrier — 54
White Sulphur Springs—R — holes
  Three scenic courses at stately, plush resort. Sam Snead head pro.

2 Lakeview C.C. — 18/72
Morgantown—PR — 6,650
  Tough course. Open to guests of adjoining Lakeview Inn.

3 Canaan Valley G.C. — 18/72
Dryfork—R — 6,300
  State-owned golf and ski resort in highlands. Cabins and camping.

4 Pipestem G.C. — 18/72
Pipestem—R — 6,215
  Scenic course amid lakes, hills and valleys. State park resort with lodge. Also 18-hole par-3 layout.

4 Glade Springs — 18/72
Beckly—PR — 6,584
  Condo villas and wooded homesites surround rolling George Cobb creation.

5 Oglebay Park Speidel G.C. — 18/71
Wheeling—PU — 6,500
  R. T. Jones toughie.

Virginia

1 The Homestead — 54
Hot Springs—R — holes
  Three great courses of varying difficulty. Upper Cascades a gem. One of America's great resorts.

2 Ole Monterey G.C. — 18/71
Roanoke—SP — 6,387
  Front nine hilly, back level. Motels nearby.

2 Lakeview G. & C.C. — 18/66
Roanoke—R — 5,000
  Tight and rolling with five par-3s. Motel, cottages, apartments.

3 Golden Horseshoe G.C. — 18/71
Williamsburg—R — 6,750
  Tough Trent Jones test in Colonial Williamsburg restored town. Also short 9-holer. Williamsburg Inn adjoins.

3 Kingsmill G.C. — 18/71
Williamsburg—R — 6,900
  Pete Dye course in 3,000-acre resort development. Open late '74.

4 Red Wing Lake G.C. — 18/72
Virginia Beach—MU — 6,387
  George Cobb course with large greens. Water on 11 holes. Motels nearby.

4 Cavalier G. & Yacht C. — 18/69
Virginia Beach—PR — 6,065
  Short, well-groomed course, water holes, elevated tees.

4 Kempsville Meadow G. & C.C. — 18/72
Virginia Beach—SP — 6,900
  Wooded, with interesting water holes, fine greens.

4 White Sands G. & C.C. — 18/71
Virginia Beach—SP — 6,500
  Tight, well-bunkered. Motel adjoins club.

4 Bide-A-Wee G.C. — 18/72
Portsmouth—SP — 6,331
  Very wooded. 13 doglegs, 6 water holes. Chandler Harper owner and host pro.

4 Lake Wright G.C. — 18/70
Norfolk—R — 6,131
  Fairly straight course built around Lake Wright. Motel adjoins.

5 The Tides Inn G.C. — 18/72
Irvington—R — 6,505
  Tree-lined, narrow fairways, with many twists, turns and dips. Water on 9 holes.

6 Sheraton Fredericksburg G.C. — 18/72
Fredericksburg—PU — 6,650
  Nice Edmund Ault course, just off Route 95. Large greens, long par 80. Motor lodge.

6 Bryce Mountain Resort — 18/71
Basye—R — 6,320
  Another Ed Ault course in all-season resort. Condos and rentals. 2,500 ft. landing strip.

7 Shenvallee Lodge & G.C. — 18/70
New Market—R — 5,758
  Weekend player's course. Few trees. Small hotel, motel adjoin.

8 Ingleside Augusta G.C. — 18/72
Staunton—R — 6,609
  Rolling terrain. Straight, beautifully conditioned.

Pennsylvania

1 Riverside Inn & C.C. — 18/70
Cambridge Springs—R — 6,104
  Lush, demanding course. Fine old resort inn.

2 Indian Lake G. & C.C. — 9/36
Indian Lake—SP — 3,250
  Arnold Palmer design, his first. Motel, private airstrip adjoin.

2 Seven Springs G.C. — 18/71
Champion—R — 6,685
  Spectacular views, course cut out of woods in resort development. Five-million-dollar lodge.

3 Bedford Springs Hotel & G.C. — 18/74
Bedford Springs—R — 6,753
  Scenic layout in Allegheny Mountains. Also pitch 'n putt course.

4 Hershey C.C. — 36/73-71
Hershey—R — 6,696-6,515
  Older West course, rugged and beautiful. New East course a bear when stretched to 7,240 yards. Hotel guests and members only.

4 Parkview G.C. — 18/70
Hershey—SP — 6,135
  Fine public layout. Twice site of National Publinx tournament.

4 Hotel Hershey G.C. — 9/34
Hershey—R — 2,680
  Pleasant, easy course next to hotel. Wooded. Hotel guests only.

4 Spring Creek G.C. — 9/36
Hershey—SP — 2,316
  Spring Creek wanders through fairly flat course. Accent on short game.

5 Host Farm Resort — 18/72
Lancaster—R — 6,250
  Gently rolling fairways, good water holes. Also very good 9-hole executive-length course.

5 Overlook G.C. — 18/70
Lancaster—SP — 6,200
  Fairly level, well-bunkered course with many beautiful old willow trees.

6 Downingtown Inn G.C. — 18/72
Downingtown—R — 6,975
  Course in good condition. Inn guests only. Some roll, good par-3s.

6 Malvern G.C. — 18/71
Downingtown—SP — 6,365
  Open year-round. Flat first nine, rolling back nine.

6 Ingleside G.C. — 18/72
Thorndale—SP — 6,795
  Open, rolling course with water on 9 holes.

7 Tamiment Resort & C.C. — 18/72
Tamiment—R — 6,538
  Rolling, challenging Trent Jones layout. Stretches to 7,110 yards. Splendid hotel.

7 Vacation Valley — 9/35
Echo Lake—R — 3,000
  Sporty course, tee off from side of mountain on two holes. Complete resort facilities. Nine holes being added.

7 Mt. Manor Inn & G.C. — 27/71-36
Marshall's Creek—R — 6,350-3,206
  Flat, wide open course. Water on 7 holes. Newer 9 hilly. Also 2 par-27 executive-length nines.

7 Shawnee Inn & C.C. — 27/72-36
Shawnee-on-Delaware—R — 6,540-3,135
  Fred Waring's pleasant golf spa amid mountain scenery. Tricky and testing.

7 Glenbrook C.C. — 18/72
Stroudsburg—SP — 6,535
  Sporty course with small greens, some water.

7 Fernwood G.C. — 27/72-29
Bushkill—R — 6,700-1,000
  Elaborate year-round resort. Open to guests 'n hotel.

8 Skytop Lodge — 18/71
Skytop—PR — 6,370
  Sporty, with lovely view. Strictly for members and lodge guests.

8 Buck Hill Inn & G.C. — 27/72-34
Buck Hill Falls—R — 6,295-3,070
  Pleasant, rolling layout amid trees and beautiful scenery.

8 Mo-Nom-O-Nock Inn G.C. — 9/35
Mountainhome—R — 3,015
  Hilly course overlooking scenic valley. No golf cars.

8 Pocono Manor Inn & G.C. — 36/72-72
Pocono Manor—R — 6,295-6,675
  East course very picturesque. West course plays tougher. No bunkers.

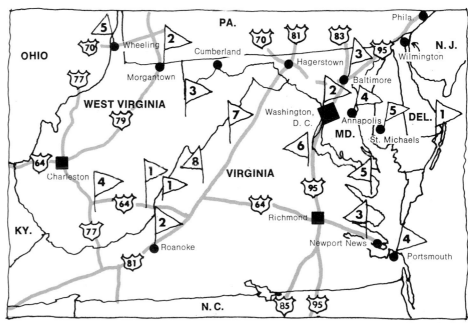

8 Pocono Farms C.C.   9/36
   Tobyhanna—R   3,200
     New course designed by Art Wall, surrounds lake. Second nine under construction. Golf house. Many accommodations nearby.

9 Le Chateau C.C.   18/72
   White Haven—R   6,675
     Rolling Geoffrey Cornish course near hotel. 8 water holes.

10 Shadowbrook C.C.   18/70
   Tunkhannock—SP   5,655
     Motel accommodations. Situated along creek in Endless Mountains.

11 Standing Stone Public G.C.   18/70
   Huntingdon—PU   6,698
     Designed by Geoffrey Cornish with a number of lakes.

12 Toftrees C.C. & Lodge   18/73
   State College—R   7,880
     Edmund Ault design carved out of central Pennsylvania's rolling woodland.

New Jersey

1 Atlantis C.C.   18/72
   Tuckerton—R   6,575
     Long, narrow fairways, big greens, four water holes. Motel adjoins.

2 Playboy Club Hotel   27/70-35
   Great Gorge (McAfee)—R   6,905-3,350
     Spectacular George Fazio course in gently rolling mountain valley with dramatic quarry holes. Plush 700-room hotel.

New York

1 Thousand Islands Club   18/72
   Alexandria Bay—R   6,433
     Scottish-type course in St. Lawrence area. Atmosphere relaxed.

2 Whiteface Inn G.C.   18/72
   Lake Placid—R   6,445
     Rolling, hilly course in Adirondacks. Tight wooded fairways.

3 7 Keys G.C.   18/70
   Loon Lake—R   5,600
     Sporty course with resort accommodations in Adirondack Mts.

4 Saratoga Spa G.C.   18/72
   Saratoga Springs—MU   6,319
     Fine test. Also short 9-hole course.

5 Sagamore G.C.   18/72
   Bolton Landing—R   6,400
     Old, well-preserved resort on Lake George. Open in summer only.

6 Stevensville C.C.   18/72
   Swan Lake—R   6,470
     Several water holes and many bunkers. Very scenic. Good test.

6 Grossinger Hotel & G.C.   27/71-36
   Grossinger—R   6,406-3,186
     Year-round mountain resort. Re-done by Joe Finger with some great holes.

6 Lochmor G.C.   18/71
   Loch Sheldrake—SP   6,470
     Well-conceived layout, beautiful scenery. Two holes are hilly.

6 Kutsher's Hotel & C.C.   18/72
   Monticello—R   6,638
     Fairly narrow Bill Mitchell layout in rolling forest.

6 Tennanah Lake G.C.   18/72
   Roscoe—R   6,750
     Hotel resort course.

6 Concord Hotel   45
   Kiamesha Lake—R   holes
     Championship 18, one of world's toughest, stretches to 7,600 yards. Fine entertainment.

6 Tarry Brae G.C.   18/72
   So. Fallsburgh—MU   6,615
     Tough course in pastureland and forest overlooking scenic Echo Lake.

6 Nevele Hotel & C.C.   18/71
   Ellenville—R   6,390
     Pleasant resort course. 400-yard 18th hole built along lake.

7 Dyker Beach G.C.   18/71
   Brooklyn—MU   6,502
     Most famous of New York's public courses. Gets heavy play.

8 Bethpage State Park   90
   Farmingdale, L.I.—MU   holes
     Variety of state-owned courses. Black course toughest.

9 The Otesaga   18/72
   Cooperstown—R   6,372
     Interesting course adjoining resort facilities with inn and cottages.

10 River Oaks C.C.   18/72
   Grand Island—SP   6,400
     Desmond Muirhead course in resort complex. Hotel planned.

10 Ransom Oaks C.C.   18/72
   Amherst—PU   6,315
     Flat Robert Trent Jones course near Buffalo with large lakes. Stretches to 6,880 yards.

11 Bergen Point G.C.   18/72
   Bergen Point—PU   7,030
     Bill Mitchell course. Lodging facilities nearby.

11 Riverton G.C.   18/72
   Henrietta—PU   6,800
     Ed Ault course open summer '74. Large greens. Trees and lakes.

12 Montauk G. & Racquet C.   18/72
   Montauk—PR   6,860
     Resort with true links-type course, wind. Villas available.

Connecticut

1 Heritage Village C.C.   18/72
   Southbury—R   6,300
     Comfortable, rolling course in retirement development. Modern inn.

2 Tunxis Plantation C.C.   27/72-36
   Farmington—SP   6,685-3,238
     Scenic, gently rolling course. Motel nearby.

3 Lyman Meadow G.C.   18/72
   Middlefield—SP   6,320
     Robert Trent Jones course. Grill and cocktail lounge.

4 Norwich Inn G.C.   18/71
   Norwich—R   6,425
     Challenging course adjoins inn.

5 Shennecossett C.C.   18/72
   Groton—MU   6,512
     One of northeast's oldest courses, designed by Donald Ross.

Massachusetts

1 The Island C.C.   18/70
   Martha's Vineyard—R   6,018
     Overlooks Nantucket Sound. Sporty, with breezes. Motel adjoins.

2 Coonamesset G.C.   18/72
   Hatchville—R   6,507
     Pine-studded course with strong lake breezes, watered fairways.

2 Clauson's Inn & Golf Resort   18/72
   Hatchville—R   6,507
     Pine tree-lined irrigated fairways, large lake, wind blows often.

2 C.C. of New Seabury   36/72-70
   Mashpee—SP   6,909-6,150
     Tough Seaside course closed to public July, August. Green course open year-round. Inn.

2 Pocasset G.C.   18/72
   Cape Cod—MU   6,300
     Hilly, especially back 9. Elevated greens on most holes.

3 Falmouth C.C.   18/72
   Cape Cod—MU   6,400
     Flat, open course. Five water holes on back 9. Par-3 13th surrounded by water and sand.

4 Dennis Pines G.C.   18/72
   Cape Cod—MU   6,500
     Tight, challenging course with trees bordering every fairway. Four water holes.

4 Bass River G.C.   18/72
   Cape Cod—MU   6,200
     Front 9 wooded, back 9 open. First 6 holes border river. Second oldest course on Cape.

5 International G.C.   18/72
   Bolton—PR   6,855
     Stretches to 8,275 yards. A real monster.

6 Jug End G.C.   18/72
   So. Egremont—R   6,250
     Tight, scenic course with new nine. Heritage House adjoins.

7 Trull Brook G.C.   18/72
   Tewksbury—SP   6,350
     Picturesque course bordered by river. Fine condition.

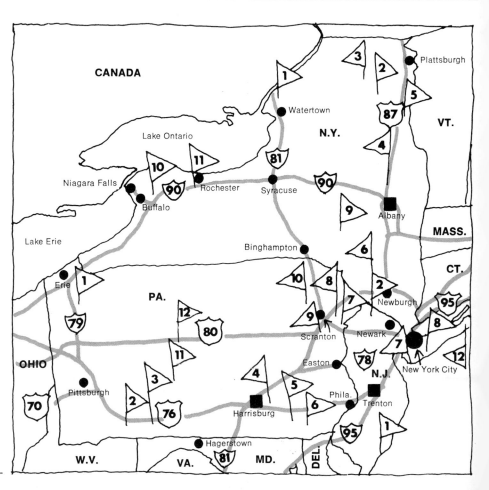

8 Pleasant Valley C.C.   18/72
Sutton—SP   6,857
    Tight, demanding course open to guests of
    Pleasant Valley Motel. Pro tour site.

Vermont

1 Mount Snow G.C.   18/72
West Dover—R   6,482
    Very rolling course at 2,000 feet. Operated
    by famous ski area. Site of '73 Women's Trans-
    Miss., 7/30-8/4.

1 Haystack   18/72
Wilmington—R   6,140
    Spectacular mountain scenery and rustic charm
    mark this Desmond Muirhead course in recrea-
    tion-resort community.

2 Lake Morey Inn & C.   18/69
Fairlee—R   5,700
    Site of annual Vermont Open. Lake-side lay-
    out, rolling, well-kept.

3 Crown Point C.C.   18/72
Springfield—SP   6,218
    Flat, pretty course open to guests.

4 Equinox Hotel & C.C.   18/72
Manchester—R   6,558
    Rolling course, superbly groomed. Hotel a fav-
    orite of U.S. Presidents since Civil War days.

4 Manchester C.C.   18/72
Manchester—PR   6,724
    "Member" hotels and lodges extend guest priv-
    ileges to this attractive layout by Geoffrey
    Cornish.

4 Stratton Mountain C.C.   18/72
Stratton Mountain—P   6,195
    Pretty test, designed by Geoffrey Cornish.
    Stratton Mtn. Inn nearby.

5 Quechee Club   18/72
Quechee Lakes—R   6,778
    Geof Cornish course on Ottauquechee River.
    Water, birch groves and gullies. Residential
    resort.

5 Woodstock C.C.   18/69
Woodstock—SP   5,939
    Robert Trent Jones course. In beautiful valley
    with wandering brook near Woodstock Inn.

6 Sugarbush Inn G.C.   18/72
Warren—R   6,741
    Trent Jones course in dramatic mountain set-
    ting, replete with water and forests. Front 9
    replete with water.

7 Basin Harbor C.   18/72
Vergennes—R   6,018
    Broad, rolling fairways bordered by woodland
    and Lake Champlain. Traditional New England
    resort. 3,000-ft. landing strip.

8 Stowe C.C.   18/72
Stowe—R   6,025
    Large, well-trapped greens. Meandering stream
    on six holes. Open to guests of Stowe member
    lodges.

New Hampshire

1 Five Chimneys G.C.   9/37
Province Lake—SP   3,235
    Lakeside course crossing Maine border.

2 Wentworth By The Sea   18/70
Portsmouth—R   6,179
    Links on inlet of Atlantic designed by Geof-
    frey Cornish, three holes play over ocean. Also
    9-hole par-3 course.

3 Bald Peak Colony C.   18/72
Melvin Village—PR   6,211
    Course slopes from mountain top to shores of
    Lake Winnipesaukee.

4 Lake Sunapee C.C.   18/71
New London—R   6,600
    Rolling terrain. Motel and cabins. Restaurant.

5 Lake Tarleton Club   18/72
Pike—R   6,226
    One of New England's first courses. Five
    lakes on 5,500-acre resort.

6 The Maplewood   18/72
Bethlehem—R   6,209
    Beautiful views of the White Mountain Range
    dominate. Course features par-6, 635-yard hole
    with tree-lined fairways.

6 Sunset Hill House & C.   9/34
Sugar Hill—R   2,600
    Famous resort in superb setting.

7 Jack O'Lantern C.C.   9/36
Woodstock—R   3,020
    Flat valley course along river, recently built.

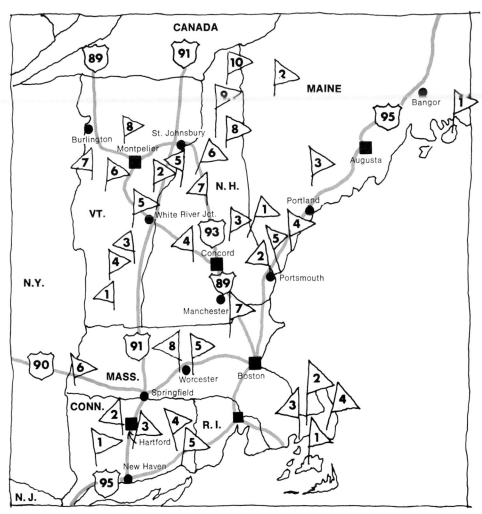

8 Crawford House G.C.   9/35
Crawford Notch—R   3,400
    Rolling course on slopes of Mt. Washington,
    highest peak in Northeast.

8 Mt. Washington Hotel & C.C.   18/71
Bretton Woods—R   6,189
    Donald Ross layout enhanced by frequent
    slopes and swales.

9 Waumbek Inn & C.C.   18/72
Jefferson—R   6,104
    One of New Hampshire's finest courses, a
    frequent tournament site; at base of White
    Mountains.

9 Mountain View House & C.C.   9/35
Whitefield—R   2,915
    Slightly hilly course. One of finest resorts in
    New England.

10 The Balsams G.C.   18/72
Dixville Notch—R   6,350
    Famous old resort with Donald Ross moun-
    taintop 18. Also executive 9.

Maine

1 Kebo Valley C.   18/70
Bar Harbor—SP   6,209
    Narrow, tree-lined course, small greens. Big
    clubhouse, restaurant.

2 Bethel Inn G.C.   9/36
Bethel—R   3,069
    Short nine-hole layout in picturesque country.
    Full facilities.

3 Poland Spring G.C.   18/71
Poland Spring—R   6,464
    Beautiful views. Oldest 18-hole resort course
    in U.S.

4 Webhannet G.C.   18/70
Kennebunk Beach—SP   6,200
    Lush seaside links. Level fairways. Adjoins At-
    lantis Hotel.

5 York G. & Tennis C.   18/70
York Harbor—PR   6,203
    Fine seaside course. For guests of nearby
    Marshall House.

Canada

British Columbia

1 Fairmont Hot Springs G.C.   18/70
Fairmont Hot Springs—R   6,510
    Surrounded by mountain grandeur and vistas of
    the Columbia Lake and Valley.

2 Victoria Golf Club   18/69
Victoria—SP   5,958
    British Columbia's oldest course, established in
    1893. Five water hazards. 104 bunkers.

2 Uplands Golf Club   18/70
Victoria—SP   6,228
    Site of 1972 Canadian Senior Championship.
    Wind always a factor.

Alberta

1 Waterton National Park G.C.   18/71
Waterton Park, Alberta—R   6,103
    Rolling course with Rockies as background.
    Campsites.

2 Banff Springs Hotel & G.C.   18/71
Banff, Alberta—R   6,729
    Breathtakingly beautiful Stanley Thompson
    course, almost a mile above sea level with spec-
    tacular mountain backdrop.

3 Jasper Park Lodge G.C.   18/71
Jasper, Alberta—R   6,590
    Hewn from slopes of Rockies. Manicured greens
    and fairways are aligned with separate moun-
    tain peaks. 200 miles northwest of Calgary.

Saskatchewan

1 Murray Municipal Golf Club   18/72
Regina, Saskatchewan—PU   6,842
    Hilly with fully watered greens and fairways.
    Located 15 miles northeast of downtown Regina.

2 Waskesiu Lake Golf Club   18/70
Prince Albert Nt'l Park, Saskatchewan—PU   6,059
    Rolling course cut out of wooded terrain. Well
    trapped. 225 miles north of Regina.

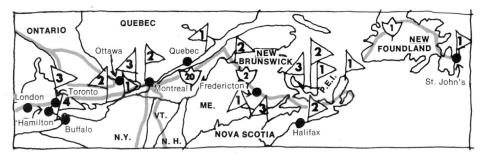

Manitoba

1 Falcon Beach G.C.   18/72
    Whiteshell Provincial Park, Manitoba—R   7,020
    Creek runs through course, coming into play on
    holes 2, 8, 16. Accommodation and campsites.

2 Clear Lake Golf Course   18/72
    Riding Mountain National Park—PU   6,272
    Located some 175 miles northwest of Winnipeg.
    One of Manitoba's most testing layouts.

Ontario

1 Upper Canada G.C.   18/72
    Crysler Farm Battlefield Park, Ontario—R   6,908
    Rolling fairways, large greens yield a pic-
    turesque setting. Complete facilities. Operated
    by St. Lawrence Parks Commission.

2 Glen Lawrence G. & C.C.   18/71
    Kingston, Ontario—SP   6,584
    Fine test of golf with water coming into play on
    seven holes. Front nine flat, back nine rolling.

3 Don Valley G.C.   18/71
    Toronto, Ontario—MU   6,298
    Difficult municipal course 10 miles from down-
    town Toronto. Don River traverses course and
    enters play on 10 holes.

4 Whirlpool Golf Course   18/72
    Niagara Falls, Ontario—PU   6,946
    Scenic layout opposite famous whirlpool with
    view of gorge. Rolling terrain, well treed, many
    traps.

Quebec

1 Manoir Richelieu G.C.   18/70
    Point-au-Pique, Quebec—R   6,120
    Overlooks St. Lawrence. Elevators on some
    holes for access to tees.

2 Carling Lake Club   18/72
    Montreal, Laurentian Foothills   6,650
    Challenging Howard Watson course with many
    tricky holes.

2 Gray Rocks Inn & G.C.   18/72
    Ste. Jovite, Quebec—R   6,445
    Hilly, wooded course in the Laurentians.

2 Le Chantecler G.C.   18/70
    Ste. Adele, Quebec—R   6,060
    Panoramic views of the Laurentians with many
    scenic holes.

3 Le Chateau Montebello   18/70
    Montebello, Quebec—R   6,110
    Near Laurentian Mountains, ravines and valleys
    provide natural hazards. Secluded by a dense
    border of pine and spruce woods.

New Brunswick

1 Algonquin G.C.   18/71, 9/31
    St. Andrews, New Brunswick—R   6,170-2,200
    Rolling seaside courses.

2 Edmundtson Golf Club   18/73
    Edmundston, New Brunswick—PR   6,666
    Plays long with one par-3 hole over railway line.
    Also, a 5-hole par-3 junior course.

Nova Scotia

1 Cape Breton Highlands Golf Links   18/72
    Cape Breton Highlands National Park—R   6,475
    Course spreads over six miles amid valleys
    and mountains.

2 Oakfield C.C.   18/73
    Grand Lake—SP   6,781
    Site of 1971 Canadian Amateur Championship.
    Lakeside setting insures breeze at all times.

3 The Pines Hotel & G.C.   18/71
    Digby, Nova Scotia—R   6,204
    Two water holes on rolling terrain.

Prince Edward Island

1 Brudenell G. & C.C.   18/72
    Brudenell Resort, Cardigan   6,000
    Prince Edward Island—R
    Situated on banks of Brudenell River, in rural
    setting. Nine water holes.

2 Belvedere Golf and Winter Club   18/72
    Charlottetown—SP   6,372
    Flat, well-bunkered course laid out in triangular
    system so you are never far from clubhouse.

3 Green Gables G.C.   18/72
    Cavendish—R   6,410
    Seaside links. Tight, windswept. Inn adjoins.

Newfoundland

1 Bally Haly G. & C.C.   18/70
    St. John's—SP   6,000
    Hilly course with tight fairways, good turf.

Mexico

1 Santa Anita C.C.   18/72
    Guadalajara—PR   6,617
    In residential development. Guests of some
    hotels may play. Southwest of city.

1 Guadalajara C.C.   18/72
    Guadalajara—PR   6,400
    Oldest, best conditioned course in area. Need
    introduction to play.

2 Bosques de San Isidro G.C.   18/72
    Guadalajara—PR   6,819
    Fine new rolling L. Hughes course in resort
    community north of city. Villas to rent.

3 Club Atlas G.C.   18/72
    Guadalajara—SP   6,804
    Good test by Joe Finger. Affiliated with some
    Guadalajara hotels.

4 Pueblo Club Las Hadas   9/36
    Manzanillo—R   3,494
    Unusual new ocean resort with one of Pete
    Dye's finest courses. Second nine open '74.

5 Pierre Marques G.C.   18/72
    Acapulco—R   6,334
    Lush, palm-bordered Percy Clifford course in
    magnificent setting. Also 9-hole par-3. Superb
    hotel.

5 Tres Vidas G.C.   36/72-72
    Acapulco—PR   6,271-6,500
    Two Robert Trent Jones courses in exclusive
    rich man's resort on beach 15 miles south of
    Acapulco.

5 Princess G.C.   18/72
    Acapulco—R   6,400
    Sporty Ted Robinson layout next to huge new
    Princess Hotel. Fairly tight with palms, 8 water
    holes.

Jamaica

1 Rose Hall G.C.   18/72
    Montego Bay—R   6,900
    Adjacent to 510-room Hotel Rose Hall sched-
    uled to open July '74. Course plays around natu-
    ral waterfall.

1 Ironshore G. & C.C.   18/72
    Montego Bay—R   6,615
    Course by Canadian Bob Moote. Small greens
    with emphasis on strategy.

1 Half Moon-Rose Hall C.C.   18/72
    Montego Bay—R   6,593
    Manicured course near Half Moon Hotel. Wind
    often a factor.

1 Tryall G. & B.C.   18/71
    Sandy Bay—SP   6,324
    Nine seaside holes, nine inland. In beautiful
    setting.

2 Runaway Bay G.C.   18/72
    Runaway Bay—R   6,562
    Designed in two circles. Open to hotel guests.
    Also 9-hole, par-3 course.

3 Upton G. & C.C.   18/71
    Ochos Rios—SP   6,540
    Rolling, inland, close to Ocho Rios complex.
    Tree-lined fairways. Chiseled from mountainside.

4 Constant Spring G.C.   18/68
    Kingston—SP   5,474
    Short but cute. First nine inland; second nine
    has sea view. Greens are hard and fast.

4 Caymanas G.C.   18/72
    Spanish Town—SP   6,540
    Wide-ranging course. Fine clubhouse. Six
    miles from Kingston.

Virgin Islands

1 Fountain Valley G.C.   18/72
    St. Croix—R   6,909
    Course opened in 1966. Many tropical trees,
    7 water holes.

1 Estate Carlton Hotel & C.C.   9/36
    St. Croix—R   3,173
    Sporty 9-holer with 18 tees . Revamped in 1966.

1 The Reef G.C.   9/35
    St. Croix—R   3,136
    Plush, new private resort with hillside con-
    dominiums and fine beach.

2 Mullet Bay G.C.   18/70
    St. Maarten—R   5,300
    Beautiful Joe Lee layout at hotel.

Puerto Rico

1 Dorado Del Mar Hotel & G.C.   18/72
    Dorado—R   6,964
    Excellent course by ocean. Palm-lined.

1 Dorado Beach Hotel C.   36/72-72
    Dorado Beach—R   6,425-6,525
    Two fine Robert Trent Jones courses near ocean;
    carved out of tropical jungle. A Rockresort.

1 Cerromar Beach Hotel   36/72-72
    Dorado Beach—R   6,480-6,450
    R. T. Jones brought lots of water into play on
    these 2 Rockresort courses. Chi Chi Rodriguez,
    golf director.

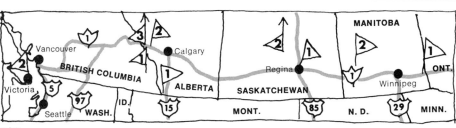

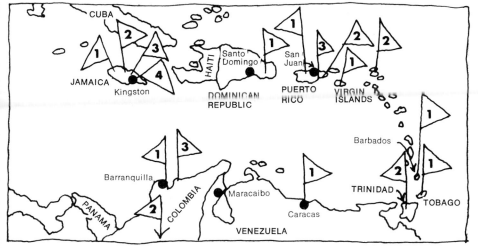

2 Fortune Hills G.C. — 9/36
Freeport—R — 3,250
  Joe Lee course. Rolling terrain. Second nine being built.

Abaco

3 Treasure Cay Beach Hotel & G.C. — 18/72
Abaco—R — 6,932
  Big greens, plenty of sand, undulating fairways, 4 miles private beach.

Great Harbour Cay

4 Great Harbour Club — 18/72
Berry Islands—SP — 6,565
  Rolling course on a real "out-island." Lush, tropical setting. Hotel.

New Providence

5 Paradise Island G.C. — 18/72
Nassau—R — 6,545
  Attractive course with lots of water, doglegs, sand. Large hotels nearby; casino.

6 Sonesta Beach Hotel & G.C. — 18/72
Nassau—R — 6,505
  Old Nassau G.C. course now owned by Sonesta.

7 South Ocean G.C. — 18/72
Nassau—R — 6,568
  Joe Lee course on ocean. May be island's best. Stunning second nine.

7 Coral Harbour G.C. — 18/70
Nassau—R — 6,710
  Hotel has folded, but course remains open.

Eleuthera

8 Cotton Bay Club — 18/72
Rock Sound, Eleuthera—PR — 6,594
  Fine test perched atop bluff.

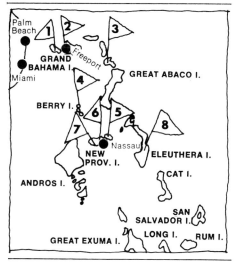

Tahiti

Golf D'Atimaono — 18/72
Papeete — 6,946
  Designed by Bob Baldock. The basically flat course is a fun challenge amid beautiful flowers, trees and water.

Bermuda

1 Port Royal G.C. — 18/71
Southampton—PU — 6,541
  Fine Trent Jones course on ocean along cliff. Water, wind, sand. Good test.

2 Princess G. & Beach C. — 18/54
Southampton—R — 2,630
  Par-3 course gives accuracy a fair test. Affiliated with Princess Hotel.

3 Riddell's Bay G. & C.C. — 18/68
Warwick West—PR — 5,660
  Skirts ocean. Many trees. Open by appointment. Dogleg 8th a beauty.

4 Belmont Hotel & G.C. — 18/70
Warwick—R — 5,717
  Interesting course though short. Well bunkered. Fun to play.

5 Queen's Park G.C. — 9/35
Devonshire—PU — 2,826
  Some good-sized holes including 540-yard fourth.

---

2 El Conquistador Hotel & C. — 18/72
Las Crobas—R — 6,625
  Picturesque, hilly course; view of Atlantic and Caribbean.

3 Palmas Del Mar — 18/72
Humacao—R — 6,600
  From hill to short, Ron Kirby-Gary Player course winds through coconut groves and cane fields.

Trinidad-Tobago

1 Tobago G.C. — 18/72
Tobago—R — 6,900
  Scenic John Harris course for guests of Mount Irvine Bay Hotel.

2 St. Andrews G.C. — 18/67
Trinidad—R — 5,564
  Picturesque H. S. Colt layout in Maraval Valley. Club founded in 1870.

Dominican Republic

1 Cajuiles G.C. — 18/72
La Romana—R — 6,500
  Superb, tough Pete Dye course climaxed by rocky ocean holes called "Teeth of the Dog."

Barbados

1 Sandy Lane G.C. — 18/72
Barbados—R — 6,632
  Inland at Sandy Lane estate. Magnificent views of the Caribbean.

Colombia

1 Club Lagos de Caujaral — 18/72
Barranquilla—R — 6,585
  Striking new Joe Lee course overlooking Caribbean with 50-unit golf lodge.

2 Los Lagartos C.C. — 18/72
Bogota—PR — 6,800
  Good little test that is regular stop on the Caribbean tour.

2 San Andres Club — 18/72
Bogota—SP — 6,755
  Attractive and testing Stanly Thompson layout on island near Bogota. Casinos and hotels.

---

2 El Rincon G.C. — 18/72
Bogota—PR — 6,700
  Very exclusive club with Robert Trent Jones course. Stretches to 7,400 yards. Visitors may play with introduction.

2 C.C. of Bogota — 18/72
Bogota—PR — 6,650
  Old, established Charles Banks course in plush surroundings. Introduction required.

3 Santa Marta G.C. — 18/72
Santa Marta—R — 6,600
  A beach and mountain resort with new course by Mark Mahannah.

Venezuela

1 Caracas C.C. — 18/71
Caracas—PR — 6,552
  Pleasant, sporty course situated in the heart of the city.

1 Valle Arriba G. Club — 18/70
Caracas—PR — 6,163
  Enjoyable, short and fairly hilly course within a good residential area, played on Caribbean tour.

The Bahamas
Grand Bahama Island

  Guests at Oceanus, Lucayan Beach, Holiday Inn, Coral Beach Hotels may obtain guest privileges at Lucayan C.C., Shannon G. & C.C., Bahama Reef C.C. and other courses in the area.

1 Grand Bahama Hotel & C.C. — 18/72
West End—R — 6,800
  Rolling fairways, 7 ponds, 70 bunkers. Pine-bordered fairways.

2 Lucayan C.C. — 18/72
Freeport—R — 6,859
  Fine test. Site of 1971 Bahamas National Open.

2 King's Inn & G.C. — 36/72-72
Freeport—R — 6,600-6,700
  Both layouts feature wide fairways, big greens and many pines.

2 Shannon G.& C.C. — 18/72
Freeport—R — 6,554
  Joe Lee course with pine-bordered, rolling fairways. 13th a spectacular par-3.

2 Bahama Reef C.C. — 18/72
Freeport—R — 6,788
  Located in hotel, beach resort area, lighted driving range, par-3.

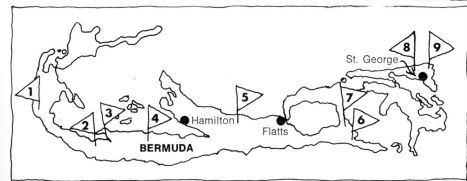

6 Mid-Ocean Club   18/71
    Tucker's Town—PR   6,519
      Site of many tournaments. Three sets of tees. On ocean. Fine course.

7 Castle Harbor G.C.   18/71
    Tucker's Town—R   6,180
      Rolling, spectacular course adjoining Castle Harbour Hotel and Club.

8 St. Georges Hotel & G.C.   9/34
    St. Georges—R   2,455
      Relatively simple course with some hills and dales.

9 Holiday Inn G.C.   9/27
    St. Georges—R   1,201
      Par-3 course with vistas. Overlooks Fort St. Catherine.

Spain

1 Costa Brava G.C.   18/71
    Santa Cristina de Aro—R   5,850
      Part of large recreation-estates development on coast near Gerona. Designed by Hamilton Stutt.

1 G.C. of Pals   18/73
    Playa de Pals—SP   6,490
      Laid out over sand dunes by British designer F. W. Hawtree. 90 miles from Barcelona. Hotels nearby.

1 Real Cerdana G.C.   18/71
    Cerdana-Puigcerda—R   6,440
      Hotels and golf chalets adjoin course.

2 G.C. of Terramar   18/70
    Sitges—R   6,080
      Seaside resort with hotel about 25 miles from Barcelona.

2 El Prat   18/72
    Prat de Liobregat—R   6,215
      Flat, challenging ocean-side course cut uniquely through umbrella-pine forest.

3 El Saler   18/72
    Valencia—R   6,600
      Government-operated course. Designed by Spanish architect Javier Arana.

4 La Manga Campo de Golf   36/71-72
    Near Cartagena   6,455-6,855
      Palms line fairways, ravines, lakes. By Robert Dean Putnam. Gary player is playing pro.

4 Club de Golf Villa Martin   18/72
    Torrevieja—R   6,700
      Rolling fairways lined with pines, olive trees. Opened early 1973. Ramon Sota, pro.

5 Club de Golf El Candado   9/35
    El Palo—PU   2,296
      Simple, but good short iron practice.

5 Campo de Golf de Malaga   18/72
    Malaga—R   6,442
      Oldest course on Southern Coast. Excellent hotel adjacent to course.

6 El Paraiso G.C.   18/72
    Estepona—R   6,460
      Course designed by Ron Kirby and Gary Player slopes from foothills to beach. Opened early '73.

6 Club Atalaya Park   18/72
    Marbella—R ·   6,935
      Long and wide with lovely view of nearby Sierra Bermeja Mountains. Complete facilities, impressive clubhouse.

6 Golf Club Guadalmina   18/72
    Marbella—R   6,824
      Long established Costa del Sol course alongside hotel and ocean.

6 Nueva Andalucia Golf Club   36 holes
    Marbella—R
      Tough Robert Trent Jones course flanked by mountains and the sea. Second course to open soon. Small golf hotel at course. Andalucia Plaza Hotel and other hotels nearby.

6 Rio Real Golf Club   18/72
    Marbella—R   6,706
      Pretty course with narrow fairways. Marvelous clubhouse. Hotel Los Monteros nearby.

6 Sotogrande   18/72
    Guadiaro—R   6,596
      Magnificent Robert Trent Jones layout set amid cork forests and lakes. Villas adjacent to lovely clubhouse. Also 18-hole par-3 course. Additional 18 open 1974.

6 Club de Golf Campamento   9/36
    San Roque   2,977
      Ordinary 9-holer on road from Gibraltar to San Roque.

6 Pueblo Cortes de Golf   18/72
    Marbella—R   6,450
      Course by Gary Player combines natural beauty with tree-lined fairways and lush, rolling greens.

7 Pineda de Sevilla   9/35
    Seville—PR   3,125
      Nice change of pace when visiting historic city.

8 La Herreria   18/73
    El Escorial—PR   6,615
      Lovely scenery backed by mountains and San Lorenzo Monastery, a must for tourists.

8 Real Club de Campo   18/72
    Madrid—PR   6,725
      Scene of '65 Canada Cup and '70 Women's World Amateur team matches. Also 9-hole course.

8 Real Club Puerta de Hierro   36/72-72
    Madrid—PR   6,860-5,900
      Oldest club on Spanish mainland (1904). Long and hilly. Site of 1970 Eisenhower Matches.

9 Real Pedrena G.C.   18/70
    Santander—SP   6,160
      On a peninsula in the middle of the bay. Designed by Colt, Allison. Club has accommodations.

10 Jaizkibel   18/72
    San Sebastian—PR   6,075
      Situated in spectacular mountain country.

11 Golf Club Son Vida   18/68
    Mallorca   6,077
      Only 18 holes in Balearic Island.

Morocco

1 Marrakech G.C.   18/72
    Marrakech—SP   6,233
      Flat layout wanders through orange groves. Good greens. Hotels in Marrakech.

2 Royal Mohammedia G.C.   18/73
    Mohammedia—R   6,370
      Established, interesting seaside links. Always windy. Casablanca hotels.

3 Royal Golf Rabat G.C.   18/73
    Dar-Es-Salem Rabat—R   6,825
      Robert Trent Jones course, exceptionally long and difficult in improbable locale.

Portugal

1 Palmares G.C.   18/73
    Near Lagos, Algarve—PR   Near 7,000
      Five dune holes along ocean prime feautre, part of housing development. By Frank Pennink.

2 Penina G.C.   27/73-36
    Near Portimao, Algarve—R   6,800-3,200
      Designed by Henry Cotton. Very long championship course. Golf hotel and complete facilities.

3 Vilamoura G.C.   18/73
    Albufeira, Algarve—R   6,500
      Rolling fairways and especially greens. Magnificent clubhouse, apartments and hotels.

4 Vale do Lobo G.C.   18/72
    Almansil, Algarve—R   6,610
      Spectacular holes wind along rugged oceanside terrain. Henry Cotton design. Villas available.

5 Monte Gordo   36 holes
    Monte Gordo—R
      Designed by Henry Cotton. Hotel and casino.

6 Estoril G.C.   18/69
    Estoril—R   5,689
      Championship course through rolling hills, and fragrant pine forests. Vistas of ocean and mountains.

7 Oporto G.C.   18/71
    Silvalde—R   6,800
      Seaside course. Sand dunes, undulating terrain and stiff sea breezes add to difficulty.

Ireland

1 Portmarnock G.C.   18/73
    Dublin Bay—R   7,093
      Ireland's greatest course and one of the world's best. Towering sandhills and many demanding par-4's. Cozy clubhouse.

1 Royal Dublin   18/73
    Bull Island, Dublin City   6,657
      Spacious fairways, diversified holes, fierce roughs. One of finest clubhouses in Ireland.

2 Woodbrook G.C.   18/72
    Emerald Isle   6,700
      Views of sea and mountains from every hole, lush new clubhouse.

3 Baltray G.C.   18/72
    Drogheda, Co. Louth   6,693
      A favorite course of Irish golfers, offering golf amid breath-taking seascapes.

4 Carlow G.C.   18/72
    Carlow   6,279
      Commonly regarded as Ireland's finest inland course. Moorland turf, brand new clubhouse.

5 Killarney G.C.   18/72
    Killarney   6,300
      Golf course is a memorable experience. Lakeside golf.

6 Waterville Golf Links   18/73
    Waterville — R   7,116
      Great golf on challenging links course opened 1972 at Waterville Lakes Hotel. All resort facilities and activities. Modern clubhouse. Great trout and salmon fishing.

7 Ballybunion G.C.   18/72
    Ballybunion, Co. Kerry   6,417
      A tremendous golfing challenge, set in picturesque range of sand dunes. Special distinction among Irish golf courses.

8 Lahinch G.C.   18/71
    Lahinch   6,434
      Rugged in character, beautiful in scenic layout. Sandhills, sandpits, rough hills provide fierce challenge. Extra large greens and tees.

9 Co. Sligo G.C.   18/70
    Rosses Point   6,435
      Natural hazards demand powerful hitting. Modern conveniences and facilities. Dog-leg holes frequent.

10 Royal Portrush G.C.   18/73
    Portrush   6,809
      Relentless challenge for the best of golfers. Narrow curving fairways and great sandhills.

11 Royal Co. Down G.C.   18/71
    Newcastle   6,647
      Stern test. Sandhills, ridges and valleys mean trouble.

England

1 Royal Lytham & St. Annes G.C.   18/74
    St. Anne's-On-The-Sea—SP   6,635
      Sea not visible but dunes affect play. 200 sand traps. Hotels nearby.

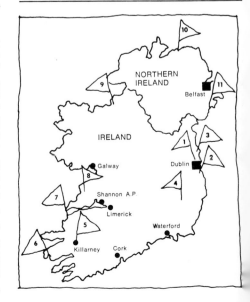

2 Royal Birkdale G.C.   18/74
  Southport—SP   6,844
    Sandy rough, willow scrubs offer tough obstacles. Resort area.

2 Southport & Ainsdale G.C.   18/73
  Southport—SP   6,625
    Seaside golf, gentle rolls, towering sandhills. Resort area.

2 Formby G.C.   18/74
  Frooulifieiu—SP   6,803
    Seaside links, good greens, thick forests. Resort area.

3 Royal Liverpool G.C.   18/75
  Hoylake—PR   6,940
    Rugged, seaside championship test. Founded in 1869. Need letter.

4 Ganton G.C.   18/75
  Scarborough—SP   6,823
    Inland, with gorse and heather. Great condition.

5 Moortown G.C.   18/73
  Leeds—SP   6,604
    On peaty moorlands, with plenty of gorse, heather, streams, trees. Many other courses nearby.

6 Woodhall Spa G.C.   18/74
  Woodhall Spa—SP   6,822
    Sand-based, but inland. Heather, gorse.

7 Lindrick G.C.   18/73
  Worksop—SP   6,541
    Good moorland golf. Great condition. Curtis and Ryder Cup sites. Restaurant.

8 Little Aston G.C.   18/73
  Streetly—SP   6,689
    Sand, gravel, subsoil, weaves through trees. No ladies Saturdays. Restaurant.

9 Berkshire G.C.   18/74
  Ascot—SP   6,379
    Rolling, tree-lined inland course. Par-yards Red course. Also Blue course (72—6,244). Lunch only. Hotels nearby.

9 Denham G.C.   18/72
  Denham—SP   6,357
    Varied, secluded setting. Pleasant clubhouse. Lunch only.

9 Sunningdale G.C.   18/72
  Sunningdale—PR   6,490
    Superb inland course; heather, gorse, pines. Scenic. Par-yards Old course. Also New course (73—6,487), a test. Restaurant. Need member introduction.

9 Walton Heath G.C.   18/74
  Tadworth—SP   6,735
    Championship caliber, sand-based, almost seaside golf. Par-yards Old course. Also new course (73-6,516).

9 Wentworth C.   18/75
  Virginia Water—PR   6,936
    Stiff challenge on sandy sub-soil, with heather, gorse. Lunch only. Par-yards West course. Also East course (72—6,209) and Short (64—3,486). Hotels nearby. Need letter.

10 Prince's G.C.   18/74
  Sandwich—SP   6,681
    Good seaside test. Restaurant. Hotels nearby.

10 Royal St. George's G.C.   18/72
  Sandwich—PR   6,633
    Great summer golf on links terrain. Lunch only. Hotels nearby. Need letter.

10 Royal Cinque Ports G.C.   18/72
  Deal—SP   6,689
    Dune runs clear across seaside course. Restaurant.

11 Littlestone G.C.   18/73
  Littlestone—SP   6,346
    Good place for family outing. Seaside. Lunch only, but good hotels nearby.

11 Rye G.C.   18/72
  Rye—PR   6,483
    Best course in Sussex. Links character. Good "winter" course. Restaurant. Hotels nearby. Need member introduction.

12 Burnham & Berrow G.C.   18/73
  Burnham-On-Sea—SP   6,624
    Seaside links, gently undulating. Lunch only.

13 Manor House Hotel G.C.   18/69
  Moretonhampstead—R   6,245
    Pleasant resort course. Manor House Hotel adjoins.

14 Royal N. Devon C. (Westward Ho!)   18/72
  Devon—SP   6,532
    Famous seaside course, founded in 1864. Home of J. H. Taylor. Restaurant.

15 St. Enodoc G.C.   18/72
  Rock—SP   6,605
    Natural, seaside golf, giant sand hills. Restaurant.

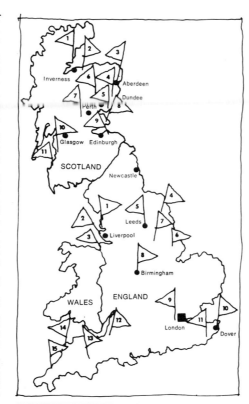

Scotland

1 Royal Dornoch G.C.   18/72
  Dornoch—SP   6,485
    Classic Scottish seaside course, set amidst dunes. Restaurant. No Sunday play. Resort hotel nearby.

2 Nairn G.C.   18/71
  Nairn—MU   6,342
    Seaside course, with gorse, heather. Sea always in view. Restaurant.

3 Royal Aberdeen G.C.   18/72
  Aberdeen—PR   6,384
    Opened in 1780. Rolling fairways wind through dunes. Restaurant. 20 municipal putting courses in city. Need letter.

4 Montrose G.C.   36/71-66
  Montrose—MU   6,396-4,863
    Splendid links in ancient setting. Course goes back to 17th century. Hotels nearby.

5 Carnoustie G.C.   18/74
  Carnoustie—MU   7,103
    Famous seaside course, where Hogan won '53 British Open. Water, wind and sand. Hotel at course. Burnside course nearby.

6 Blairgowrie G.C.   18/73
  Rosemount—SP   6,490
    Pines, birches line inland course's fairways. Good turf. Each hole secluded. Restaurant.

7 Gleneagles   18/72
  Perthshire—R   6,597
    Beautiful moorland golf, with pines, streams. Par-yards is King's course. Also 2 others (Queen's, 6,102; Wee, 2,625). Gleneagles Hotel features restaurant, tennis, swimming.

8 Royal & Ancient G.C.   72
  St. Andrews—MU   holes
    Old Course, at 6,591 yards, par 73, is "home" of the game, golf in its most natural state. Also, New Course, 6,542 yards; Eden, 6,250 yards; Jubilee, 6,005 yards. Golf museum, restaurant. Many hotels nearby.

9 Gullane G.C.   18/72
  Gullane—SP   6,461
    Seaside golf. Course winds around hills. Par-yards is No. 1. Also 2 others (No. 2, 5,952; No. 3, 5,008). Restaurant. Hotels nearby.

9 Hon. Co. of Edinburgh Golfers   18/74
  Muirfield—PR   6,806
    "Club" moved to Muirfield in 1891. Great seaside golf, slender fairways. British Open, Amateur site. Hotels nearby. Need member introduction.

9 North Berwick G.C.   18/71
  North Berwick—SP   6,335
    Sea, sand and wind, a true links. 2 other courses plus 9-holer in area. Restaurant. 2 resort hotels nearby.

10 Western Gailes G.C.   18/72
  Gailes—PR   6,580
    Sand dunes, heather, whins spice play. Lunch, ten only. Mon only.

10 Troon G.C.   18/72
  Troon—PR   6,533
    Championship, seaside links. Founded in 1878. Restaurant. Second course nearby. Need letter of introduction.

10 Prestwick G.C.   18/72
  Ayrshire—PR   6,571
    British Open started here in 1860. Founded in 1851. Seaside links. Lunch available.

11 Turnberry G.C.   18/73
  Turnberry—R   6,835
    Good seaside golf. Par-yards is Ailsa course. Arran course adjoining, 6,653 yards. Turnberry Hotel at course.

Italy

Olgiata G.C.   27/72-34
Rome—SP   6,833-3,092
  Course winds over undulating countryside. Large, well-bunkered greens.

Villa d'Este G.C.   18/70
Montorfano—Como   6,070
  Narrow, wooded course in Italy's beautiful Lake Como region. Hotel 8 miles away.

Sardinia

Pevero G.C.   18/72
Costa Smeralda   6,874
  R. T. Jones course in White Mountains overlooks bay on rocky coast. Part of new international resort owned by Aga Khan.

Greece

1 Corfu G.C.   18/72
  Corfu—R   6,768
    Greek island course has lakes and stream in play on 13 holes.

2 Glyfada G.C.   18/72
  Glyfada—R   6,715
    Built amid groves of mature evergreen. Playable year-round.

Belgium

Royal Zoute Golf Club   18/72
Knokke-Le Zoute   6,300
  Links-type course in delightful resort town. Windy, many bunkers, but fair test.

Switzerland

Crans Golf Club   27/73-34
Crans sur Sierre   7,135-2,715
  Alpine links course situated above Sierre; Rhone Valley. 5,000 feet above sea level. Open May to October.

Davos G.C.   18/69
Davos-Dorf   5,717
  Open June to October. Many hotels nearby.

Engadine Golf Club   18/70
St. Moritz   6,289
  Alpine course open June to September in famed resort town. Beautiful views. Good test.

Lucerne G.C.   18/71
Lake Lucerne   5,625
  Course surrounded by majestic Swiss Alps. Gently rising slopes; very scenic. Hotels nearby. Open April to October.

Golf Club de Geneve   18/72
Geneva   6,689
  Open March to December. Practice area available. Restaurant and bar on site. Accommodations nearby.

Israel

Caesarea G. & C.C.   18/72
Caesarea—R   6,500
  Course built on undulating dunes overlooking the Mediterranean Sea. Also 9-hole putting green and driving range.

great courses charts

Of all the golf courses in the world, of all the great ones pictured and described in this book, a handful stand above the rest by virtue of their fame, their design and their influence on the game or the tradition of great events regularly staged there. In this special section we publish charts of five such courses, detailed diagrams of the layouts of Augusta National, the Georgia beauty; the Old Course at St. Andrews; Pine Valley, the New Jersey demon; Pebble Beach and Cypress Point, the neighboring California marvels.

Because we had space to publish only five charts, we had to decide on those with the broadest appeal. Although other editors might have chosen differently, we felt that if a majority of the world's golfers were polled and asked to select the five golf courses they most would like to play, these five would emerge at the top of the list.

Perhaps each reader of this book will have the good fortune to play all five courses, but in the meantime we hope this section will add a dimension of vicarious enjoyment and appreciation of these truly outstanding courses.

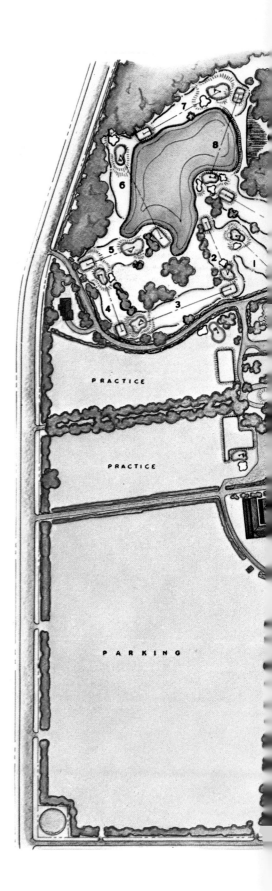

AUGUSTA NATIONAL SCORECARD*

Hole	Par	Yards	Hole	Par	Yards
1	4	400	10	4	470
2	5	555	11	4	445
3	4	355	12	3	155
4	3	220	13	5	475
5	4	450	14	4	420
6	3	190	15	5	520
7	4	365	16	3	190
8	5	530	17	4	400
9	4	420	18	4	420
	36	3,485		36	3,495

Totals: Par 72, Yards 6,980.
*Yardage for the 1974 Masters changed to 7,020 by increasing the length of the third and 10th holes.

Augusta National

The spacious, parkland layout of Augusta National, site of the Masters each April, rolls majestically through the Georgia pines. The famous Amen Corner (holes 11, 12 and 13) is at the upper right. At the upper left, above the clubhouse, is the beautiful par-3 course, cunningly designed by George Cobb, which Masters' contestants play each year before the tournament begins.

The Old Course, St. Andrews

Golf's spiritual home, the Old Course at St. Andrews, Scotland, is and odd looking piece of ground, narrow and congested having been formed over the decades by the forces of nature. Half the holes play out, and half back providing maximum exposure over the barren linksland from the elements converging off the Firth of Forth (below left) and River Eden (above right.)

ST. ANDREWS (OLD COURSE)
SCORECARD

Hole	Par	Yards	Hole	Par	Yards
1	4	374	10	4	338
2	4	411	11	3	170
3	4	405	12	4	312
4	4	470	13	4	427
5	5	567	14	5	560
6	4	414	15	4	413
7	4	364	16	4	380
8	3	163	17	4	466
9	4	359	18	4	358
	36	3,527		36	3,424

Totals: Par 72, Yards 6,951

Pine Valley

The heroic and often frightening character of Pine Valley, where fairways are "islands" between thick forests and sandy wasteland, is readily seen on this perspective drawing which appears on the placemat used in the club's dining room. Many believe this to be America's premier golf course, not so much because of its toughness but because it has so many first class, memorable holes.

PINE VALLEY SCORECARD

Hole	Par	Yards	Hole	Par	Yards
1	4	427	10	3	145
2	4	367	11	4	399
3	3	185	12	4	382
4	4	461	13	4	446
5	3	226	14	3	185
6	4	391	15	5	603
7	5	585	16	4	436
8	4	327	17	4	344
9	4	432	18	4	424
	35	3,401		35	3,364

Totals: Par 70, Yards 6,765.

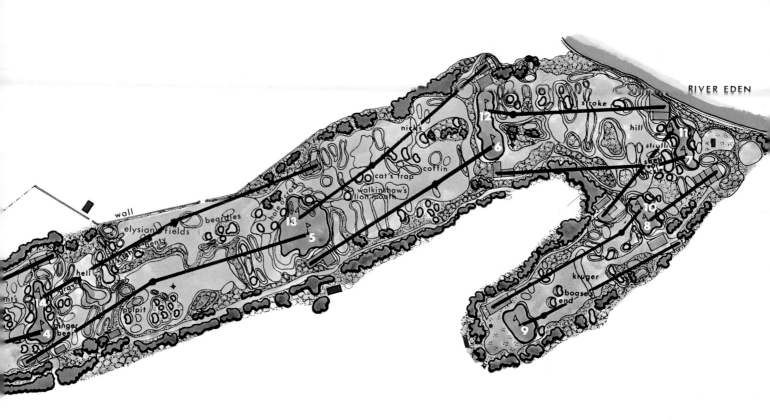

Pebble Beach

The famous ocean holes of Pebble Beach, six through 10, 17 and 18, are built along craggy bluffs overlooking Carmel Bay, giving Pebble Beach its unique and dramatic appeal. The inland holes are of a gentler disposition, though several of them, notably 13 and 14, are very good indeed and a testament to the amateur design work of Jack Neville and Douglas Grant.

PEBBLE BEACH SCORECARD

Hole	Par	Yards	Hole	Par	Yards
1	4	385	10	4	436
2	5	507	11	4	380
3	4	368	12	3	205
4	4	325	13	4	400
5	3	180	14	5	555
6	5	515	15	4	406
7	3	120	16	4	400
8	4	425	17	3	218
9	4	450	18	5	540
	36	3,275		36	3,540

Totals: Par 72, Yards 6,815.

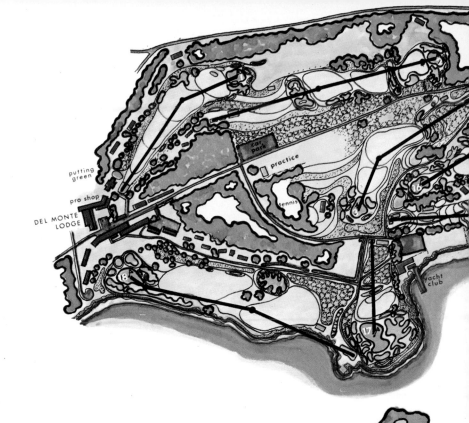

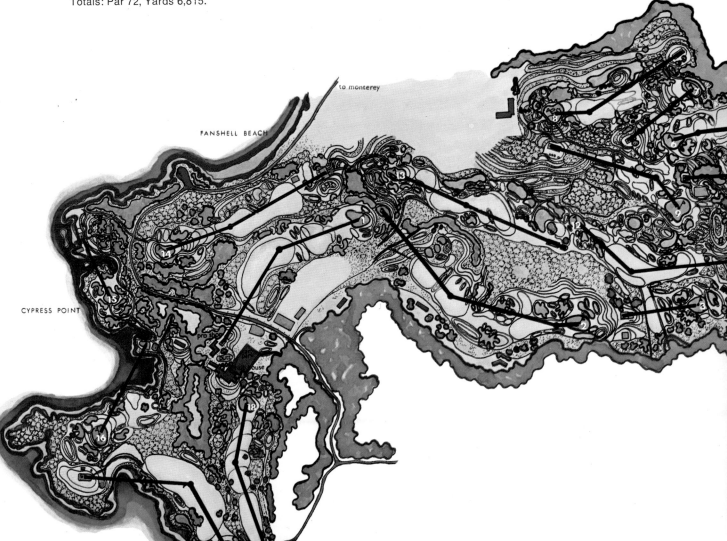

268

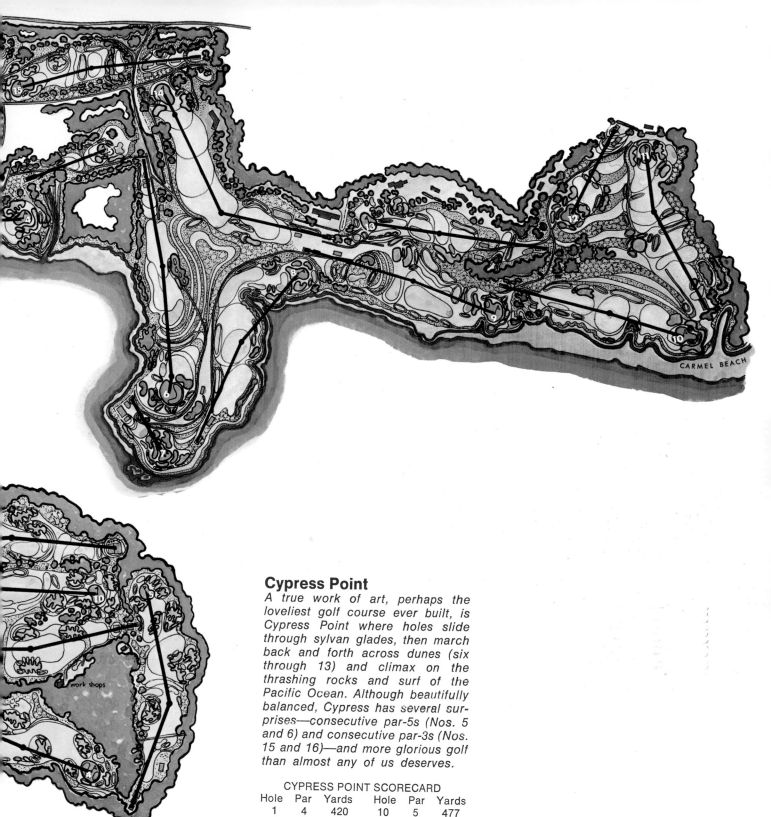

CARMEL BEACH

work shops

Cypress Point

A true work of art, perhaps the loveliest golf course ever built, is Cypress Point where holes slide through sylvan glades, then march back and forth across dunes (six through 13) and climax on the thrashing rocks and surf of the Pacific Ocean. Although beautifully balanced, Cypress has several surprises—consecutive par-5s (Nos. 5 and 6) and consecutive par-3s (Nos. 15 and 16)—and more glorious golf than almost any of us deserves.

CYPRESS POINT SCORECARD

Hole	Par	Yards	Hole	Par	Yards
1	4	420	10	5	477
2	5	544	11	4	433
3	3	161	12	4	411
4	4	384	13	4	361
5	5	490	14	4	387
6	5	521	15	3	139
7	3	160	16	3	233
8	4	338	17	4	375
9	4	291	18	4	339
	37	3,309		35	3,155

Totals: Par 72, Yards 6,464.

acknowledgments

EDITORIAL

Unlike a work of fiction, a volume of this sort is possible only with the help of many individuals contributing a needed word, a picture or a missing shred of information. In the Foreword to *Great Golf Courses of the World,* individual credit has been given to members of the Golf Digest staff for their various contributions and throughout the book by-lines appear at the beginning or end of all articles. This acknowledgment section is further devoted to the non-staff by-liners and the many other individuals, including photographers, who made contributions to this volume.

The following non-staff writers authored important chapters and some background on them is deserved:

Herbert Warren Wind (The Architect Makes the Golf Course Great, p. 16) is long-time writer for *The New Yorker* and author of the *Story of American Golf, The Complete Golfer* and *Herbert Warren Wind's Golf Book.*

Carl G. Staelin (Inverness, p. 66), past president, the Inverness Club (1965-66), is vice president—law and secretary, Owens-Corning Fiberglas Corporation, Toledo.

Raymond Jacobs (St. Andrews, p. 182) is the respected golf writer for the Glasgow Herald, Scotland, and a contributing columnist to golf publications in Britain.

Thomas Crow (Australia, p. 210) was formerly Australian golf champion and sales director, Precision Golf Forgings, Australia, when request for his editorial assistance was made. He is now president of Cobra Golf Inc., San Diego.

The following individuals, all affiliated with national golf associations, provided helpful research assistance, general information and statistics:

Howard Clark, president, and Fred Corcoran, tournament director, International Golf Ass'n

Alexander M. Radko, director, eastern region and national research director USGA Green Section

Janet Seagle, librarian and museum curator, United States Golf Ass'n

Dave Zink, executive director, Canadian Professional Golfers' Ass'n

The following individuals provided extensive help, research and background materials for the sections indicated:

U.S. COURSES

Donald E. Casey, president, Chicago Golf Club, for photographs and material on Chicago Golf

Joseph Hoover Jr., Joseph Hoover and Sons, for photographic film of many courses

Carlton S. Young, Manager, Myopia Hunt Club, for vintage photographs of Myopia, and Alexander N. Stoddard, Publisher, Essex County Newspaper, for background information on Myopia

The help of dozens of club managers and presidents of golf courses and clubs in the United States who edited material for accuracy is also gratefully acknowledged.

MEXICO

Adrian Morales Carillo, General Manager, and Emilio Zambrano, Editor, *Playgolf Internacional,* Mexico City, for background material, and Ruth Weimar, librarian, Robinsons, Inc., for researching availability of photographs

EUROPE

Henry Cotton, former British Open champion and director of golf, Penina Golf Hotel, for background material on Portugal and Samuel E. Stavisky & Associates, Inc., for photographs of Portuguese golf courses

Donald Swaelens, Royal Waterloo Golf Club, Belgium, for material and photos of various European golf courses

JAPAN

Yasuo Haruyama, former president of *Golf Monthly,* Japan, Takeaki Kaneda, Asian Manager of *Sports Illustrated,* Japan, and Mr. Nakajima, Kanematsu-Gosho Ltd., Japan, for material on Japanese courses, and Kenzo Murai, Japan Airlines, New York, for translating Japanese background material

GREAT GOLF IS EVERYWHERE

Louie Reyes, former publisher, *Golf Digest,* Philippine Edition, for background information on Asian courses

Special Thanks to:

Helene K. Marer, Marer Associates, for indexing this book

Jack Barnett, former vice president, *Golf Digest,* for his early organizational efforts

Francine Delphia, librarian, *Golf Digest,* for her continued research assistance throughout the production of this book

PHOTO AND ART

We wish to acknowledge Craven and Evans for the original design concept of *Great Golf Courses of the World* and to John Newcomb, Art Director, *Golf Digest,* for imaginatively implementing that concept to meet changing needs, also to Laura Duggan and Susan Crane for their art assistance in the final stages of production. The following list includes all the staff and contributing photographers and the page numbers on which their photos appear:

Jacket, John Newcomb; 2-3, Roy Attaway; 12, Frank Gardner; 13, Anthony Roberts; 15, Marvin Newman; 17, courtesy United States Golf Ass'n; 18-19, William Brooks; 21, courtesy Chicago Golf Club; 22-23, Cal Brown; 24, John Hemmer; 25, courtesy United States Golf Ass'n; 26-27, Lester Nehamkin; 31, Cal Brown; 32 (Dick Wilson), courtesy Joseph Lee; 34-35, 36, 37, 40-41, 44, Cal Brown; 46, 47, 48, courtesy Chicago Golf Club; 49, courtesy Philadelphia Cricket Club; 51, courtesy Myopia Hunt Club; 53, James Brooks; 55, John Alexandrowicz; 56, John Newcomb; 59, Frank Gardner; 61, Hank Morgan; 63, courtesy The Olympic Club; 65, Richard Coddington; 67, courtesy Inverness Club; 69, Bill Richards; 71, courtesy Cherry Hills Country Club; 73, courtesy The Country Club; 75, courtesy Oakland Hills Country Club; 76, Joseph Sterling; 79, John P. May; 81, 82, 83, 84, 85, 86, Paul Barton; 89, Roy Attaway; 91, courtesy Firestone Tire & Rubber Co.; 93, Cal Brown; 95, courtesy Champions Golf Club; 97, J. Smith; 99, courtesy Southern Hills Country Club; 101, 102-103, courtesy Sea Pines Co.; 105, Al Panzera; 107, 108, courtesy Del Monte Properties Co.; 110-111, Jerry Claussen; 112, Hugh Morton; 113, courtesy Concord Hotel; 113 (Wood-stock, Equinox), Peter Miller; 115, Larry Keighley; 115, courtesy Hershey Hotel; 117, courtesy The Greenbrier; 118, courtesy The Homestead; 120-121, courtesy Brandon Advertising Agency; 123, Roy Attaway; 124, courtesy Pine Needles Lodges & Country Club; 125, Charles Smith; 126-127, courtesy Sea Palms Golf & Country Club; 128, courtesy Sea Island Co.; 129, Fred Baldwin; 130, courtesy Sea Pines Co.; 130, courtesy The Hilton Head Co.; 133, courtesy Doral Country Club; 134, courtesy Walt Disney World Co.; 134, Cal Brown; 135, Paul Barton; 136, courtesy Innisbrook Golf & Country Club; 137, Paul Barton; 138-139, courtesy Grand Hotel; 140-141, Ken McVey; 142, courtesy Desert Island Country Club and Milton Jones Advertising Agency; 142, courtesy The Wigwam; 144, 146-147, Cal Brown; 149, courtesy La Costa Resort Hotel & Spa; 151, 152, Howard Gill; 153, Hank Morgan; 157, courtesy Castle Harbour Beach & Golf Club; 159, courtesy Shannon Golf & Country Club; 161, Bob Gelberg; 162-163, courtesy Jamaica Tourist Board; 165, 166-167, 168, Paul Barton; 170-171, Graetz Bros. Ltd.; 173, courtesy Hamilton Golf & Country Club; 174, courtesy Canadian Pacific; 176-177, Howard Gill; 178-179, Anthony Roberts; 183, Frank Gardner; 184, courtesy United States Golf Ass'n; 187, Frank Gardner; 189, H. W. Neale; 191, Frank Gardner; 193, Robin Gray; 195, H. W. Neale; 197, Frank Gardner; 198, courtesy The Scotsman Publications, Ltd.; 201, Frank Gardner; 202, W. Croft Jennings Jr.; 203, Frank Gardner; 206-207, Anthony Roberts; 208, courtesy Waterville Lake Hotel; 210-211, 212, Thomas Crow; 213, Peter Henderson; 215, Peter Parkinson; 216, John Hadley; 219, courtesy New Zealand Tourist Board; 220-221, 223, 224-225, Nikkan Sports Golf (formerly Golf Monthly); 227, G. Thompson; 228-229, 231, 232, courtesy Shell Oil Co.; 232-233, Cabell Robinson; 235, Cal Brown; 237, David Hamilton; 237, courtesy Vale do Lobo Golf Club; 238, London Daily Express; 239, 240-241, courtesy Shell Oil Co.; 288, John de Garmo.

SELECTION PANEL FOR AMERICA'S 100 GREATEST TESTS OF GOLF

The following are members of the regional selection panel who assist the editors of Golf Digest magazine in nominating and selecting golf courses in the United States to the list of America's 100 Greatest Tests of Golf (pages 40-44). The panel is composed of leading amateur and professional players, and experienced golfing experts from every region of the country.

ALABAMA
  Amateurs: Nolan S. Hatcher, Florence; Bob Lowry Jr., Huntsville
ARIZONA
  Amateurs: Edward L. Keating, Tubac; Dr. Ed Updegraff, Tucson
  Professional: Johnny Buila, Phoenix
ARKANSAS
  Amateur: Walter A. Dowell, Texarkana
  Professionals: Tommy Bolt, Cherokee Village; Pete Fleming, Hot Springs
CALIFORNIA
  Amateurs: John Dawson, Palm Desert; Cecil Dees, Glendale; Adrian French, Los Angeles; Bob Roos, Hillsborough; Dan Sheehan, West Covina; Jack Westland, Pebble Beach
  Professionals: Billy Casper, Chula Vista; Mac Hunter, Pacific Palisades; Tal Smith, Oakland; Dave Stockton, San Bernardino
COLORADO
  Amateurs: James English, Denver; Mark Schreiber, Denver
  Professionals: Dow Finsterwald, Colorado Springs; Paul Runyan, Denver; Fred Wampler, Denver
CONNECTICUT
  Amateurs: Jerry Courville, Norwalk; Jim McArthur, Greenwich; Sam Petrone, Cos Cob; Dick Siderowf, Westport
  Professionals: Billy Farrell, Greenwich; Mike Krak, Darien
FLORIDA
  Amateurs: Dexter Daniels, Winter Haven; Christopher Dunphy, Palm Beach; Howard Everitt, Jupiter; Downing Gray, Pensacola; Robert Kiersky, Delray Beach; Dr. John Mercer, Sarasota; John K. McCue, Winter Park
  Professionals: Bobby Cruickshank, Delray Beach; Bob Toski, Miami
GEORGIA
  Amateurs: Dewey P. Bowen, Atlanta; Jim Gabrielson, Atlanta; Charles Harrison, Marietta; Hobart L. Manley Jr., Savannah
  Professionals: Tommy Aaron, Pine Mountain; Davis Love Jr., Atlanta
HAWAII
  Amateurs: Merrill Carlsmith, Hilo; John Roberts, Honolulu
  Professional: Jerry Johnston, Maui
ILLINOIS
  Amateurs: Charles Eckstein, Hazel Crest; A. L. "Jim" Miller, Chicago
  Professionals: Bill Erfurth, Glencoe; Bob Goalby,

Belleville; Dick Hart, Hinsdale; Bill Ogden, Glenview

INDIANA
Amateurs: H. E. Danby, Indianapolis; Ed Tutwiler, Indianapolis
Professionals: Sam Carmichael, Martinsville; Mickey Powell, Columbus

KANSAS
Professional: Stan Thirsk, Shawnee Mission

KENTUCKY
Amateur: Jim O'Hern, Goshen

LOUISIANA
Professionals: Luca Barbato, Lafayette; Fred Haas, Gretna

MARYLAND
Amateur: Ralph Bogart, Kensington
Professional: Deane Beman, Bethesda

MASSACHUSETTS
Amateurs: Ted Bishop, Boston; Joseph Morrill Jr., Great Barrington
Professionals: Paul Harney, Sutton; Richard Stranahan, Longmeadow

MICHIGAN
Amateurs: Tom Draper, Troy; Peter Green, Franklin; Glen Johnson, Grosse Ile
Professionals: Gene Bone, Walled Lake; Bob Gajda, Bloomfield Hills; Al Mengert, Birmingham

MINNESOTA
Amateur: Neil Croonquist, Minneapolis
Professional: Corky Dahl, St. Paul

MISSISSIPPI
Amateur: Mickey Bellande, Biloxi
Professional: Johnny Pott, Ocean Springs

MISSOURI
Amateurs: Bob Cochran, St. Louis; Hord Hardin, St. Louis
Professional: Leland (Duke) Gibson, Kansas City; E. J. (Dutch) Harrison, Chesterfield; Bob Rosburg, Chesterfield

NEBRASKA
Professional: Merle Backlund, Grand Island

NEW HAMPSHIRE
Amateur: Henry J. Robbins, Portsmouth
Professional: Gene Sarazen, New London

NEW JERSEY
Amateurs: P. J. Boatwright, Far Hills; J. Wolcott Brown, Sea Girt
Professionals: Pat Schwab, McAfee; Babe Lichardus, Scotch Plains

NEW YORK
Amateurs: Don Allen, Rochester; Peter Bisconti,

Mt. Vernon; Joe Dey Jr., New York
Professionals: Gene Borek, East Norwich; Bill Collins, Purchase; Tom Nieporte, Locust Valley; Sam Urzetta, Rochester

NORTH CAROLINA
Amateurs: Bill Harvey, Greensboro; Dale Morey, High Point; Billy Joe Patton, Morgantown; Richard Tufts, Pinehurst; Sonny Ridenhour, Kernersville
Professional: Lanny Wadkins, Clemmons

OHIO
Amateur: Roger McManus, Hartville
Professionals: Walker Inman, Columbus; Frank Wharton, Akron

OKLAHOMA
Amateur: Charles Coe, Oklahoma City
Professional: Labron Harris Sr., Stillwater

OREGON
Amateur: George Beechler, Florence

PENNSYLVANIA
Amateurs: Fred Brand Jr., Pittsburgh; William Hyndmann III, Huntingdon Valley
Professionals: Skee Riegel, Jamison; Bob Ross, Flourtown; Art Wall Jr., Honesdale; Lew Worsham, Oakmont

SOUTH CAROLINA
Amateur: Des Sullivan, Myrtle Beach
Professional: Randy Glover, Summerville

TENNESSEE
Amateurs: Mack Brothers, Nashville; Lew Oehmig, Chattanooga; Curtis Person Sr., Memphis
Professionals: Joe Campbell, Knoxville; Cary Middlecoff, Memphis

TEXAS
Amateurs: David (Spec) Goldman, Dallas; Webster Wilder, San Antonio
Professionals: Jimmy Demaret, Houston; Byron Nelson, Roanoke; Henry Ransom, Wheelock

VIRGINIA
Amateur: Marvin Giles III, Richmond
Professional: Chandler Harper, Portsmouth

WASHINGTON
Professionals: Jim McLean, Seattle; Jerry Mowlds, Vancouver

WEST VIRGINIA
Amateur: William Campbell, Huntington
Professional: Sam Snead, White Sulphur Springs

WISCONSIN
Professionals: Bobby Brue, Milwaukee; Manuel de la Torre, Milwaukee

index

Only golf course designers and golf courses (excluding those listed in the Course Directory pages 243-263) mentioned in the book are indexed. Famous players are also indexed where the text refers to them as golf course designers.

Photographed at Portmarnock, Ireland